Comme

MW00460484

"John Schwarz's book *What's Christianity All About?* offers a good overview of the Bible. It also provides a brief sketch of the history of Christianity, sets forth important Christian beliefs, suggests ways for Christians to deepen their faith and, last, offers some guidelines for Christian living. For those serious about Christianity and the desire to understand it better, this book is a good place to begin."

N. T. (TOM) WRIGHT
Research Professor of New Testament and Early Christianity
University of Saint Andrews, Scotland

"*What's Christianity All About?* is a much-needed book that provides information to whet readers' appetites. It also opens wide the doors to help us see and imagine the future into which the triune God is calling us even now."

SARAH S. HENRICH
Professor of New Testament, Luther Seminary

"*What's Christianity All About?* is a both a guidebook for inquirers and beginners and a refresher course for the casual. It contains brief surveys of the Christian Bible, Christian beliefs, Christian history, Christian living and Christianity alongside other faiths. Brisk, exact and user-friendly, it merits a very wide ministry and will bring clarity of focus wherever it goes."

J. I. PACKER
Board of Governors Professor of Theology, Regent College

"John Schwarz writes as a layman, and he writes so that laypersons can understand. However, what he writes shows the result of serious biblical scholarship. This is a good read for those who want to know what the Bible is all about and Jesus' relevance to the modern world."

TONY CAMPOLO
Professor Emeritus, Eastern University

"John Schwarz is a careful thinker, a lover of the faith, an equipper of the church. He has devoted himself to making an understanding of Christian Scripture and thoughts available on a broad scale. I am grateful for his work."

JOHN ORTBERG
Senior Pastor, Menlo Park Presbyterian Church

"The most appropriate description that I can think of for John Schwarz's book is *multum in parvo*, that is, a great deal in a small space. For here we are given a succinct summary of the contents of the Bible, a brief history of Christianity, an introduction to other religions, together with outlines of both Christian belief and behavior. John Schwarz has succeeded in giving us a mine of information, some skillful overviews, and in areas of controversy, a fair statement of the different options."

JOHN R. W. STOTT
Former Rector Emeritus, All Souls Church, London

"*What's Christianity All About?* is an excellent road map for those starting out on the Christian journey. It is a good primer on the Bible, one that paints a picture of the big story of God at work in the world and shows how the different parts of the Bible fit together. I warmly recommend it to those who want to understand what it means to be a follower of Christ."

LEIGHTON FORD
President, Leighton Ford Ministries

"*What's Christianity All About?* by John Schwarz combines an encyclopedic breadth of information and insights—and materials not usually found in overviews and surveys of the Bible—with an easy-to-read style. I can think of no other introduction, intended for the lay reader, that does the job as well."

PATRICK R. KEIFERT
President, Church Innovations Institute

"For years, as I traveled around the world to teach and preach, I have searched for a simple, readable but comprehensive introduction to the Bible, Christianity and world religions, one that is understandable to all, but especially to my Chinese audiences and readers. I could not find one until I came across John Schwarz's book, *What's Christianity All About?* I am surprised by its simple elegance, but also by its broad coverage and pertinent information. I hope that one day it will be available in the Chinese language."

SIMON YIU CHUEN LEE
Senior Pastor, Richmond Chinese Alliance Church

"*What's Christianity All About?* is concise, readable, fascinating, accurate and, above all, compelling to both believers and nonbelievers who know little of the Bible and the life of Christ. I want this book to be a companion to everyone who reads the Bible because it opens doors of understanding to the Christian faith."

JERRY WHITE
President Emeritus, The Navigators

"*What's Christianity All About?* is a must read for anyone looking for an informed overview of the Bible, Christian traditions and the continuing imperative for evangelism. Schwarz, long a lay teacher, provides an easy-to-read guide to basic facts, themes and dates pertaining not only to the foundation and development of the church, but also to simple but important clues for living the Christian life amid the challenges of a confusing world. I highly recommend this book.

CAIN HOPE FELDER
Professor of New Testament, Howard University School of Divinity

"John Schwarz has written a "manual" for Christians, whether they're skeptics examining the faith or believers wanting to know more. As someone active in youth ministry, I see many Christians today who have not been taught the fundamentals of the faith. Whether it is broad themes or specific questions, the answers are probably in this book—and in straightforward language all can understand and apply."

"If you want an overnight read that will give you a good foundational underpinning of the Christian faith, this is the book. I studied theology for seven years on my way to becoming a deacon in the Catholic Church. *What's Christianity All About?* is a book that I wish I had read at the beginning of my studies."

"For those who have never done any serious Christian study, *What's Christianity All About?* is a good place to begin. John Schwarz, a layman, has produced an extremely lucid bird's-eye view of the Bible, the history of Christianity and its doctrines, reasons for faith and guidelines for Christian living and witness in today's world. If you are wondering what to give to people who are starting their Christian walk, this is it."

"*What's Christianity All About?* is a breath of clarity and simplicity and a thoroughgoing explanation of the essence of Christianity. For me, as someone who grew up in the church and discovered, at age thirty-three, that I didn't have a clue about the true nature of the Christian faith, this book was spot on. As a follower of Christ, I come across people inside and outside the church who totally miss what it means to be a Christian. They would be aided by John Schwarz's book, which organizes, explains and distills what others have made complicated and mysterious."

WHAT'S
CHRISTIANITY
ALL ABOUT?

John Schwarz

WIPF & STOCK · Eugene, Oregon

What's Christianity All About?
Its Scriptures, History Beliefs and Practices

Scripture quotations are from the *New Revised Standard Version*
of the Bible, copyright © 1989, Division of Christian Education
of the National Council of Churches of Christ in the United States
of America. Used by permission.

Cover Design: Spunk Design Machine
Interior Design: James Monroe Design and Luz Design

Image Credits:
Luz Design: pages 1, 69, 117, 145, 201 and 245
Wikipedia Commons: page 219
istockphotos: pages 21 and 95
Simon Dewey/Altus Fine Arts: page 43

Wipf & Stock
An Imprint of Wipf and Stock Publishers
199 West 8th Avenue, Suite 3
Eugene, Oregon 97401

www.wipfandstock.com

ISBN 13: 978-1-4982-2537-3

Manufactured in the United States of America

Dedication

This book is dedicated to scholars and pastors who taught, guided and directed me over the years, beginning in the late 1970s. I read their books, several were classroom teachers, and many edited and critiqued my writings. Collectively, they formed in me much of what appears in this book. Bob MacLennan was the teaching minister at Colonial Church in Minneapolis in the late 1970s; Bob was my first Bible teacher. Roy Harrisville taught New Testament classes at Luther Seminary in Saint Paul for thirty-five years; Roy has been my *Doktor Vater* (doctor father), friend and a careful reader of everything I have written. Norman Dodman founded the Nairobi Bible Training Institute; Norman taught me to see Christianity from a developing world perspective when I lived in Kenya in the 1980s. Ward Gasque was one of the founders of Regent College, an international school of theology in Vancouver, British Columbia; Ward introduced me to Regent College, opened many helpful doors, and encouraged me in my writings. John Stott, who died in 2011, was a pastor, author and the founder of John Stott Ministries (now Langham Parternship), on whose board I was privileged to serve for many years; John modeled for me what it means to be a Christian. N.T. (Tom) Wright is the former Anglican Bishop of Durham (England) and now research professor of New Testament and early Christianity at the University of Saint Andrews in Scotland; Tom sharpened my thinking during the filming of five Christian education programs we did over the years 1999–2004.

Contents

Preface

I grew up in the Episcopal Church, where I was an acolyte as a young boy and confirmed as a teenager, after which I was not involved in the church. When I was in college, I was influenced by classes I took in philosophy and humanities and by teachers who challenged my thinking. I began to wonder if Christianity's truth claims were true. I assumed, without any real basis for doing so, that some were certainly questionable. When I graduated from college and began working in the business world, I had colleagues and clients who were Christians, people whose lifestyle and confident faith I much admired. I read books about Christianity and asked lots of questions and came to believe in the Christ of Christianity, which started me on my Christian walk.

When I became a believer I didn't know much about the Bible or the history of Christianity or what Christians believe. I decided some years later that I would write the kind of book I wished someone had given to me when I began asking questions about Christianity.

My first book was *Word Alive! An Introduction to the Christian Faith*, which Bethany House Publishers printed in 1993 as a 10-chapter resource guide for an in-church Christian education program, which included DVD presentations on each of the chapters by Tom Wright, Martin Marty, Tony Campolo and others. I later wanted to see if I could get the book published and asked John Stott for a commendation. I told John that if he thought the book was worthy of an endorsement, I would send him, gratis, copies of the book for John Stott Ministries. John sent me the commendation on page two of the commendations, and then asked for 30,000 books for evangelical pastors and teachers in the majority world. In 1999, Bethany published Word Alive! under the title *The Compact Guide to the Christian Faith* for sale to bookstores and churches. In 2001, I expanded the Compact Guide, which Bethany and Baker Books (after Baker acquired Bethany) published as *A Handbook of the Christian Faith*. As the books grew in popularity, foreign publishers asked Bethany for permission to translate and publish the Handbook in French, Spanish, Portuguese, Hindi, Korean and other languages. *What's Christianity All About?* is a revised, shortened version of the Handbook.

The book has two halves. The first five chapters have to do with the structure, formation and message of the Bible; the Old Testament story of God's creation and covenants and the rise and fall of Israel; Jesus and the first-century world in which he lived and carried out his ministry; the Gospel testimonies to Jesus' life, death and resurrection; and the story of Paul and others who spread the gospel—the good news of Jesus—throughout the Roman Empire. The second five chapters have to do with the history of Christianity; the bottom-line beliefs of Christianity; a comparison of Christianity with other religions and belief systems; growing one's faith through prayer, study, service and evangelism; and guidelines for Christian living from the Ten Commandments, the Sermon on the Mount and Jesus' parables. The book has discussion questions at the end of each chapter that relate the material in the chapter to everyday life.

What's Christianity All About? reflects an orthodox view of the Scriptures. Where there are disagreements regarding the interpretation of words and passages, I set forth the different ways that scholars have understood the text. Where there were differences in spelling, the dating of events, matters of geography and the translation of Hebrew, Greek and Latin words, I used a "majority rule" approach. The scriptural quotations in the book are from the *New Revised Standard Version* of the Bible.

In an effort to make the book easy to read, I amplified materials parenthetically rather than cluttering up the text with footnotes. Several of my quotes and statements lack source citations. They come from personal notes I scribbled to myself over the years before I had any thought that one day I would write this book.

There may be things in the book you will not agree with. A friend of mine who has spent his life teaching the Bible and theology and was the president of a seminary said, "I have learned more from people who disagreed with me than from those who didn't. They caused me to reexamine my positions and beliefs. Sometimes I had to admit that they had stronger arguments for their positions than I had for mine." You may find this to be true in your case as well.

I am a layman, not an academic, and asked the following people to review and comment on what I had written: Roy A. Harrisville Jr., professor emeritus, Luther Seminary, a widely-published author and mentor; J. Andrew Overman, theologian, archaeologist and chair of the classics department, Macalester College; Grayson J. Carter, associate professor of church history, Fuller Seminary Arizona; and Lee Martin McDonald, president emeritus, Acadia Divinity College, and past president, Institute for Biblical Research.

What's Christianity All About? is an introduction to Christianity, not a textbook. Those who want to know more about the Bible, the first-century Greco-Roman-Jewish world, Jesus' life and ministry, the individual Gospels, Christianity in America, Islam, prayer and other topics can find information about each on Wikipedia and other internet sources.

John Schwarz
Advent 2015

1

The Story and Message of the Bible

What is Christianity all about? It's not about the church or the creeds or the sacraments. It is about Jesus Christ, about his life, death and resurrection, about uneducated fishermen, tax collectors and others we'll never know who launched a movement in his name in the rough and tumble Roman-run pagan world of the first century to become the largest religion in the world with, today, more than two billion adherents who love, follow and serve him.

The Bible: The Unknown Book

Some may think it strange to start a book on Christianity with the story of the Bible. If Christianity is about Jesus, why not start with the Gospels? The reason we are starting with the Bible is to explain how the world's need for—and God's plan of—salvation came to be written and collected in the books that comprise the Judeo-Christian Scriptures. This chapter sets forth the Bible's structure, theme and translations and offers some suggestions for reading the Bible.

Biblical Literacy

The Bible is the best-selling book of all time. According to a 2002 Gallup poll, nearly every American (93 percent) owns one—in fact, many own several versions or translations (according to the Barna Group, the average American family owns three Bibles). Yet for many people the Bible is an unknown book: often prominently displayed, but seldom read and hardly ever studied. In polls and surveys, 60 percent of American Christians could not name five of the Ten Commandments and less than 50 percent could name the four Gospels. Twelve percent of adults thought Noah's wife was Joan of Arc and 50 percent thought the cities of Sodom and Gomorrah were husband and wife. A Gallup pollster asked a group of people who preached the Sermon on the Mount. The No. 1 response was Billy Graham. Many Bible-owning Christians are, sadly, biblically illiterate.

Stephen Prothero, chair of the religion department at Boston University, said, in an article in *USA Today*, that if Americans were given a test on religion, most would fail.

What Is the Bible?

So what is the Bible? It is a book that tells about God's love for us and his will for our lives. It is the story of God's covenants with Abraham, Moses and David and his plan of salvation, which reaches its climax in Jesus of Nazareth. It is God's recorded words to the patriarchs and prophets of Israel in the Old Testament and Jesus' words and the letters of Paul and others in the New Testament. It is the story of God saving Israel from the Pharaoh's army in Egypt and Jesus' saving death to reconcile us with God. It is a manual that tells us how to live Christianly in the world, a book that is "useful for teaching, for reproof, for correction and for training in righteousness so that everyone who belongs to God may be proficient [and] equipped for every good work" (2 Timothy 3:16–17).

"The Bible," an anonymous writer said, "is the traveler's map, the pilgrim's staff, the pilot's compass, the soldier's sword and the Christian's charter. It should fill the memory, rule the heart and guide the feet. It should be read slowly, frequently and prayerfully."

The Bible's Structure and Formation

The English word *Bible* comes from the Greek word *biblia*, meaning books—though not all of the books are technically "books." In the Old Testament, the Psalms are a collection of poems and prayers and the Proverbs are a collection of wise sayings. In the New Testament, the majority of the books are letters.

The Christian Bible has two major divisions or halves. The first and much longer half is the Old Testament, the story of God's creation of "the heavens and the earth" and calling Israel to shower his blessings on all the world; the rise and fall of Israel in the Promised Land; the call of Elijah, Amos, Isaiah, Jeremiah and others to speak God's word to the people of Israel; and the books of Psalms, Proverbs, Job and others.

The New Testament is the shorter half of the Bible. It is the story of Jesus' public ministry, sacrificial death and bodily resurrection, and the outward movement of the good news to cities throughout the northern Mediterranean world.

In addition to the Old and New Testaments, there are the apocryphal or *deuterocanonical* (second canon) books that were written during the interim between the Old and New Testaments. One finds these books in Roman Catholic and Eastern Orthodox Bibles, but not in most Protestant Bibles.

The word *testament* comes from the Latin *testamentum*, meaning "oath" or "covenant." The Old Testament contains the covenant that God made with Israel at Mount Sinai when he said to Moses: "Now therefore, if you obey my voice and keep my covenant, you shall be my treasured possession out of all the peoples" (Exodus 19:5). Several centuries later he told the prophet Jeremiah: "The days are surely coming . . . when I will make a new covenant . . . It will not be like the covenant that I made with their ancestors [when I brought] them out of the land of Egypt" (Jeremiah 31:31–32). Jesus instituted the new covenant at the Last Supper when he told his disciples: "This cup that is poured out for you is the new covenant in my blood" (Luke 22:20).

The books in the Old and New Testament *canons*—from a Greek word meaning "measuring stick" or "rule" or "approved list"—are the books that were accepted by the rabbis and church fathers as Holy Scripture. They were written over a 1,200-year period, between 1100 BC and AD 100; by more than forty different authors, some of whom are known but many of whom are not, especially in the Old Testament; from places like Jerusalem, Babylon, Corinth, Ephesus and Rome.

According to the Wycliffe Bible Translators, the New Testament has been translated into 3,000 languages and 75 percent

of the world's population has access to the whole or some part
of the Bible in their own language.

The Old Testament

Christians differ on the number of books in the Old Testament
portion of their Bibles. There are thirty-nine books in Protestant Bibles; forty-six books in Catholic Bibles (the additional
books come from the Septuagint, discussed below); and fifty
books in Eastern Orthodox Bibles (the Catholic Old Testament
plus 1 Esdras, 3 Maccabees, the Prayer of Manasseh and Psalm
151). There are four sections or divisions in the Christian Old
Testament.

The **Pentateuch** comprises five foundation books: Genesis,
Exodus, Leviticus, Numbers and Deuteronomy. These books
tell the story of God creating "the heavens and the earth"; calling Abraham to be a blessing to "all the families of the earth";
rescuing the enslaved Israelites in Egypt; giving the Ten Commandments to Moses on Mount Sinai, along with rules and codes
of conduct to guide Israel in living as God's chosen people; and
the gradual molding of Israel into a nation.

The **historical books** are the books of Joshua, Judges, Ruth,
Samuel, Kings, Chronicles, Ezra, Nehemiah and Esther. They
trace the history of Israel over a period of some 800 years, beginning with the Israelites' entry into the Promised Land (Canaan)
under Joshua in 1250 BC; the settlement of the land during the
250-year period of the Judges; the united kingdoms under kings
Saul, David and Solomon (1020–920 BC); the split and division
of the land into the kingdoms of Israel and Judah; the defeat of
Israel by the Assyrians in 721 BC and Judah by the Babylonians
in 586 BC; the exile of the Judeans in Babylon; and the return of
the exiles to Israel in 538 BC and the restoration of Jewish life

in the mid-400s BC.

The **prophetic books** are the collected writings of the four major or longer prophets—Isaiah, Jeremiah, Ezekiel and Daniel—and twelve minor or shorter prophets, some of the more familiar of whom are Hosea, Joel, Amos, Jonah and Micah. In the Jewish Bible, the minor prophets are one book, called The Book of the Twelve.

The **devotional and wisdom literature** are the books of Job, Psalms, Proverbs, Ecclesiastes and the Song of Solomon. In Christian Bibles, these books precede rather than follow the prophets. For purposes of this book, they are at the end of the overview of the Old Testament because they are not part of the Bible's "salvation history" story.

The New Testament

The New Testament is the story of good news—the good news that Jesus both announced and embodied in his own person— the good news that those who believe in his saving, sacrificial death will be forgiven of their sins and deemed righteous on the day of judgment.

The New Testament canon has twenty-seven books, also divided into four sections.

The **Gospels** of Matthew, Mark, Luke and John are the written testimonies to the life, teachings, saving death and resurrection of Jesus.

The Acts of the Apostles is the story of the persecution of the early Christians by Jews who rejected Jesus' messiahship, and Paul's conversion, missionary travels, church planting and final journey to Rome, covering the years 30 to the early 60s.

The **letters** are Paul's nine letters to churches in Rome, Corinth, Galatia, Ephesus, Philippi, Colossae and Thessalonica and his pastoral letters to Timothy, Titus and Philemon; the anonymous letter to the Hebrews; and the seven general letters of James, 1-2 Peter, 1-2-3 John and Jude.

The **Revelation to John** is a series of apocalyptic visions about the sovereignty of God and his coming victory and triumph over the forces of evil.

The New Testament writings were gathered together in the second century. There seems to have been general agreement on the books in the New Testament canon by the end of the century, except for the anonymous letter to the Hebrews, three of the general letters, and the book of Revelation. According to New Testament scholar I. Howard Marshall, the forming of the canon "was not so much a confirming of authority by the church upon the books as it was a recognition of the authority which the books inherently possessed." The canon in its present form was first mentioned in an Easter letter by Athanasius, the bishop of Alexandria, in the year 367, though agreement on the books in the canon must have occurred much earlier.

The Order of the Books

In the Hebrew Bible, the books appear more or less in chronological order. This is not true of the New Testament. Paul, who was martyred in Rome in the mid-60s, wrote all of his letters before any of the Gospels, the first of which, most scholars believe, was written between the years 65 and 70. Paul's letters, with one minor exception, are arranged in descending order by length, not by date. Romans is first in line because it was Paul's longest letter, though it was the last of his nine church letters. And though Matthew is the first book in the New Testament, most scholars believe that Mark was the first Gospel, not Matthew.

The Acceptance of the Books

The basis on which books were accepted into the canon was threefold. First, the author must have been an apostle or have had a close association with an apostle, like Mark with Peter and Luke with Paul. Second, the writings had to be consistent with the church's teachings about Jesus. Third, the writings had to have enjoyed church-wide acceptance. We wish we knew more about how the books were received and accepted into the canon, but we don't. Canon scholar Lee Martin McDonald, in his book *Formation of the Bible*, says, "There are no ancient documents that tell us [how this was done]."

The Manuscripts

Christians have good reason to be confident of the authenticity of the New Testament. More than 5,000 Greek manuscripts have been found, including near-complete manuscripts dating from the mid-300s. One is the *Codex Sinaiticus*, discovered by the German biblical scholar Constantine von Tischendorf at a monastery near Mount Sinai in 1844, which is now in the British Museum in London. Another is the *Codex Vaticanus,* now in the Vatican Library in Rome.

The first books in the New Testament were written within a generation of Jesus' death (Paul's first letter is dated around the year 50, twenty years after Jesus' death). The number and dating of the New Testament books contrasts with the miniscule number and late dating of the writings of Plato, Aristotle, Julius Caesar and others in antiquity, which scholars universally accept as authentic. In his book *Can We Trust the New Testament?,* British scholar John A. T. Robinson calls the New Testament "the best-attested text of any writing in the ancient world."

The Canonical Gospels

The central narrative of the New Testament is the public ministry, salvific (saving) death and bodily resurrection of Jesus of Nazareth, which are contained in the four canonical Gospels. (I use a lower case 'g' when referring to the gospel or good news and an upper case 'G' when referring to one of the four Gospels.) Some ask why there are only four Gospels, because there were Gospels other than those that made their way into the New Testament canon, such as the apocryphal Gospels of Peter, Philip and Thomas. With regard to this question, the Gospels that did not make it into the canon were judged not to have been apostolic in origin (most were written in the second, third and later centuries); were not considered doctrinally orthodox; and had not been accepted by the church at large.

As to why there are four Gospels and not one, the church fathers felt that our understanding of Jesus would be richer and deeper with all four, rather than only one, or with a harmonized Gospel such as Tatian's *Diatessaron* (fourfold), which appeared in the latter half of the second century and remained popular for centuries. The early church fathers chose to keep the Gospels separate because they were inspired by the Holy Spirit (2 Timothy 3:16), rather than replace them with Tatian's human-only composition. The fact that Tatian chose the four canonical Gospels for his composite Gospel testifies to the widespread acceptance of Matthew, Mark, Luke and John over rival Gospels that were beginning to circulate.

The Apocrypha

The Apocrypha are books that are included in Catholic and Eastern Orthodox Bibles, but not in most Protestant Bibles. Alexander the Great (356–323 BC)—the great military commander and conqueror—introduced Greek language and culture in areas he conquered. Over time Greek became the *lingua franca* (common language) in Europe, Asia Minor and North Africa. Sometime around the year 280 BC, seventy-two Jewish elders and scribes, six from each of the twelve tribes, were sent from Jerusalem to Alexandria, Egypt, which had the largest Jewish community in the ancient world, to translate the Pentateuch into Greek so that it could be read by Alexandrian Jews. According to legend, when they finished their translations there was not a single discrepancy between them! The Greek scriptures were called the *Septuagint*, from the Latin *septuaginta*, meaning "seventy," the nearest round number for the seventy-two translators. The Septuagint is often abbreviated with the Roman numerals LXX.

The Septuagint became the Bible for Jews living outside Palestine and for Greek-speaking Christians in the early church, and it was the version from which the authors of the books of the New Testament most often quote.. The Septuagint includes several books that are not in the Hebrew Bible, among them Tobit, Judith, 1 and 2 Maccabees, three additions to Daniel, additions to Esther, the letter of Baruch, Jeremiah's secretary, the Wisdom of Solomon, and Ecclesiasticus.

When Jerome translated the Hebrew Scriptures into Latin around the year 400, he included several of these books in his translation, with a caution from rabbis with whom he worked that they were not to be considered on the same level as the books in the Hebrew canon. At the Council of Trent (1545–1563), the Roman Catholic Church accepted the additional books into its Old Testament canon.

When Martin Luther and the Reformers translated the Bible into German, French, English and other languages, they either omitted these books or put them in a separate section called the *Apocrypha*, from a Greek word meaning "things hidden," because they had not been received into the Hebrew Bible.

The deuterocanonical books of the Maccabees shed light on the years between the two Testaments. Other books in the Apocrypha let us see the development of Jewish thinking regarding the afterlife, which is only briefly alluded to in the Hebrew Scriptures.

The Theme and Message of the Bible

Students of the Bible claim there is a unifying theme or meta-narrative (grand story) from Genesis to Revelation. Some say the theme is that of *covenant*—the three covenants God made with Israel (with Abraham, Moses and David) and through Jesus with all humankind. Others say the theme is *salvation history*, the progressive revelations of God so that all might come to the knowledge of the truth and be saved (1 Timothy 2:4). Still others say the theme is *promise and fulfill-ment*—God's promise of a Messiah from the house of David (2 Samuel 7) and the fulfillment of this promise in Jesus of Nazareth.

The central truth claims of Christianity are that Jesus was God incarnate (God in the flesh); that he died a sacrificial death to reconcile us with God; and that he was raised from the dead to confirm his mission. Is there any evidence that Jesus was raised from the dead? The surest evidence is the witness of those who were martyred for their faith. Why is this evidence? Because, as Paul Little said in his book *Know What You Believe,* "People will die for what they believe is true [that Jesus rose from the dead], but no one willingly dies [as did Peter, Paul and others throughout the Roman Empire] for what they know is false."

When Lord Nelson defeated Napoleon's French fleet in the Battle of the Nile in 1798, he told the British Admiralty that *victory* was not a big enough word for what he had accomplished. When Christians talk about Jesus' victory over death on Easter morning, *victory* is not a big enough word for what he accomplished.

The Formation and Translations of the Bible

The stories that make up the Bible were passed down orally from generation to generation, and then written on scrolls like the Isaiah scroll that Jesus read from in the synagogue at Nazareth (Luke 4:17-21). Orality and memory were important and valued in the ancient world, and even today with many people able to memorize the entire New Testament. Luke, in the opening verses of his Gospel, tells us that "many have undertaken [to remember and pass on] events that have been fulfilled among us" and that he has decided "to write an orderly account of such things."

The books in the New Testament were written on papyrus made from stalks of the papyrus plant that grew along the Nile River. Strips of papyrus were overlaid and pasted together and smoothed with a piece of ivory or a shell. The Roman scholar Pliny the Younger said the characteristics sought in papyrus were "fineness, stoutness, whiteness and smoothness." The other principal writing material was parchment, which was made from the skins of goats, sheep and calves. Parchment was more available than papyrus, which grew only in Egypt; it was more durable than papyrus; and both sides could be used for writing. It is estimated that the Codex Sinaiticus required the skins of 360 goats and sheep. Ink was made from carbon-based chimney soot, which was mixed with gum water.

Writing instruments were made from reeds, which had to be continually sharpened. Pens made from bird's feathers, which were sturdier, did not appear until the seventh century. Letter writers like Paul used professional stenographers, who took

shorthand before putting the writer's words in final form. Letters were sent by a relay system similar to that employed in the
early days of the United States, with postal stations and horses
that could travel fifty miles a day.

It was not until the second century that Bibles were produced with pages that could be turned, called *codices*. The
earliest Bibles were written in capital letters, with no spacing,
chapters or verses. The *Geneva Bible*, published in Geneva in
1560, was the first Bible in which the text was divided into both
chapters and verses. With the invention of the printing press
by Johann Gutenberg in 1456, the production of Bibles moved
from handwritten pages to movable type.

The early church's Bible, as mentioned, was the Greek Septuagint. As the church moved west there was need for an accurate
Latin translation of the Bible, which was completed by Saint
Jerome (347–419) in 405. Jerome's translation came to be called
the *Vulgate*, from a Latin word meaning "common" or "ordinary."
It became and remained the official Roman Catholic Bible until
well into the twentieth century, and it was the first Bible to be
printed, the *Gutenberg Bible*.

The first Bible in English was completed by followers of
John Wycliffe (1330–1384), who translated the Latin Vulgate
into English in 1382. After England split with Rome (1534),
many new translations began to appear—so many that King
James I of England commissioned a committee of forty-seven
scholars and churchmen to produce an "authorized" version,
known today as the *King James Version* of 1611. The KJV became
the Protestant Bible of the English-speaking world until well
into the twentieth century, and its popularity continues even
today.

The last century saw more than one hundred new English
translations. The principal reason was that new information
was gleaned from archaeological discoveries, like the Dead

Sea Scrolls, discovered in 1947, the most important manuscript find in the twentieth century (some 900 manuscripts). Another was twelve Coptic-language codices discovered at Nag Hammadi in Upper Egypt in 1945. The most important manuscript at Nag Hammadi was the Gospel of Thomas, which is popular today among biblical scholars, but is not a Gospel per se: it is a collection of 114 sayings of Jesus, with no narrative structure or mention of Jesus' death and resurrection.

Other reasons for new translations were the need to update certain words in the Bible, such as "Thee" and "Thou"; to reflect continuing advances in biblical research and scholarship; and to make the Bible more gender inclusive.

Revelation, Inspiration and Authority

The Bible is called the "Word of God," which is a figure of speech because God did not dictate the Bible, as Muslims believe the angel Gabriel did the Koran. Rather, he communicated with those entrusted with the task of putting pen to papyrus through visions and dreams (Numbers 12:6) and through encounters with prophets and apostles whom God called to speak his word. The authors, though, were humans, and had different oral and written sources (see Luke 1:1–4), and wrote for different audiences, which accounts for occasional differences in their writings. Three teachings that relate to the Bible are revelation, inspiration and authority.

General and Special Revelation

It is said that religion is humankind's attempt to reach God, and that Judaism and Christianity are God's words and revelations to humankind. *General revelation* refers to God's universal revelation in nature (the stars, other planets, the animal kingdom) to all persons everywhere since the beginning of time (Romans 1:20). *Special revelation* refers to God's special words and acts, among them, calling Abraham to "Go from your country . . . to the land that I will show you" (Genesis 12:1); leading the Israelites out of Egypt; giving the Ten Commandments to Moses on Mount Sinai; speaking to Israel through the prophets ("Thus says the Lord"); sending the angel Gabriel to tell Zechariah in the temple that he would have a son (John the Baptist, Jesus' forerunner) and telling Mary that she was favored to bear God's son; and the coming of Jesus in the "fullness of time." The Bible is the written witness to God's *special* revelatory words and acts.

The Inspiration of the Bible

The Bible is the vehicle or medium through which God's word comes to us. The divine selection of those who wrote the scriptures, and their guidance by the Holy Spirit to assure the faithful transmission of their testimonies, is called *inspiration*. Some believe that every word in the Bible is inspired, a view called *verbal inspiration*. Those in this camp believe the Bible is inerrant, meaning without error in all regards, even as to matters of history and science. They say that admitting to the possibility of errors in the Bible is the first step down the slippery slope to unbelief. A softer view is *limited inerrancy*, the view that the Bible is without error in all that it teaches, but not everything in the Bible is meant to be understood as "teaching." Others believe that the Bible *contains* the word of God (regarding salvation), which allows for some latitude in interpreting the text. Evangelicals prefer the word *infallible*, meaning that the Bible is trustworthy in its affirmations regarding Jesus, most importantly, his virginal conception, sacrificial death and bodily resurrection.

The Authority of the Bible

The bedrock belief of post-Reformation Christians, especially, evangelicals, is that the Bible is "the Word of God written." As such it is authoritative in matters of orthodoxy (Christian beliefs) and orthopraxy (Christian practice). Christians down the ages have understood the Bible's teaching and authority differently, each group thinking they alone have it right, which is one reason Protestantism is so diverse. The Bible, though, is not a book of dogmas and rules. It is the story of God's love, grace and forgiveness. Unfortunately, the church today is less interested in the Bible's "authority" than in social justice, missions, evangelism and other matters.

The Bible's obituary is totally unwarranted, though some wonder if Moses wrote all five books of the Pentateuch; if the four Gospels were written by those for whom they are named; and if Paul authored all thirteen letters attributed to him. Christians accept the Scriptures as authoritative because they were received into the canon by the early church councils.

Another challenge is the way people read the Bible. According to the authors of *American Grace*, adults who read the Bible literally has declined from 66 percent in the 1960s to 30 percent today. Many read the Bible as a metanarrative or grand story, with a beginning (God creating the "heavens and the earth" in Genesis 1-2); an ending (the "new heaven and new earth" coming down from heaven in Revelation 21-22); and lots of stories in between—histories, prophecies, poetry, stories of God speaking and people 'doing.' The purpose of many of the stories, like many of Jesus' parables, is to teach us about God and ourselves and how to be God's 'image bearers' on earth.

New Testament theologian Donald Bloesch, in *Essentials of Evangelical Theology*, said, "There are many roads by which man seeks to come to God, but there is only one road by which God comes to man, and that road is Jesus Christ." The story of the road from Father Abraham to Jesus is set forth in God's revelations to prophets, apostles and others who wrote, under the inspiration of the Holy Spirit, what John A. T. Robinson called "the best-attested text of any writing in the ancient world."

Reading the Bible

The British New Testament scholar N. T. (Tom) Wright (b. 1948) said, in his book *Scripture and the Authority of God*, that reading the Bible is central in our understanding of God and his truth and in developing "the moral muscle to live in accordance with the gospel of Jesus when everything seems to be pulling the other way."

In her book *Be Still and Know*, Millie Stamm tells the story of a famous actor who was being honored at a banquet. After dinner an old clergyman asked him to recite the Twenty-third Psalm, the best known and most popular of the Psalms. The actor said that he would be glad to, on condition the clergyman do the same. Impressively, the actor recited the psalm, holding his audience spellbound. When he was finished, the clergyman did the same, and there was not a dry eye in the room. After a moment of silence, the actor said, "I reached your ears, but this man reached your hearts. I know the psalm, but he knows the shepherd." Many people, like the actor, read the Bible as beautiful literature. Others, like the clergyman, read the Bible as the revealed Word of God. The following are some suggestions for reading the Bible.

First, the Bible should be read with an open mind and with the expectation that God will speak, through his word, to our hearts and minds. The Bible, someone said, is God's "telephone line" to us.

Second, the Bible is one continuous story of salvation, from Genesis to Revelation. It begins with God's call of Abraham to be the father of a people who would bring God's word and blessing to all nations, and his special covenants with Moses and David. It reaches its fulfillment in the birth, life, death and resurrection of Jesus.

Third, the Bible was written some 2,000 years ago and is, in places, hard to understand. William Booth (1829-1912), the founder of the Salvation Army, was once asked what he did when he came across something in the Bible he didn't understand. Booth said, "I do the same thing I do when eating a fish: I put the bones on the side of the plate and get on with the good meat."

Fourth, the Bible has different literary forms, which should be read in ways consistent with each book's *genre*. There are books of history (Kings, Chronicles and Acts), prophecy (Isaiah, Jeremiah, Amos and others), collections of poetry (the Psalms), wisdom literature (Proverbs and James) and several letters.

Lastly, the Bible is its own commentary, meaning that the New Testament interprets the Old. For instance, when Jesus "declared all foods clean" in Mark 7:19, he overruled the laws regarding clean (kosher) and unclean foods in Leviticus 11.

Popular Bible Translations

As mentioned, there have been several new translations and revisions of the Bible in the last thirty or so years. The following are comments on six popular, widely-used Bibles. In buying a Bible, buy a study version with introductions to the books, commentaries on the text, maps and so forth.

- The *New Revised Standard Version* (NRSV, 1989) is a revision of the Revised Standard Version (RSV, 1952). It is considered by many to be the most faithful rendering of the Greek text. Following the dictates of the National Council of Churches, which sponsored the revision, the NRSV is "as literal as possible, as free as necessary." One change from the RSV is the avoidance of masculine-oriented language when referring to people in general. The NRSV is the most ecumenical Bible, used by Roman Catholics, Protestants and the Eastern Orthodox.

- The *Good News Translation* (GNT, 1976) was published by the American Bible Society, initially for non-native English speakers in Africa and the Far East. It is a sixth-grade reading level paraphrase, rather than a word-for-word translation. The GNT avoids technical religious terms, is popular with youth and those learning English, and is used by both Protestant and Catholic churches and by evangelistic organizations.

- The *New International Version* (NIV, 2011) is an update of the original NIV (1978), which was a completely new translation by a trans-denominational team of biblical scholars sponsored by the International Bible Society. The NIV is the most popular English translation of the Bible in terms of sales, according to the Christian Booksellers Association. It is intentionally conservative in scholarship and translation and widely used by evangelicals.

- The *New Living Translation* (NLT, 1996), which was completed by a team of ninety evangelical scholars from various denominations, is published by Tyndale House Publishers. The NLT is easy to read and is popular with both young and old alike. It translates words and terms into English (weights, time, measures, metaphors), avoids technical theological terms, and uses "gender-inclusive" language.

- The *English Standard Version* (ESV, 2001) is another revision of the Revised Standard Version. It follows a literal translation philosophy (it is even more literal than the NIV), while taking into account the grammar and syntax of current literary English. Like other modern translations, it removes "thee" and "thou" and replaces obsolete words with contemporary English words.

- *The Message* (2002) is a single-author translation by Eugene Peterson. Its uniqueness is Peterson's personal interpretation of the Bible's stories and his use of modern-day American words and terms.

Discussion Questions

1. Which version of the Bible do you use? Do you read the Bible daily, weekly—for instance, on Sunday—or only once in a while? What is your favorite Bible verse or verses?

2. How would you explain the Bible to someone who didn't know anything about its message or teachings?

3. In reading about the Bible in chapter 1—its structure, theme, formation, translations, inspiration and authority—what are some things that were new to you?

2

The Hebrew Scriptures

God entered into a covenant with the Israelites at Mount Sinai. Because Christians believe that God made a new covenant, which Jesus instituted at the Last Supper, they refer to the covenant God made with Israel as the *old* covenant. If God made a new covenant, some wonder why we need to read the old covenant? Because Jesus came to fulfill God's covenantal promises to Israel, which are recorded in the Old Testament. The story of salvation did not begin with Jesus' birth in Bethlehem. It began 2,000 years earlier with God's call of Abraham in the Mesopotamian city of Haran.

The Two Testaments

The Bible is divided into two parts of unequal length, with Jesus coming in between, as it were. Christians say the Old Testament looks forward to Jesus and the New Testament looks back to Jesus. The first part is the story of God's covenant with Israel; the second part tells how the covenant was fulfilled in Jesus. Richard Hays, the dean of Duke Divinity School, in his book *Reading Backwards*, says, "The Gospels teach us how to read the OT ... and the OT teaches us how to read the Gospels." In recent years some have found the terms *old* and *new* misleading, as though the New Testament is somehow superior to the Old Testament. To avoid this, some scholars refer to the Old Testament as the Hebrew Scriptures or the Hebrew Bible.

The Pentateuch: Creation, Fall, Election and Covenants

The story of Israel becoming a nation is contained in the first five books of the Bible, which Jews call the Torah, from the Hebrew word *tora*, meaning "instruction" or "the law." The Torah contains Israel's formative/foundational books, much like the Gospels in the New Testament. It is Israel's "fundamentals of the faith." In the Christian Old Testament, the first five books are called the Pentateuch, from the Greek words *penta* (five) and *teukhos* (scrolls).

The Pentateuch is the story of God electing Israel to be his people (the call and covenant with Father Abraham); speaking to Israel's patriarchs and leaders (Abraham, Moses and others); rescuing Israel from her bondage in Egypt (the Exodus); and entering into a covenant with Israel at Mount Sinai (the Mosaic Covenant).

God told Moses to tell the people of Israel: "If you obey my voice and keep my covenant, you shall be my treasured possession out of all the peoples" (Exodus 19:5). Moses sealed God's Sinaitic Covenant with the blood of oxen, "dashing" half of the blood on the altar of the Lord and the other half on the people (Exodus 24:5–8). (Jesus sealed God's new covenant with his own blood.) The Torah is central to Jewish worship and is read aloud in its entirety each liturgical year. The five books of the Torah or Pentateuch are as follows.

Genesis

Genesis is the story of the creation of the universe, planet Earth, vegetation, living creatures and humankind; the "fall" of Adam and Eve; the stories of Cain and Abel, Noah and the flood and the tower of Babel; the call of Abraham to go to a new land; and family stories of Abraham, Isaac, Jacob and Joseph. The book of Genesis—the English translation of a Greek word meaning "birth" or 'beginning"—lays the foundation for the biblical story of creation, de-creation (the downward fall) and re-creation (God's plan of restoration). Genesis is about the beginning of everything except God, who had no beginning.

Stephen Prothero, in his book *Religious Literacy*, said Genesis has been "the most influential book in American life," with its stories of creation, Adam and Eve, the Garden of Eden, the serpent, Cain and Abel, Noah and the ark, Joseph and his family, and the Pharaoh in Egypt.

Exodus

The book of Exodus contains the birth and call of Moses; the ten plagues; the Exodus (the "going out") from Egypt; God's covenant with Israel at Mount Sinai; and the Decalogue (Ten Words) or

Ten Commandments. Exodus tells the story of God's deliverance of Israel through the Red Sea, the great salvation event of the Old Testament, and is, for Jews, the center of the Hebrew Bible.

Leviticus

The Levites were the priestly descendants of Levi, one of the twelve sons of Jacob. The book of Leviticus contains instructions pertaining to religious offerings; clean (kosher) and unclean food; codes of behavior; and *Yom Kippur*, the day of atonement, the most solemn day in the Jewish calendar, the day when Israel confesses her sins, both "seen and unseen" so that she may be reconciled with God (similar in importance to Good Friday). Leviticus contains God's command to "Love your neighbor as yourself" (19:18), which Jesus said was the second greatest commandment (Mark 12:31).

Numbers

The fourth book in the Pentateuch is about the census (numbering) and organization of the twelve tribes of Israel into a united community or nation; God's call to take possession of Canaan, the land promised to Abraham's descendants; and Israel's forty years of wandering in the Sinai wilderness as God's judgment for their failing to do so. The book of Numbers contains the Aaronic blessing: "The Lord bless you and keep you [and] make his face to shine upon you [and] give you his peace" (6:24–26).

Deuteronomy

Deuteronomy is the *deutero* (second) telling of Israel's covenant relationship with God, because most of the elders had died during their forty years in the wilderness. It contains the

Shema, Israel's great confession of faith: "Hear, O Israel: The Lord is our God, the Lord alone" (6:4), which Jesus said was the greatest commandment (Mark 12:28–30); and Moses' farewell instructions to the twelve tribes before their entry into the land of Canaan; and Moses' death.

The Prologue to the Biblical Story

Genesis 1–11 is the prologue or preamble to the biblical story, the period *before* history, much like chapters 4–22 in the book of Revelation look ahead to the period *beyond* or *after* history. The major stories in the prologue are as follows.

The Two Creation Accounts

There are two creation accounts in Genesis. The first (1:1–2:3) is a careful, orderly, systematic statement about the creation of the heavens and the earth, the vegetation, living creatures, and man and woman. Did God create "the heavens and the earth" in six literal *days,* as set forth in Genesis 1:1–31? Or, as astronomers today believe, 13.7 billion years ago? The opening chapter of Genesis is not about the *how and when* of creation; it is about the *who* of creation—about the One behind creation, the One who brought everything into being, the One we call God the Father. Christian faith does not require the belief that God created "the heavens and the earth" in six 24-hour days.

The second creation account (2:4–25) is the story of God forming man, breathing into him the gift of life, and making woman from one of his ribs. The story of God breathing life into man is the story of God imparting a non-material soul into humankind, which makes humans different from all other creatures. It also makes it possible for humans, who were created in the spiritual image and likeness of God (Genesis 1:26), to have a personal relationship with God.

The two creation accounts are clearly different, which can be seen in the different stages of creation, with the vegetation coming before the creation of humankind in the first account and after humankind in the second. One way to look at the two accounts is to recall the opening scene in the movie *The Sound of Music*. The camera comes in over the Alps and zeroes in on Maria as the focal point of the story. Genesis 1 opens with the universe, and then, in Genesis 2, zeroes in on Adam and Eve as the focal point of the story.

John Stott (see epilogue), in his commentary on Paul's letter to the Romans, said, "It is fashionable nowadays to regard the biblical story of Adam and Eve as a 'myth,' a story whose truth is theological but not historical. The scriptures intend us to accept their historicity because the biblical genealogies trace the human race back to Adam. We don't know whether God formed Adam 'from the dust of the ground' and 'breathed into his nostrils the breadth of life,' or whether this is the Bible's way of saying that he was created out of an already existing hominid. The vital truth is that, though our bodies are related to the primates, our fundamental identity is that we are related to God."

There is a disagreement today between young- and old-earth creationists. The young-earthers say the universe is approximately 4,000 years old. Where did this number come from? It came from James Ussher (1581-1656), the Archbishop of Ireland, from his study of the genealogies in the early chapters of Genesis. According to Ussher, God "created the heavens and the earth" at 6 pm on Sunday, October 23, in the year 4004 BC. Ussher's dating was incorporated into a copy of a Bible printed in 1701 and came to be accepted with the same reverence as the Bible itself . This contrasts with the old-agers, who, guided by science, believe that the earth is 4.5 billion years old and in the gradual mutation and evolution of living creatures over thousands and millions of years.

The Downward Fall

Genesis 1 and 2 are usually read together. Many think Genesis 2 should be read with Genesis 3 and subsequent chapters as the story of the Downward Fall. In Genesis 2, Adam was put in the garden to till and cultivate the land, with one prohibition: he was not to eat from "the tree of the knowledge of good and evil." First Eve, and then Adam, disobeyed God and ate from the tree (humankind's so-called "original sin"). The story does not identify the fruit. Some say it was an apple and that it got caught in Adam's throat, which is why we call the bump in our throat an Adams Apple. Everything went downhill from there, with God sending a great flood over the face of the earth.

The Genesis fall stories are about the universality of sin and God's judgment of sin. They conclude with the story of the building of a tower to humankind's glory rather than to God's glory. God confuses their tongues—makes them *babble*—and scatters them far and wide.

Abraham: Israel's Founding Father

Former Princeton Theological Seminary scholar Bernhard Anderson, in his book *Understanding the Old Testament,* said: "The stories of the primeval history set forth the human predicament in universal terms—the predicament of peoples estranged from God and scattered over the face of the earth in confusion and strife. These stories provide the prologue to the special place of Israel in God's history-long, world-embracing plan."

The balance of the Bible is the answer to the prologue, the story of God's acts in history to save his people, a history sometimes referred to as "salvation history"—the story of God working out his plan of salvation through Abraham and Moses, the judges and the prophets, David and the kings, Jesus and the apostles, and Paul and the church.

God's plan of salvation begins with Abraham—God so loved the world that he called Abraham—whom he blessed to be a blessing to others. (With Abraham, we move from pre-history to history-history.) Abraham was born in Ur of the Chaldeans (ca. 2000–1800 BC) in present-day Iraq. Ur was a Summerian city whose people were literate, manufactured copper and glass, had wheeled vehicles, and practiced astronomy, medicine and mathematics. Abraham's family later moved to Haran in present-day Syria, near the Turkish border. We are not told why God called Abraham. According to later rabbinic writings, God called many, but only Abraham responded. The working out of God's plan of salvation continues through the rest of the Old Testament and all the way to the end of the New Testament—from Genesis 12 to Revelation 22.

Abraham's descendants were to bring God's blessings to all peoples and nations on earth (Genesis 12:3). Abraham's wife Sarah, however, was old and barren. God's grace overcomes her barrenness and she bears a son, who is named Isaac. The theme of barrenness occurs throughout the Old Testament, and also in the New Testament with Elizabeth, the mother of John the Baptist.

Genesis 22 is the story of God's command to Abraham to sacrifice Isaac, his beloved son, to see if he is trustworthy—if he is the one to carry forward God's plan of salvation. He tells Abraham to take Isaac "to the land of Moriah and offer him there as a burnt offering [a *holocaust*] on one of the mountains that I will show you." (According to

2 Chronicles 3:1, Mount Moriah is the site where Solomon later built "the house of the Lord in Jerusalem.") Abraham takes Isaac to Mount Moriah and gathers wood and builds an altar on which he places Isaac. God sees that Abraham is faithful and trustworthy and provides a ram instead for the sacrifice. In his letters to the Galatians and Romans, Paul lifts up Abraham as one who, by faith, obeyed God and was justified, that is, made right with God.

God enters into a covenant with Abraham, electing him to be the father of Israel. The sign of the covenant was circumcision. (For most Christians, the sign of belonging to God is baptism.) God makes two further covenants, one with Moses at Mount Sinai (Exodus 19:3-6), along with the Ten Commandments; another with David, promising that a son of his would rule over a kingdom that would have no end (2 Samuel 7:16).

Isaac has twin sons, Esau and Jacob. The ancestral line continues through Jacob, whose name is changed to *Israel* by an angel of the Lord (Genesis 32:28). Jacob's sons become the Twelve Tribes of Israel. Joseph, Jacob's eleventh and favorite son, is sold into slavery by his jealous brothers. He is taken to Egypt, where he interprets the Pharaoh's dreams and becomes the second-ranking official in the land. A famine in Canaan brings Jacob and his family to Egypt, where Joseph feeds and cares for them, after which they settle in Goshen in northern Egypt.

"Calls" in the Bible

In the Bible, God calls Abraham and others to be agents in his plan of salvation. The German Old Testament scholar Claus Westermann (1909-2000), in his book *A Thousand Years and a Day,* said that God's calls have several common ingredients.

- The purpose of the calls is to send the one called on a mission: Abraham to Canaan, Moses (who was in Midian) back to Egypt, Jonah to Nineveh, Samuel to Saul and then to David, Paul to the Gentiles.

- The one called was not looking to be called: Abraham was with his family in Haran (in antiquity, one did not leave home while his father was still living), Moses was tending Jethro's flock in Midian, Samuel was apprenticing with Eli, Isaiah did not consider himself worthy, Jeremiah thought he was too young, Paul was pursuing Christians in Damascus.

- The call came from beyond: in a voice to Abraham, in a burning bush to Moses, in visions to the prophets, by the angel Gabriel to Zechariah in the Temple and to Mary in Nazareth, in a dream to Joseph about Mary's pregnancy, in a dazzling light to Paul on the road to Damascus, in a vision to Ananias.

- The call changed the destinies of large numbers of people: Abraham and his family moved to Canaan, Moses led the Israelites out of Egypt, Joshua led the Israelites in their invasion and settlement of Canaan, David exercised kingship over the northern and southern kingdoms of Israel and Judah, Paul planted churches and evangelized Gentiles.

- The one called did not respond for his own glory, but for the glory of the one who called him, namely, God.

Although some, such as Jonah, tried to resist their calls, most often the response was: "Here I am," as with Abraham's response to God's summons to sacrifice Isaac (there are two "Here I am" responses in Genesis 22, one to God, the other to "an angel of the Lord"), Moses' response at the burning bush (Exodus 3:4), Samuel's answers during his apprenticeship under Eli (there are three "Here I am" responses by Samuel in 1 Samuel 3:4-8), Isaiah's response to God's query, "Whom shall I send?" (Isaiah 6:8), and that of Ananias in Damascus (Acts 9:10).

Moses: Israel's Deliverer and Lawgiver

Some 600 years after Abraham, the Israelites were living as slaves in Egypt. God hears their cries for help and calls Moses at a burning bush (a bush that burned but was not consumed) to lead the Israelites out of Egypt. The date of the Exodus—Israel's deliverance from bondage—was either 1290 BC, the majority view, based on archeology; or 1446 BC, based on 1 Kings 6:1 ("In the four hundred eightieth year after . . . "). The Exodus is the single most important event in Israel's history. Every year at Passover the story is retold: the story of the angel of death, who struck down the firstborn of the Egyptians, but *passed over* the homes of the Israelites (Exodus 11-12).

After God sent ten plagues on Egypt, the Pharaoh—the Hebrew word for the ancient king of Egypt—allowed the Israelites to leave. Moses led the Israelites through the Red Sea to Mount Sinai. The Bible says "Red Sea," but the route out of Egypt was more likely through the Sea of Reeds—the words *yam suf* in the Hebrew Scriptures—in northern Egypt (the Red Sea is at the southern end of the Sinai Peninsula). When the Israelites arrived at Mount Sinai, God entered into a covenant with them and gave Moses the Ten Commandments.

Moses was the preeminent leader of Israel, the one who molded the twelve tribes into a nation. When Winston Churchill became the prime minster of England in 1940, he said, "My whole life has been but a preparation for this moment." When God called Moses at the burning bush, Moses could have said the same thing. First, his early years with his biological mother, whom Pharaoh's daughter unknowingly retained to care for her own son, made him aware of his Jewish heritage. Second, his education in Pharaoh's household prepared him to confront the Pharaoh—most likely Ramesses II, who reigned from 1279 to 1212 BC—when he was called by God to do so. Third, his years in the Midian desert (southeast of Sinai), to which he fled after killing an Egyptian who had beaten a fellow Israelite, enabled him to guide and lead the Israelites to Mount Sinai, where they received God's law and commandments.

It is said that the New Testament was written after the followers of Jesus had experienced the risen Christ—that is, from the other side of the cross. The same might be said of the Old Testament: it was written after the Israelites had experienced the God of Abraham, Isaac and Jacob—that is, from the other side of the Red Sea.

The Historical Books:
The Rise and Fall of Israel

The historical books trace the history of the Israelites from their entry into Canaan—the land promised to Abraham's descendants (Genesis 12:6-7)—in the thirteenth century BC, to the return of the exiles to Israel and the restoration of Jewish life in the fifth century BC. Geographically, the land of Israel was (and is today) very small, not quite 300 miles north-to-south and, at its widest point, 75 miles east-to-west—similar in size and shape to the state of Vermont. Why was Canaan the Promised Land? Perhaps because it sat at the crossroads of the world, between the continents of Asia, Europe and Africa, where Israel would be God's "light to the nations" (Isaiah 42:6).

Joshua and the Judges

Israel's history in Canaan begins with the call of Abraham to go "to the land that I will show you" (Genesis 12:1). In 1250 BC (based on an Exodus date of 1290 BC), Joshua, Moses' successor, leads the Israelites into Canaan, where they secure footholds in the central hill country. The story of Israel taking possession of the land continues for another 250 or so years, during the "tribal confederacy." (Israel did not take full control of the land until the reign of David around the year 1000 BC.) During the confederacy, Israel was led by a series of judges, who were not jurists but charismatic leaders like Deborah and Gideon, whom God called to lead Israel when it was attacked by warring peoples like the Philistines. Samson is the most famous person during the period of the Judges, but he was not a "judge."

The United and Divided Kingdoms

The Israelites wanted a king to lead them against their enemies (1 Samuel 8:19-20). Saul, a successful military commander, was Israel's first king (1020-1000 BC). He was followed by David, Israel's greatest king, who ruled from 1000 to 960 BC. David was a boy hero who, with five small stones, slew the Philistine giant, Goliath; a great military strategist and leader who defeated Israel's enemies and secured her borders; a charismatic politician who was able to unite the twelve tribes into one nation, with its capital in the city of Jerusalem; and a lover of God, who wrote psalms and repented after his affair with Bathsheba (Psalm 51). David came from the tribe of Judah (Jacob's fourth son), the *remnant* tribe that was entrusted with the mission of bringing God's message of salvation to the world. Through the prophet Nathan, God made a covenant with David that a descendant of his would rule over "a kingdom that would have no end" (2 Samuel 7:12-16). In the Gospel of Luke, the angel Gabriel tells

Mary that her son will inherit "the throne of his ancestor David [and] of his kingdom there will be no end" (Luke 1:32–33).

David was followed by Solomon (960–920 BC), his son by Bathsheba. Solomon taxed the people both monetarily and physically (building his temple, his most famous legacy), married non-Jewish foreigners, and "did what was evil in the sight of the Lord" (1 Kings 11:6). After his death the United Kingdom split in two. The ten northern tribes became the Kingdom of Israel; the two southern tribes (Judah and Benjamin) became the Kingdom of Judah. The Assyrians defeated the Northern Kingdom in 721 BC and assimilated the Israelites into the Assyrian population, resulting in the Ten Lost Tribes of Israel. The Babylonians defeated the Southern Kingdom in 586 BC and hauled its leaders off in chains to Babylon. Before and during the defeat of Judah, Jews began leaving Palestine in the *Diaspora*, a Greek word meaning "dispersion," and settled elsewhere in the Mediterranean world, resulting in the majority of Jews in the first century living outside Palestine.

The Exile in Babylon

The exile in Babylon (587–539 BC) severely tested Israel's faith. Solomon's Temple, the sign or symbol of God's presence among his people, had been destroyed; and David's dynasty, which was to last forever, had come to an end. *What happened?* What happened had been foretold by the prophets: God would judge and punish the Israelites if they disobeyed the covenant he made with them at Mount Sinai, and if they did not live as a people of justice and righteousness.

In the year 539 BC, the Persians defeated the Babylonians. The Persian king, Cyrus, issued an edict that allowed the Jews to return to their homeland. (When the United States recognized Israel as an independent state in 1948, President Truman said, "I am Cyrus.") After the Exile, the term *Jew* became a designation for those from or identified with Judah. The exiles who returned found their country in shambles. It took men like Nehemiah, who rebuilt the walls around Jerusalem, and Ezra, who reinstituted Jewish religious life, to strengthen the faith of those who returned and took up residence in the Promised Land.

The Voice and Message of the Prophets

During the period of the united and divided kingdoms, the Israelites became a decadent, faithless, disobedient people. God sent prophets ("one who speaks for another") to exhort the leaders to return the Israelites to the Mosaic Covenant, and to prophesy dire consequences if they refused to do so. The prophets were prominent during the time of the kings; they faded out in postexilic Israel when kings no longer who ruled Israel.

There were two kinds of prophets in ancient Israel. Prophets such as Nathan, Elijah and Elisha, whose lives and words are woven into the biblical narratives, are called speaking or *narrative* prophets. Those whose words were written down and collected by their disciples, to be remembered and passed on, are called writing or *canonical* prophets. We often think the prophets spoke (prophesied) mainly about the future, but this was only a minor part—perhaps only 10 percent—of their words to Israel. Their message was "forth-telling" rather than "fore-telling"—a call to the Israelites to return to the Mosaic Covenant. Four important prophets were the following.

Elijah was the most important of the pre-canonical prophets, the one who appeared with Moses on the Mount of Transfiguration (Mark 9:5). Elijah did not die. He was taken to heaven in a "whirlwind" in the 800s BC (2 Kings 2:11). The prophet Malachi prophesied that Elijah would return to announce the Day of the Lord (4:5). (Orthodox Jews are still waiting for this to happen.) Jesus referred to John the Baptist as the "Elijah figure" sent to announce the Messiah (Matthew 17:12–13 and Luke 7:24–28).

Amos was the first prophet whose words were recorded in a book that was named for him. Amos was a herdsman from Tekoa, south of Jerusalem. He spoke out against the Northern Kingdom's oppression of the poor and its false worship, saying that what God wants is for "justice to roll down like waters, and righteousness like an ever-flowing stream" (5:24). Scholars consider Amos the greatest of the twelve minor prophets in terms of personality and message.

Isaiah was a man of culture and learning who lived in Jerusalem in the 700s BC. Isaiah answered God's call: "Whom shall I send, and who will go for us?"(6:8). Some think there were two Isaiahs: Isaiah of Jerusalem, chapters 1–39, whose words were written before the exile; and Isaiah of Babylon, chapters 40–66, which imply a situation after the exile. This may be interesting to scholars, but, as the nineteenth-century evangelist Dwight L. Moody said, "What's the use of talking about two Isaiahs when most people don't know there is one?"

The book of Isaiah has prophecies that the followers of Jesus interpreted as messianic: The sign of salvation will be a son born of a "virgin" (7:14; Matthew 1:23); the Spirit will anoint him "to bring good news" to the poor (61:1; Luke 4:17–19); he will come as a suffering servant to bear the sin of many (53:12; Mark 10:45). Isaiah's prophecies underlie important events in Jesus' life—especially his suffering at the hands of others (52:13–53:2) and his sin-bearing death—and is, for Christians, the center of the Jewish Bible.

Jeremiah lived 100 years after Isaiah, in the last years of the Southern Kingdom of Judah; he is considered the second most important prophet. Jeremiah spoke out against the military policies of important kings of Judah, resulting in his frequent arrest, punishment and imprisonment. The British scholar William Neil said, "Jeremiah's chief contribution lies in his own life, which bears a closer resemblance to Jesus than any other Old Testament figure." What we remember most about Jeremiah, however, is his prophecy of a new covenant (31:31–34), which Jesus instituted at the Last Supper.

By some counts there are more than 400 messianic prophecies in the Old Testament. While many are open to more than one interpretation, they all point to something more to come, something still ahead, something yet to happen, which the New Testament interprets as having occurred in Jesus of Nazareth— his virginal conception, Davidic heritage, wondrous acts, and suffering death for "the sin of many" (Isaiah 53:12).

The Wisdom and Devotional Literature

There are five books in the Old Testament that the Christian Bible calls Wisdom and Devotional Literature (the Jewish Bible calls them the Writings). Two of these, Psalms and Proverbs, are collections of poems, prayers and sayings, without a single author; the other three are not central to the Bible's salvation history story. Job is first in line because its setting is earlier than the other four. Psalms and Proverbs are next, and in this order because David, the patron of psalmic literature, preceded his son Solomon, the patron of wisdom literature. The other two books are Ecclesiastes, the pessimistic reflections of an old man, who writes that only in God can one find meaning in life; and the Song of Solomon, so called because Solomon's name appears six times in the book, though he never speaks. The most important of these books are Psalms, Proverbs and Job.

The Book of Psalms

The Psalms have been called Israel's soul music (in ancient Israel, the Psalms were meant to be sung). In contrast to other writings in the Old Testament, the Psalms are Israel's words and songs to God, rather than God's words to Israel. The entire book of Psalms is read through in shifts each day at the Wailing Wall in Jerusalem where, it is believed, God resides in some mysterious way. It is difficult to date the Psalms because they do not deal with specific events in Israel's history to which they can be related. The dates probably range from the United Kingdom through the period of the Exile. David is given credit for writing 73 of the 150 Psalms, but a Psalm *of* David can also mean a Psalm *for* or dedicated to David. In Jesus' day, the Psalms were not numbered; they were known by their first line, like our hymns are today. Psalm 23 would have been called "The Lord is my Shepherd."

Broadly speaking, the Psalms are prayers and petitions to God for help; hymns of praise to God for choosing Israel and delivering her from her enemies; and hymns that extol God's greatness and holiness. A unique feature of the Psalms, also seen in the Proverbs, is the parallelism and rhyming of thoughts, with the second line reinforcing the first. The book of Psalms is called the Psalter, from a Greek word meaning "stringed instrument," because the Psalms, as mentioned, were meant to be sung. The Psalter is the longest book in the Bible, the most quoted Old Testament book in the New Testament, and is used by churches for responsive readings and by believers for personal devotions.

The Book of Proverbs

The book of Proverbs is filled with wisdom about how to live in the world, even the twenty-first century world. Pastor and author Eugene Peterson, in his preface to the book of Proverbs in *The*

Message, says wisdom is "being skillful in honoring our parents and raising our children, handling our money and conducting our sexual lives, going to work and exercising leadership, using words well and treating friends kindly, eating and drinking healthily, and cultivating emotions and attitudes that make for peace." Peterson says the book of Proverbs concentrates on these matters more than any other book in the Bible.

All together, there are some 500 proverbs (sayings) in the book, which are attributed to Solomon because of his legendary wisdom (1 Kings 4:29–34). Most scholars, however, believe the book is anonymous because there are eight clearly discernible collections of sayings in the book. The individual proverbs have to do with wisdom, hard work, honesty, self-control and sexual temptation. The book of Proverbs is seldom read or quoted in church.

The Book of Job

Job is a folktale-like story, both at the beginning (the wager) and the end (restoring Job's fortunes). It is a story about a wealthy Bedouin chieftain who was wise and just and revered God. Because of a wager between God and Satan to test Job's love for God, Job loses everything—his flocks, his children, even his health (painful, festering sores). The book of Job is a discussion about the justice of God. If he is all-powerful and all-loving, why do the righteous suffer? And why do some suffer more than others? Job pleads with God for an answer to his plight, which never comes. (We often hear about someone having "the patience of Job," but Job is anything but patient.)

Finally, at the end of the book, God speaks to Job out of a whirlwind, though he never tells Job about his wager with Satan, which was the cause of his misfortune, nor does the author satisfy his readers: no reason is given for the suffering of the righteous. Rather than answering Job, God reminds him who he is: the One who laid the foundations of the earth, and made the light and the darkness, and the wind and the rain, and the creatures of the world (38-42). Humbled, Job says, "I have uttered what I did not understand" (42:3), confessing, perhaps, what he said in the first chapter: "Naked I came from my mother's womb, and naked shall I return; the Lord gave, and the Lord has taken away; blessed be the name of the Lord" (1:21).

"Your Majesty, the Jews!"

The great Swiss theologian Karl Barth (1886-1968), in his book *Dogmatics in Outline*, tells a story about Frederick the Great (1620-1688), who asked his personal physician, Dr. Zimmerman, "Can you name me one proof of the existence of God?" Zimmerman replied, "Your Majesty, the Jews!"

Barth said, "By that he meant that if one wanted to ask for a proof of God, for something visible and tangible, that no one could contest, which is unfolded before the eyes of all men, then we should have to turn to the Jews. Quite simply, there they are to the present day. Hundreds of little nations in the Near East have dissolved and disappeared in the huge sea of nations; [only] this one tiny nation has maintained itself . . . If the question of God is raised, one need merely point to this simple historical fact. For in the person of the Jew there stands before our eyes the witness of God's covenant with Abraham, Isaac and Jacob, and in that way with all of us. Even one who does not understand Holy Scripture can see this reminder."

Barth's comments, of course, do not prove the existence of God, any more than Thomas Aquinas's "five ways" prove the existence of God. But it is a fact that the tiny nation of Israel inhabits today the same land that God promised and gave to the Israelites some 4,000 years ago, which seems like more than just an interesting coincidence.

Judaism and Christianity

According to the *World Christian Encyclopedia* (2001), there are 14 million Jews in the world. Thirty percent live in Israel and 40 percent in the United States. The first Jews came to North America in 1654, but the real influx came following the pogroms (organized massacres) in Russia in the 1800s.

Orthodox Judaism is the smallest and most legalistic form or expression of Judaism. It forbids all commerce, travel, cooking, letter writing and other activities on the Sabbath; follows the Hebrew Bible's dietary laws; and has male-only rabbis. Men wear head coverings and men and women do not sit together in worship services.

Reform Judaism began in Germany in the early 1800s to "reform" Judaism to bring it into the mainstream of society. Reform Jews do not regard the Torah as "law" but as teaching and open to interpretation. In the United States, Reform worship services are in English; rules regarding the Sabbath are relaxed; dietary laws are generally not observed; and men and women sit together during worship.

Conservative Judaism began in Europe, but is largely an American phenomenon. It is a middle path between the legalism of Orthodox Judaism and the progressive liberalism of Reform Judaism. In recent years it has moved more to the left (Reform) than to the right (Orthodox).

According to a recent (2008) Pew Report on "Major Religious Traditions in the United States," 41 percent of American Jews are Reformed, 29 percent are Conservative, 12 percent are Orthodox, and 18 percent are unaffiliated.

Judaism and Christianity have many similar beliefs: both believe in a supreme, sovereign God, in the centrality and authority of Scripture, and in an afterlife. The principal differences are, first, Judaism believes that God revealed himself in the Torah, not in a person. Second, that God is pure spirit, which precludes his incarnation in a human. Third, that God is one single person, not triune. Fourth, that men and women have inclinations to do good and evil, but are not sinful because of Adam's fall in the Garden. Fifth, that salvation comes through righteous living and faithfulness to the Mosaic Covenant, not through Christ's salvific death on the cross.

Discussion Questions

1. God called Abraham and others to be agents in his plan of salvation. Has God ever called you? What was his call? What has happened since he called?

2. The Israelites believed that God was involved in their lives, and in the nation Israel, and in the world. Do you think that God is active and involved in the world today? In what ways?

3. Do you ever send psalmic messages to people who are suffering or recovering from a medical procedure or tragedy? Google has colorful psalmic notes that you can send over the internet.

3

The World, Life and Ministry of Jesus

The Old Testament is a story in search of an ending, which comes with Jesus of Nazareth. People have managed to do away with many things, but not Jesus. He remains a compelling figure—often misunderstood, sometimes disparaged, but forever remembered and proclaimed in books, icons, statues, paintings, hymns, songs, stained glass windows, billboards, bumper stickers, chapels, WWJD bracelets and, well, almost everywhere you look. We date our calendars with his birth, capture him in art and music, and use his teachings as reference points in talking about matters of social justice.

The Gospels' *Sitz im Leben*

In reading the Gospels, it is important to know the *Sitz im Leben*, the "life setting" or back story behind the Gospels. The pages that follow look at the world of Jesus and his public life to give us the context for the next chapter on the Gospels.

There is little mention of Jesus outside the New Testament, other than by the first-century Jewish historian Josephus (37-100) and the first-century Roman historians Tacitus, Suetonius and Pliny the Younger. Few in the first century were interested in what was happening in a remote corner of the empire among the Jews, but no professional historian today denies that Jesus lived and died in the first third of the first century.

In an anonymous piece about Jesus, called *One Solitary Life*, the writer says: "All the armies that ever marched, and all the navies that ever sailed, and all the parliaments that ever sat, and all the kings that ever ruled—put together—have not affected the life of men and women on this earth as much as this one solitary life."

The Intertestamental Period

The years following the return of the Jewish exiles from Babylon in 538 BC is a period of religious history that remains in the shadows. The walls around Jerusalem were rebuilt under the supervision of Governor Nehemiah; a modest temple was erected, referred to by scholars as the Second Temple; Jewish religious life was reestablished by Ezra, a Jewish priest and scribe; and the Hebrew Scriptures were gathered together, though the final Jewish canon was not agreed upon until the second century AD.

In 336 BC, at the age of twenty, Alexander the Great succeeded his father, Philip of Macedonia, who was assassinated. He invaded Palestine in 332 and Persia in 331 and became the ruler of the largest empire the world has ever known. Alexander was a pupil of Aristotle and he loved everything Greek. His dream was to unify East and West: he introduced Greek language, culture and philosophy wherever he was victorious; he encouraged his soldiers to marry women from among the conquered peoples; and he founded Greek cities like Alexandria in Egypt, where he is buried. The world became so Hellenized (*Hellas* was the name of ancient Greece) that the Hebrew Scriptures had to be translated into Greek so they could be read by Jews in Alexandria and elsewhere in the Mediterranean world, resulting in the Greek Septuagint mentioned in chapter 1.

Alexander died of typhoid fever or malaria in Babylon at the young age of thirty-three. Because he had no legal heir, his empire was divided among his generals. In the East, Seleucus became the ruler of Syria and Babylonia; Ptolemy became the ruler of Palestine and Egypt (Queen Cleopatra, who committed suicide in 30 BC, was the last of the Ptolemies). The Seleucids were landlocked and wanted access to the Mediterranean Sea. In 198 BC, they defeated the Ptolemies and became the rulers of Palestine.

In 167 BC, the Seleucid king Antiochus Epiphanes banned the circumcision of newborn males, Sabbath observances, temple sacrifices, and the teaching of the scriptures, all on "pain of death"; he also made sacrifices in the temple to a pagan deity. This provoked an uprising led by Mattathias, a priest, and his five sons, the most famous of whom was Judas, who was called *Maccabeus*, a Greek word meaning the "hammer." The Maccabeans defeated the Syrians in December 164 BC and purified the temple, an event that Jews celebrate as Hanukkah, a Hebrew word meaning "dedication." (John 10:22 mentions Jesus going to the temple for "the festival of the Dedication.")

In 63 BC, the Roman army under Pompey invaded Palestine to solidify Rome's control of the perimeter of the Mediterranean Sea to assure a safe winter land route to bring food from Egypt, the breadbasket of the ancient world, to Rome. Jesus was born during the reign of Octavian, who was called Augustus, the "august one." He was the great-nephew, adopted son and heir of Julius Caesar, who had no legitimate children. Augustus ruled for forty-one years, from 27 BC to AD 14. He is considered by historians to be Rome's greatest emperor because of his organization and administration of the empire. It was Augustus who issued the decree that "all the world should be registered" for tax purposes (Luke 2:1), which sent Joseph and Mary to Bethlehem, a five-day journey by mule, where Jesus was born. (Mary did not need to accompany Joseph; she did so because of her advanced pregnancy.) How ironic that a secular king, Augustus, made it possible for the real king, Jesus, to be born where he was supposed to be, in Bethlehem. Jesus died during the reign of Tiberius (14–37), who was raised by Augustus, who married his mother, Livia.

The House of Herod

The founder of the House of Herod was Antipater, a half-Jew from Idumaea, the Old Testament land of Edom. In 48 BC, Antipater came to the aid of Julius Caesar in his civil war with Pompey for the sole control of Rome. (Caesar was victorious; Pompey was assassinated). Caesar rewarded Antipater with Roman citizenship and the governorship of Judea and granted the Jews two special privileges: exemption from military service and the freedom to worship their own God. Antipater's son, Herod, was Rome's military overseer in Galilee. In the year 37 BC, Marc Antony, the ruler of the eastern half of the Roman Empire, made Herod the King of the Jews—though he did not become "king" until he proved to Rome that he could manage the Jews, collect taxes and send them to Rome, and rule the land of Palestine.

The Jews never accepted Herod because he was an Idumean. He was called "Herod the Great" because of his great architectural achievements: beautifying the temple to win favor with the Jews (Herod's temple was grander even than Solomon's temple); building the city of Caesarea, named for Caesar Augustus, on the Mediterranean Sea, which became Herod's capital city and the official residence of Pontius Pilate and other Roman governors, and the place where Paul was imprisoned in the late 50s; and building Antonia Fortress, named for Marc Antony, where Jesus was flogged by the soldiers. He also built palace-fortresses like Machaerus on the Jordanian side of the Dead Sea, where John the Baptist was beheaded; Masada, a mountaintop fortress near the Dead Sea, the last Jewish holdout at the end of the First Jewish War; and Herodium, a town eight miles south of Jerusalem, where Herod is buried.

Herod was born in 73 BC. He ruled Israel for thirty-three years—from 37 to 4 BC. He was a brutal, ruthless ruler, one example being his "slaughter of the innocents" in Bethlehem, recorded in Matthew chapter 2; another being the murder of three of his ten wives and three of his seven sons. He must have been an efficient administrator, however, because Rome never removed him, as they did his sons.

Herod died on the eve of Passover in 4 BC at the age of 70. His empire was divided between three of his sons. *Archelaus* was given the rule of Judea and Samaria. He was an evil, oppressive ruler like his father. In AD 6, the Jews sent a delegation to Rome to complain about Archelaus and he was removed, after which Judea and Samaria were ruled by Rome-appointed governors like Pontius Pilate, the fifth governor of Judea-Samaria, a coarse, brutish man who ruled from 26 to 36. *Herod Antipas*, or Antipas, ruled Galilee and Perea until he was removed by Rome in the year 39. It was Antipas who had John the Baptist beheaded (Mark 6:14-29) for speaking out against his marriage to Herodias, his niece and his brother's wife, which was forbidden by Jewish law (Leviticus 20:21). Luke writes that Antipas had a conversation with Jesus on Good Friday (23:6-12). *Philip the Tetrarch* (ruler of a fourth) ruled the northeastern territories until his death in 34. Philip built a temple in the city of Casarea Philippi, combining his name with that of Caesar, the location of Peter's confession of Jesus as the Messiah (Mark 8:29).

Herod Agrippa I, the grandson of Herod the Great, who is called King Herod in the book of Acts, ruled the former territories of Antipas and Philip, and then all of Israel from 41 to 44. It was Agrippa who had James, the brother of the disciple John, "killed with a sword" (Acts 12:2). He was succeeded by his son, Herod Agrippa II, who is called King Agrippa in Acts 25. This Agrippa had an incestuous relationship with his sister, Bernice, and heard Paul's testimony before Paul left for Rome to appeal his case to Emperor Nero in the early 60s. Agrippa II , who died in the year 93, was the last Herodian ruler.

The First-Century World of Jesus

The following are comments on the first-century Greco-Roman-Jewish world (the lands surrounding the Mediterranean Sea) into which Jesus was born and lived out his life. Today the first-century world of Jesus is an area of active scholarly interest and research.

Economics

Palestine was an agrarian economy, with a rich variety of grains, vegetables and fruits. Wealthy landowners farmed their lands by leasing them out to tenants, sharecroppers and day laborers. In addition to farmers, there were carpenters, bakers, butchers, weavers, potters and merchants. Life was hard, with people scratching out a living as best they could. Rome levied taxes on crops and imposed duties on merchandise; Jewish law required both tithes and grain offerings. Civil and religious taxes and tithes could amount to 30 percent or more of one's income.

Society

There were three classes of people in first-century Palestine. At the top was the ruling aristocracy (1–2 percent of the population), made up of wealthy landowners and priests who officiated at the temple. Below the ruling aristocracy were the common people, and below them indentured servants. Village life was primitive and never easy and life was short (there were no cures for most illnesses and diseases). Travel was slow and by foot (fifteen to twenty miles a day). Those who lived in remote villages like Nazareth were generally more conservative, both theologically and otherwise, than those who lived in large cities like Jerusalem.

Domestic Life

The family was the basic unit. Marriage and procreation were considered family obligations ("Be fruitful and multiply," Genesis 1:28). Marriages were normally arranged by parents, often to family relatives. Because life spans were short, girls were married between the ages of twelve and fourteen, males between the ages of eighteen and twenty. Women, for the most part, were restricted to the home. Men did not converse with women in public, not even their own wives. The literacy rate was probably around 5 percent. Those who could read and write were mostly males who lived in urban centers like Jerusalem.

Religious Life

Jews were either full-blooded Jews (those born Jewish) or proselytes (those who converted to Judaism). Two other groups were the "God-fearers," those who were attracted to Judaism but never converted to Judaism; and Gentiles, a term for those who were not Jewish. The most important institution was the temple in Jerusalem, the center of the Jewish sacrificial system. Two other important institutions were the Sanhedrin, the seventy-one-member Jewish ruling council and supreme court (Numbers 11:16) and the synagogue, from a Greek word meaning "place of assembly," which was more important than the temple for Jews living outside Jerusalem. The synagogue was a place of worship, prayer, study and fellowship.

Jewish Religious Communities

The two leading Jewish branches or factions in the first century were the Sadducees and the Pharisees. In addition, there were three other communities or groups. The *Scribes* were experts in the law of Moses. They studied, taught and copied the scriptures. The *Essenes,* who are not mentioned by name in the New Testament, were ultra-conservative Jews, even more so than the Pharisees. The Essenes—the term *essene* is thought to mean "pious"—believed they were Israel's true remnant. Most were unmarried males who lived in semi-monastic communities like Qumran near the Dead Sea (the "Monks of Judaism"). Although a peaceful people, they were destroyed by the Roman Tenth Legion in the First Jewish War. Fortunately, they first placed their sacred writings in clay jars and hid them in eleven caves overlooking the Dead Sea, which were accidently discovered by a Bedouin shepherd in 1947. The Qumran scrolls are the oldest extant (existing) Jewish Scriptures, some dating back to 250 BC.

The *Zealots* were Israel's freedom fighters—heirs of the Maccabees—who many believe provoked the First Jewish War (66-70), which was brutally crushed by Rome. (Jesus' disciple Simon the Zealot, so-called by Luke, may have been an anti-Roman zealot.) Thousands of Jews were killed, thousands more were sold into slavery, and the city was razed and the temple burned, with only the Western or "Wailing" Wall left standing, which today is Judaism's most holy and sacred site. This was followed sixty years later by a Second Jewish War (132-135), a revolt that likewise was crushed, following which Rome changed the name of the land to *Palestinia*—the "land of the Philistines"—to remove the name of Israel from the land. The Jews did not regain control of their homeland until the United Nations established the State of Israel in 1948.

The Sadducees

The Sadducees were Israel's priestly party. The name *Sadducee* comes from Zadok (Greek: *Saddouk*), a priest whose descendants held office from the time of Solomon. They controlled both the temple and the Sanhedrin and were friendly and cooperated with Rome. The Sadducees believed that Jesus was a dangerous revolutionary who might provoke a riot that would bring a strong anti-Jewish response from the Roman garrison in Jerusalem, so he had to be dealt with. The Sadducees were linked with the temple; after its destruction in the year 70 they gradually disappeared from the scene.

The Pharisees

The Pharisees, the "religious" of Israel, were lay, fundamentalist Jews. According to Josephus, there were about 6,000 Pharisees in first-century Palestine, out of an estimated population of

600,000. Scholars think the name *Pharisee* means "separated one" because the Pharisees separated themselves from anything they considered unclean. The Pharisees are portrayed negatively in the Gospels as Jesus' enemies, perhaps because the Gospels were written after the Jews and Christians split apart from one another in the latter half of the first century. They were much admired by the Jewish people for their learning and piety. Nicodemus is called a Pharisee in John 3:1 and the apostle Paul calls himself a Pharisee in Acts 23:6 and Philippians 3:5. The Pharisees believed the way to honor God was to keep the law. They challenged Jesus when they felt he did not do so: when he ate with sinners, healed the unclean and broke the Sabbath.

A distinguishing difference between the Pharisees and Sadducees, who disagreed about many things, was the resurrection of the dead. The Pharisees believed in a future resurrection; the Sadducees did not (see Acts 23:6–8) because their "bible" was the Torah, which contains no mention of resurrection. The Pharisees were the most important religious group standing at the end of the First Jewish War. They took over the leadership of the Jewish community in Palestine and determined the books to be received into the Jewish canon.

The Coming of Jesus in the "Fullness of Time"

There are two Greek words for time. One is *khronos*, which denotes linear time, from which we get the word *chronology*. The other is *kairos,* which denotes the "right" or "perfect" time. Jesus came in kairos time—in the fullness of time (Galatians 4:4)—which made it possible for the good news to spread quickly throughout the Roman Empire.

- There was universal peace, prosperity and stability in the empire—the *Pax Romana* (the Peace of Rome)—that began with the reign of Augustus in 27 BC.

- There was a *lingua franca* or universal language, Greek, which made it possible for the good news to be preached everywhere in the Greco-Roman world.

- There was a good road system and safe sea routes that allowed Paul, Barnabas and others easy access to important cities in the Mediterranean world.

- There was a hunger for something other than Roman mythology and emperor worship. People wanted something that gave meaning and hope to their lives.

- There was a growing belief in one God as a result of the Diaspora, the dispersion of Jews who left Palestine before and during the fall of Jerusalem in 586 BC. According to Catholic scholar Frederick Cwiekowski, more than 150 cities in the Roman Empire had synagogues in the first century, with Jews proclaiming their faith and belief in a single, supreme, sovereign God.

In the fullness of time—a 100-year window between the beginning of Augustus's reign in 27 BC and the Roman army's mopping-up operation at Masada in AD 73 at the end of the First Jewish War—the Word of God became flesh and entered human history in the person of Jesus of Nazareth.

We don't know what Jesus looked like, but he would have been much more middle eastern looking than the fair-skinned, blue-eyed Jesus we often see in Western religious art.

Jesus' Birth

The four Gospels narrate the story of Jesus' public life from his baptism in the River Jordan to his death and resurrection in Jerusalem. The first and third Gospels, Matthew and Luke, tell us that Jesus was conceived through the power of the Holy Spirit (Luke 1:35), meaning that Jesus was God incarnate (God in the flesh) from the very moment of his conception; that his legal father, Joseph, was from the line or lineage of David, from which God's "anointed" (the Messiah) was to come (2 Samuel 7:12-16); and that he was born in Bethlehem, where the Messiah was prophesied to be born (Micah 5:2). If it were not for Matthew and Luke, we would know very little about Jesus' birth: there is no account of his birth in Mark or John or the letters of Paul.

Joseph and Mary

Joseph and Mary were the parents of Jesus. Both were from the tribe of Judah, the "remnant tribe." Joseph was his stepfather and Mary his biological mother. We know very little about Joseph; he is not mentioned after the story of Jesus at the temple when Jesus was twelve years old (Luke 2:41–52). Most scholars believe that Joseph died before Jesus began his public ministry. (In Mark 6:3, Jesus is called the son of Mary, not the son of Joseph.) If so, Jesus would have been the family's primary breadwinner.

We don't know much about Mary, either, other than that she was young, a virgin when Jesus was conceived, the cousin of Elizabeth (the mother of John the Baptist), and had found favor with God (Luke 1:28). She must have been a remarkable woman. After Jesus and Paul, she is the most prominent figure in the church, especially among Roman Catholics (she is Catholicism's most important saint). There is no way of knowing how old Joseph was when he and Mary became husband and wife.

According to marriage customs at the time, Mary would have been thirteen or fourteen, much younger than the matronly Mary we often see in Christian art.

The Matthean and Lukan Birth Narratives

Matthew's birth narrative is told from Joseph's perspective, Luke's from Mary's perspective. The two accounts have different details, which we see in manger scenes at Christmas time. Matthew's Gospel includes the story of the magi (astrologers), wise men from the East, or perhaps Jews who stayed behind in Babylon after Cyrus allowed the exiles to return to Jerusalem. (Nothing for certain is known about the maji. They are only mentioned by Matthew.) Following the "star" (Numbers 24:17 and Matthew 2:2, 9), they brought "gifts of gold, frankincense and myrrh" to the newborn Jesus (2:11). Scholars believe there were more than three maji; Matthew mentions "three" because of the three gifts. Luke's Gospel has the story of the lowly shepherds, who are told by an angel of the Lord that "to you is born this day in the city of David [Bethlehem] a Savior," following which they hurry to visit him (2:8-20).

The most striking thing about the two infancy narratives is not their differences but their complete agreement on all essential points. The principal characters are Joseph and Mary; the revelations regarding Mary's pregnancy are made to Joseph by "an angel of the Lord" and to Mary by the angel Gabriel; conception takes place between betrothal and marriage (Mary's virginity is emphasized in both accounts) and occurs through the agency of the Holy Spirit; Mary's son is to be given the name Jesus; the birth takes place in Bethlehem during the reign of Herod the Great; and the family settles in Nazareth.

Jesus' Birth Year and Date

We don't know for certain the year of Jesus' birth. It was probably 6 or 5 BC (see next section). A sixth-century monk, Dionysius Exiquous (Dennis the Small), revised the calendar in 533 to move the center of history from the founding of Rome in 753 BC to the birth of Jesus. Unfortunately, he made a calculation error. For centuries the calendar was marked off by BC (Before Christ) and AD (which does not mean After Death but *Anno Domini*, Latin for "Year of the Lord"). Today it is more common to see BCE (Before the Common Era) and CE (Common Era) because Jews, Muslims and others do not regard Jesus as the center point of history.

Another thing we don't know for certain is the day Jesus was born. The great celebratory feasts and festivals in the early church were Good Friday—called "good" because it was the day Jesus died to reconcile us with God—and Easter, from *Eostre*, an Anglo-Saxon spring goddess. (For many today, Christmas is the most widely celebrated holy day.) Jesus' birth date, which we celebrate on December 25 as Christmas—from the Old English *Christes messe*, meaning "Christ's Mass"—was established by Constantine, the first Christian emperor of the Roman Empire, in the year 336.

The association of Santa Claus with Christmas comes from Bishop Nicholas of Myra—Claus is an abbreviation for Nicholas—the patron saint of children who, according to legend, rewarded good children by putting presents in their shoes while they were asleep. Nicholas was one of the bishops at the Council of Nicea in 325.

For many centuries the Eastern church celebrated Christ's birth on January 6, the day of Epiphany—the day of Christ's manifestation to the Gentiles (the magi). This allowed the birth narratives of Luke and Matthew to be harmonized, with the shepherds from the fields visiting Jesus in the manger on the day he was born, December 25, and the traveling magi visiting the family later, after Jesus had been born, on January 6.

Brief Outline of Jesus' Public Ministry

Herod was fearful of those he considered rival claimants to his throne. When he heard that one whom the magi called the "King of the Jews" had been born in Bethlehem, he ordered the killing of "all the children in and around Bethlehem who were two years old or under" (Matthew 2:16). Herod died in 4 BC. Jesus was born one or two years before Herod's death, most likely in 6 or 5 BC. Jesus spent the first thirty-two years of his life in Nazareth. (Luke 3:23 says that "Jesus was about thirty years old when he began his work." The word *about* could easily mean that Jesus was in his early thirties when he "began his work.") Nazareth was an insignificant agricultural village in Galilee, with a population of only two or three hundred people. We know very little about Jesus' growing-up years. Scholars believe that he and his brothers worked as stonemasons and carpenters building Herod Antipas's capital in Sepphoris, a city four miles north of Nazareth that had a population of some 40,000 people. (Antipas later moved his capital to Tiberias on the coast of the Sea of Galilee.) The following is a brief outline of Jesus' public life and ministry.

- The prophet Malachi said that Elijah, who was taken directly to heaven, would return to proclaim the coming of the Lord (Malachi 3:1 and 4:5). In the year 27, John the Baptist or Baptizer, the Elijah-like messenger prophesied by Malachi, announces that Jesus is the one Israel has long been waiting for and baptizes him in the River Jordan. Jesus receives God's Spirit (Mark 1:9–11) and is led into the wilderness, where he is confronted and mocked by Satan.

- Following his testing, Jesus returns to Galilee, proclaiming:
"The kingdom of God has come near; repent and believe
in the good news" (Mark 1:15).

- Jesus appoints twelve to be his disciples and begins his
ministry, much of which occurs in and around Capernaum,
a fishing village and commercial center on the northwest
shore of the Sea of Galilee, which becomes his hometown
after he is rejected by the people of Nazareth (Matthew
4:13). The crowds are amazed at Jesus' teachings and
healings, but they do not recognize him as the hoped-for
Messiah.

- Conflicts arise between Jesus and the religious leaders
concerning Jesus' association with sinners (tax collectors,
lepers, the demon-possessed), his nonobservance of
certain Jewish rituals (washing before meals and fasting)
and breaking the Jewish law against work on the Sabbath.
After Jesus heals a man with a shriveled hand on the
Sabbath, the Pharisees and the Herodians (Jews who
favored the continued rule and policies of Herod Antipas)
conspire "how to destroy him" (Mark 3:6).

- At Caesarea Philippi, Jesus asks his disciples, "Who do
you say that I am?" Peter answers, "You are the Messiah"
(Mark 8:29). Peter gives the right answer, but he and the
disciples do not understand that Jesus will suffer and
die, even though he tells them three times that he will be
handed over to the authorities and be killed.

- Jesus journeys to Jerusalem to celebrate Passover, a
religious obligation for adult Jews who were financially and
physically able to travel to Jerusalem. He goes to the temple
on the first Monday after Palm Sunday and overturns the
tables of the moneychangers, publicly challenging the
temple priests on their own turf, which leads them to seek
ways "to kill him" (Mark 11:15–18).

- Jesus celebrates a last supper with his disciples. He washes their feet, is betrayed by Judas Iscariot, arrested by the temple guards, convicted by the Sanhedrin on grounds of blasphemy—not because he claimed to be the Messiah (many claimed to be the Messiah, both before and after Jesus) but because he claimed to be divine (Mark 14:61–63)—and is sentenced to death by crucifixion by Pontius Pilate (Rome did not allow its subject peoples the right of capital punishment, which is why the Jewish leaders had to go to Pilate).

- Jesus is scourged by the soldiers at Antonia Fortress (the Roman barracks in Jerusalem), denied by Simon Peter, crucified between two criminals, and buried in the family tomb of Joseph of Arimathea. Three days later Jesus is raised from the dead to confirm that he was and is the messianiac Son of God.

Jesus' Baptism, Testing and Disciples

The years before Jesus appeared at the Jordan—the years prior to the year 27—are referred to as Jesus' "hidden years." Jesus steps on the stage of history with his baptism by his cousin John (the two were related through their mothers, according to Luke 1:36), which launches him on his public ministry. The baptism accounts are very sparse in the Gospels: only three verses in Mark (1:9-11). The emphasis in the New Testament is not on the beginning of Jesus' public ministry, his baptism, but on the end and climax of his ministry, his death and resurrection. Scholars disagree about the meaning of Jesus' baptism. John baptized "for the repentance of sins" and Jesus was sinless. New Testament scholar Everett Harrison said that Jesus submitted to John's baptism to identify with those whom he came to save.

Following his baptism, Jesus is tested by Satan for forty days in the Judean wilderness ("tested" rather than "tempted," as Abraham was on Mount Moriah). The number *forty* is biblical shorthand for a long period of time, as in the forty days of rain during the great flood in Genesis 7:4; Moses' forty days on Mount Sinai; the spies' forty-day reconnaissance mission in Canaan; Israel's forty years in the wilderness; and the forty days between Jesus' resurrection and ascension in Acts 1:3.

Inasmuch as Jesus was alone in the wilderness, the account of his testing must have been told to the disciples at a later date, along with other personal material in the Gospels (see Mark 4:34).

The word *disciple* comes from a word meaning "student" or "apprentice." There were disciples in the Old Testament—Isaiah, for instance, had disciples (Isaiah 8:16)—but the term owes its popularity to the New Testament, where it usually refers to "one of the Twelve." Peter was the first disciple whom Jesus called (Mark 1:16-17). He is portrayed as the "chairman of the board," the one who confesses Jesus as the Messiah (Mark 8:29) and who most often speaks for the disciples. The brothers James and John are also prominent and, together with Peter, comprise the inner circle of Jesus' disciples in the Gospels and the book of Acts: they are always named first in the lists of the disciples; they alone go with Jesus to the Mount of Transfiguration; and they are asked by Jesus to pray with him in the Garden of Gethsemane at the end of his life.

It is believed that the disciples came from Galilee, with the exception of Judas Iscariot, who many scholars believe came from southern Judea. They were working men, probably middle class, and included two sets of fishermen brothers—Andrew and Peter, who were John the Baptist's disciples before they were Jesus' disciples (John 1:35–42), and James and John, the sons of Zebedee. The other eight disciples are less prominent in the Gospels. Jesus chose his disciples from among his many followers (Luke mentions seventy in verse 10:1), which Jesus commissions to be the new patriarchs of Israel.

In addition to disciples, there were also apostles, those sent forth to preach the good news. All of the disciples were apostles, but not all of the apostles were disciples. There is no indication that Paul, for instance, ever saw or met Jesus until he did so on the road to Damascus.

Jesus' Threefold Mission

What was Jesus' mission, that is, what did he come to do? First, he came *to reveal God.* He said, "The Father and I are one" (John 10:30) and "Whoever has seen me has seen the Father" (John 14:9). Paul says that Jesus was "the image of the invisible God" (Colossians 1:15). The author of the letter to the Hebrews says that Jesus was "the exact imprint of God's very being" (Hebrews 1:3).

Second, Jesus came *to announce the kingdom of God* (Mark 1:15). Scholars refer to the kingdom of God as both *already* (in Jesus, evidenced by his miracles) and *not yet* ("Thy kingdom come"). The kingdom of God does not mean a kingdom, like the United Kingdom; it means the kingly rule or reign of God. It is a spiritual concept, not a political one. New Testament scholar Oscar Cullmann said that Jesus' first coming was like D-Day, the day the Allied Forces landed at Normandy in June 1944, which signaled the beginning of the end of the war in Europe. Jesus' second coming will be V-Day, the day when he comes in power and glory to reign over the earth. As Christians, we know the decisive day—Jesus' life, death and resurrection—has come. The only unknown is the date of the final victory (V-Day), as it was when the Allied Forces landed in France in 1944.

Third, and most important, Jesus came *to redeem humankind of its sins*—for not loving God with our whole heart (Mark

12:28–30); for not obeying his commandments (1 John 5:3); for not showing love and mercy to our neighbors (John 15:12-13). Christianity regards all of the circumstances surrounding Jesus' death, including the betrayal of Judas, as necessary ingredients in God's plan of redemption, which Jesus confirms at the Last Supper when he says, regarding Judas, "It is to fulfill the scripture [that] the one who ate my bread has lifted his heel against me" (John 13:18).

Jesus' Death

Most scholars believe that Jesus was crucified on April 7 in the year 30. Why was he put to death? This is a two-part question. First, why did Jesus go to Jerusalem to celebrate Passover, knowing that he would be killed there (Mark 10:32-34)? Second, why was he put to death four days after his appearance at the temple? As to the first question, Jesus' mission was to die a sacrificial death to redeem and restore us (Mark 10:45). If he had died of an illness or old age, he would not have died for our sins.

As to the second question, why did the Sadducees want Jesus killed, and why did Pontius Pilate, knowing that Jesus was innocent (Luke 23: 13-15), agree to his crucifixion? The Sadducees were afraid that Jesus appearance during Passover would provoke an uprising that would bring a brutal response from Rome, and as Jewish leaders they would be the first casualties, so he had to be silenced. The reasons for their concern were many: Passover celebrated the deliverance of Israel from foreign rule; it was believed that the Messiah would appear during Passover; Jesus came from Galilee, an area seething with anti-Roman resentment; and Jerusalem was overflowing with tens of thousands of pilgrims who had come to celebrate Passover.

As for Pilate, he was on bad terms with the Jews for erecting emblems of Emperor Tiberius in Jerusalem (graven images) and for appropriating money from the temple treasury to build an aqueduct. The Jewish leaders said to Pilate, "If you release this man, you are no friend of the emperor" (John 19:12), implying, perhaps, that they would go to Rome to have him removed, as they had Archelaus.

Christianity presents Pilate in an unfavorable light—"crucified under Pontius Pilate"—but he must have been an effective administrator because Rome allowed him to rule the ever-troublesome Jews for ten years. Pilate would have known about Jesus, who traveled and taught throughout Palestine; and it would have been natural for him as the governor to have had a file on Jesus, whom he must have considered innocent of any charge or crime because he never arrested him—though at the end, to appease the Jews, he handed Jesus over to his soldiers, who beat and crucified him.

Jesus' death was by crucifixion, a cruel, shameful method of execution. Crucifixion was preceded by flogging to weaken the victim's strength, thereby shortening the time it would take him to die. Crosses were hung in public places. Jesus was executed at the Place of the Skull—*Golgotha* in Aramaic, a language related to Hebrew that was widely spoken in Palestine, and *Calvary* in Latin—with a sign declaring the accused's crime as a warning to others. Jesus' sign read: "King of the Jews," implying that he claimed to be a king who opposed the Roman emperor. (The Sanhedrin's charge that Jesus was guilty of blasphemy would not have warranted Roman execution.) The final humiliation came at the end: victims were stripped naked and their bodies left to scavenging birds and animals. Crucifixion, because of its inhuman cruelty, was abolished by Emperor Constantine in the year 337.

Jesus' sacrificial death is the essence of the "good news," for it is by believing in his salvific death that we are redeemed of our sins and reconciled with God. Some mistakenly think we are redeemed and justified by Jesus' resurrection. The great churchman John Stott (1921-2011), in *The Cross of Christ*, his most important book, said that it "was by [Jesus'] death, not his resurrection, that our sins were dealt with." He cites the apostle Paul, who wrote that "Christ died for our sins" (1 Corinthians 15:3). Nowhere in the New Testament, Stott says, is it written that "Christ rose for our sins." Jesus' resurrection confirmed his mission to die a perfect, efficacious, saving death to cover our sins against God and our neighbors.

Jesus' Resurrection

The New Testament has twelve separate accounts of Jesus appearing to his disciples, to Paul and to others after his resurrection. The accounts were written as fact, as something that actually occurred; they emphasize the element of surprise—no one was expecting what happened on Easter morning, even though Jesus said he would be raised on the third day (Mark 8:31, 9:31 and 10:33); and they struggle to describe Jesus' post-resurrection body, which was physical (Jesus ate, drank and spoke), but could also pass through doors.

Some question the validity of the resurrection narratives because they contain different details, which are hard to reconcile (numbers of people, names, angels, grave clothes, appearances in Galilee and Jerusalem). This, however, makes them all the more believable. If they were identical, we would be suspicious that the writers had copied one another to make their accounts all agree.

The esteemed New Testament scholar Bruce Metzger (1914–2007), in his book *The New Testament: Its Background, Growth, & Content,* tells about two different accounts of Hannibal crossing the Alps, one by the Greek historian Polybius, the other by the Roman historian Livy. Metzger says, "By no stretch of the imagination [can these two accounts] be harmonized, yet no one doubts that Hannibal most certainly arrived in Italy. Differences in the accounts of Jesus' resurrection cannot be used to prove that the resurrection did not take place."

Though the four accounts have different details, they all agree on two main points: First, that Jesus was crucified, died and was buried (the scriptures say "buried," but Jesus was not buried in the ground, as people are today; he was placed in a tomb). Second, that he was raised from the dead—the Gospels do not tell us how Jesus was raised, only that he was—and that he appeared to many people on and following Easter Sunday (see Paul's list of people to whom Jesus appeared in 1 Corinthians 15:5-8).

The Christian writer Frederick Buechner, in his book *The Magnificent Defeat,* said, "Unless something very real took place on that strange, confused [Easter] morning, there would be no New Testament, no church and no Christianity." Why not? We'll come to this later.

The Names and Titles of Jesus

We often think of Christ as Jesus' second name or surname. Originally, Christ was a title, not a name. In the ancient world there were no surnames. People were named after their father (Jesus would have been Jesus bar [son of] Joseph) or where they came from (Joseph of Arimathea) or some activity (Simon the tanner). There are some fifty names and titles for Jesus, among them Lord, Savior, Emmanuel (God with us), Rabbi, the Galilean, Master (a title of respect), the Nazarene, Son of David (a messianic title), the Carpenter, the Prophet, the Lamb of God, the Word of God (John 1:1), the Lion of Judah, and the Alpha and the Omega, the first and last letters of the Greek alphabet, meaning Jesus was the beginning and will be the end.

The three most common titles are Messiah, Son of God and Son of Man. *Messiah* comes from a Hebrew word meaning "the anointed of God" (the Greek word for Messiah is *Christos*, from which we get the English word *Christ*), which Jesus affirms or consents to in his trial before the Jewish Council on Maundy Thursday. *Son of God* is a title that expresses Jesus' unique, filial relationship with God. It was a term that did not require any special knowledge for Gentile readers, as did Messiah. *Son of Man* is a term that Jesus often used to refer to himself, as when he said, "The Son of Man came . . . to give his life as a ransom for many" (Mark 10:45). No one is certain what "Son of Man" means. Some think it refers to words spoken by the prophet Daniel about "one like a son of man coming with the clouds of heaven" (7:13, NIV); others think it was used because it had no precise meaning, as did Messiah.

After Jesus' resurrection, the above names and titles mostly disappear. Jesus is thereafter called Jesus Christ, or just Christ, as when Paul says, "We proclaim Christ crucified" (1 Corinthians 1:23). Paul's favorite title for Jesus, however, is Lord, which spoke more directly to Paul's Greco-Roman readers.

Discussion Questions

1. Jesus lived in Nazareth, where he grew "in wisdom and in years" (Luke 2:52). Looking back over your growing-up years, who and what most influenced your life and faith?

2. At Caesarea Philippi, Jesus asked his disciples, "Who do you say that I am?" (Mark 8:29). How would you answer someone who asked you, "Who is Jesus and why is he so important?"

3. How did you come to faith? Was it your parents, or friends who were Christians, or reading one of the Gospels?

4

The Gospel Testimonies to Jesus

The word *gospel* derives from the Old English word "godspel"—
God's (good) story that Jesus died that "we may not perish but
have eternal life" (John 3:16, the most popular verse in the New
Testament, sometimes called the Gospel in a Nutshell). The
move from oral stories about Jesus to written narratives—the
Gospels—occurred because of the need for authentic, first-hand
testimonies to Jesus' life and ministry by those who knew him
(his followers were dying off) and because heretical views about
Jesus were beginning to arise.

The Gospels: Then and Now

Matthew was the most popular Gospel in the early church because it was believed to have been written by one of Jesus' disciples (Mark and Luke were not disciples and John's Gospel came later); it was comprehensive in scope, with both infancy and resurrection narratives; and it was the early church's manual of Christian instruction. Mark is important today, especially among scholars, because it has the strongest claim to being closest to Jesus, and because it was used by Matthew and Luke in writing their Gospels. Luke is the most complete and orderly of the Gospels and the only one with a sequel, The Acts of the Apostles. Luke's Gospel is often used in novels, plays and movies about the life of Jesus. John's Gospel has long been a favorite of Christians because of its sublime portrait of Jesus; it is also a favorite of Bible translators because of its limited vocabulary.

The Canonical Gospels

Some read the Gospels as biographies. They are not biographies in the modern sense because they cover only the last three years of Jesus' life. But they do follow a Greco-Roman biographical format and the early Christians probably read them as such to learn about Jesus' public life. They were not written, however, to give us the details of his life. They were written to tell us the meaning of his life: his salvific death on the cross.

Who chose the four Gospels in the New Testament? For years I thought this was done at the Council of Nicaea in 325. I was wrong. The four canonical Gospels traveled together as a unit as early as the year 100. New Testament scholar Charles Hill, in his book *Who Chose the Gospels*? said, "Nobody [chose the Gospels]. They almost seem to have chosen themselves through some [self-authenticating] process of natural selection." Hill quotes Eusebius (ca. 260-340), the first Christian historian, who wrote a 10-volume *Ecclesiastical History* of the early church. Eusebius said the disciple John mentions the Gospels of Matthew, Mark and Luke and says that he is writing a Gospel of his own, which indicates there was a fourfold Synoptics-plus-John canon two hundred years before Nicaea.

The Gospel Narratives

On Christmas Eve, 1776, George Washington led his rag-tag army across the icy Delaware River to Trenton, New Jersey, in a surprise attack on Britain's Hessian mercenaries. Is the story true? There were no observers who saw Washington cross the Delaware. The reason we believe the story is true is because it was told by those who were with Washington when his army surprised the Hessians. Jesus fed 5,000 men and their families —the feeding of "the multitudes"—a story that appears in all four Gospels. The reason we believe the story is true is because it was told and passed on by those who, like Washington's soldiers, were present at and witnessed the event.

What about other stories in the Gospels? New Testament scholar Richard Bauckham, in his book *Jesus and the Eyewitnesses,* makes a strong case for the validity of the Gospel narratives, which he believes are based on the remembrances of those who personally knew Jesus and were with him during his public ministry. Biblical scholar Tom Wright said, "In a characteristic *tour de force,* Richard Bauckham draws on his unparalleled knowledge of the world of the first Christians to argue not only that the Gospels do indeed contain eyewitness testimony, but that their first readers would certainly have recognized them as such."

Beginning in the mid-60s, the various remembrances were combined into written narratives, which were later called Gospels. Most scholars believe that Mark was the first Gospel, written between 65 and 70, followed by Matthew and Luke in the 80s and John in the 90s. A minority view is that all four Gospels were written before the year 70 because they do not mention the destruction of the temple by the Romans in that year (see Luke 21:5-6).

The Authorship of the Gospels

We think because the Gospels have names—"The Gospel According to . . ."—that we know who wrote them. The Gospels, however, are anonymous: the authors did not add their names to their narratives as Paul and others did to their letters. This does not mean that we have no idea who may have written them. According to the British scholar R.T. France, "There is no evidence that any of the Gospels ever existed [without their present names], nor is there any variation in the names of those to whom they are attributed." The Gospels were named to allow readers to differentiate them one from another and for purposes of liturgical reading. During the Enlightenment (pages 133-135), questions arose concerning the authorship of the Gospels, which continue to this day.

The Structure of the Gospels

Each Gospel has a different beginning. Matthew begins with Jesus' family tree, Mark with Jesus' baptism, Luke with Zechariah in the temple, John before the creation of the world. The first three Gospels have a similar story line; John has a longer timeframe (three Passover celebrations) and a different geography (more about Jesus in Judea than in Galilee). The climax in all four Gospels is Jesus' arrest, trials, crucifixion, burial and resurrection.

The first half of each Gospel has to do with Jesus teaching throughout Galilee and Judea, interspersed with healings and miracles to show that Jesus is more than just an itinerant preacher-teacher. The second halves have to do, first, with Jesus' journey to Jerusalem, during which he prepares his disciples to carry on his mission; and second, with Jesus' passion, death and resurrection.

The Gospel Audiences

We read the Gospels as we do other written works. In the first century, which had a very low literacy rate, the Gospels were read aloud in house groups rather than privately. To help listeners follow their stories, the writers often used triads—repeating stories and sayings three times—an example being Jesus' three passion predictions concerning his coming death in Matthew, Mark and Luke.

The audiences for the Gospels were twofold. First, they were written for specific communities. Mark wrote to Roman Christians suffering persecution under Nero; Matthew wrote to Jewish Christians who believed that Jesus was the hoped-for Messiah; Luke, a non-Palestinian Gentile, wrote to an educated citizenry in Asia Minor and Europe; John wrote to Christians in Ephesus. Second, the Gospels were written for Christians throughout the Mediterranean world, with scrolls traveling over land and by sea from one city to another. There is scholarly consensus that Matthew and Luke used Mark's Gospel in writing their Gospels, and given Eusebius's history of the early church (page 70), there is good reason to believe that John had access to all three.

The Historical Jesus

The study of Jesus has become a growth industry, with new books being published every year. Stephen Prothero, in his book *God Is Not One,* says, "There are an estimated 187,000 books about Jesus in 500 different languages [including] roughly 17,000 in the Library of Congress."

The serious study of Jesus got underway in the first half of the nineteenth century with David Friedrich Strauss's book *The Life of Jesus Critically Examined* (1835). Strauss said the Gospels were collections of legends and myths, which led to Strauss losing his lectureship position at the University of Tübingen. The decades that followed saw an obsessive "quest" to find the real Jesus, which many thought could be done by stripping away the supernatural aspects of the Gospels. The result was a human-only Jesus, which opened the door to liberal Protestantism and its emphasis on religious experience as the basis for Christian faith. The quest came to an end with Albert Schweitzer's classic study, *The Quest of the Historical Jesus* (1906). Schweitzer's conclusion, after reading some sixty lives of Jesus, was that "he comes to us as one unknown."

In 1953, after a half-century of no "quests," the German theologian Ernst Käsemann led the search back to the view that much more could be known about Jesus than was previously suspected. In the 1980s, a Third Quest was begun by Tom Wright, E. P. Sanders and others. The third questers took more seriously the Jesus we find in the Gospels, especially his Jewishness, and asked: If Jesus was a mere teacher and healer, as some claim, why was he crucified? And how are we to account for the fact that within a generation of his crucifixion there were large communities of believers in his resurrection throughout the Roman Empire?

Christianity is based on a real person, Jesus of Nazareth, who lived in Palestine 2,000 years ago; who died a sacrificial death in Jerusalem to reconcile us with God; who was raised from the dead to confirm his mission; who is coming again at the end of the age to reign over planet Earth.

The Synoptic Gospels

Since the late nineteenth century, Matthew, Mark and Luke have been called the Synoptic Gospels. The word *synoptic* comes from "syn" (with or together) and "optos" (seeing, as in optics), meaning these three Gospels present a somewhat similar story.

The Priority of Mark

Scholars believe that Mark was the first Gospel to be written. One reason is because Matthew and Luke include large portions of Mark's narrative in their own Gospels—90 percent in Matthew and 50 percent in Luke—in places verbatim; also they generally follow Mark's storyline, whereas in their handling of common non-Markan material, referred to by scholars as Q (next section), they often disagree with one another. And they smooth out Mark's grammar and choppiness, soften his statements about the disciples' failure to understand Jesus, and they speak more reverently about Jesus—all of which argues for Mark's Gospel coming before the other two.

If Mark was the first Gospel, Matthew and Luke must have felt the need to tell their readers more about Jesus' life and teachings. But if Matthew and Luke were first, it is hard to see why Mark was included in the canon: he has no birth narrative, his shorter ending has no resurrection appearances, and he has no sermons and very few parables.

The Formation of the Synoptic Gospels

Mark and Peter were together in Rome at the end of Peter's life (1 Peter 5:13). According to tradition, Mark's Gospel is based on Peter's recollections of his three years with Jesus. Some fifteen years later, Matthew and Luke, using Mark as a source document, wrote their own Gospels. In addition to Mark, it seems that Matthew and Luke had in their possession another source, referred to by nineteenth-century German scholars as Q, for the German word *Quelle* (source). Some think that Q was a written document, but no Q document has ever been found. The rationale for a Q hypothesis is that Matthew and Luke contain, in common with one another, some 230 verses not found in Mark. Also, Matthew and Luke have information that each gleaned independently of the other, for instance, their different birth narratives, different sermons on the mount and on the plain, and different parables.

Mark: The Foundation Gospel

Mark's Gospel was long neglected because of its alleged incompleteness. Some think the only reason Mark was included in the canon is because the church fathers believed that it was based on Peter's remembrances of Jesus' life and teachings. Today Mark is popular among scholars because it was the first attempt to put the oral stories of and about Jesus into written form, and because it was used by Matthew and Luke in writing their Gospels. Scholars, with Mark in front of them, can see how Matthew and Luke edited Mark for their intended readers. The American novelist Reynolds Price, in his foreword to *Mark as Story*, said, "The good news according to Mark has proved the most enduringly powerful narrative in the history of Western civilization, perhaps in the history of the world."

We wish we knew Mark's sources, but we don't, other than Papias's claim that Mark was Peter's colleague and interpreter. Some have called Mark the "Gospel of Peter" because Peter is the most prominent person in Mark's narrative. Timothy Keller, in his book *King's Cross*, based on Mark's Gospel, said, "Nothing happens [in Mark] in which Peter is not present." One thing we do know is that Mark had strong Christian mentors, among them his cousin Barnabas (Colossians 4:10), with whom he did mission work in Cyprus (Acts 15:39); the apostle Paul, with whom he traveled in Asia Minor (Acts 13:13) and worked with in Rome (2 Timothy 4:11); and the apostle Peter, who refers to Mark as "my son" (1 Peter 5:13).

Mark's Gospel is action-packed, as if written to Christians hiding in the catacombs and on the run, as seen in his frequent use (some forty times) of words like *at once, immediately* and *quickly*. Mark begins his Gospel with "the good news of Jesus Christ," who he goes on to say was more that just the Messiah: he was the very "Son of God" (1:1).

John Mark

According to scholar-theologian Thomas Oden, in his book *The African Memory of Mark*, Mark was born of Diasporan Jews in Cyrene, Libya. The family later moved to Palestine and settled in Jerusalem.

Mark's Gospel was written from Rome, most likely in the years immediately following Peter's martyrdom in the mid-60s. According to Papias (60–137), the second-century bishop of Hierapolis (Asia Minor), "Mark became Peter's interpreter and wrote down accurately all that he remembered of the things said and done by the Lord, but not, however, in order" (Mark was more interested in what Jesus said and did than in his chronology).

It is unlikely that the second Gospel would have been attributed to him—he was neither a disciple nor, are we told, a follower of Jesus—unless he was, in fact, the author. According to tradition, then, the author of the first or earliest of the four Gospels was Mark, also called John Mark (Acts 12:12, 25; 15:37).

Mark was the son of Mary, a widow of some means who lived in Jerusalem (Acts 12:12). Mary's home may have been the location of the Last Supper. If so, the story of the "young man" in the Garden of Gethsemane in Mark 14:51–52 may be Mark's "secret autograph." (Some think that each Gospel has a secret autograph; others consider such notions little more than silly speculation.) Mark and Barnabas accompanied Paul on his first missionary journey (ca. 46–48), and then went off on their own.

The Christian historian Eusebius said that Mark founded the church in Alexandria, Egypt. Thomas Oden, who calls Mark the Father of African Christianity in the book above, says that he was martyred in Alexandria in the year 68 for opposing the worship of idols. In 829, Venetian merchants smuggled Mark's bones out of Egypt in clay jars and buried them in Saint Mark's Basilica in Venice.

Structure and Audience

The Lutheran theologian Martin Kähler calls Mark's Gospel "a passion narrative with an extended introduction." The word *passion* refers to Jesus' agony from his arrest in the Garden of Gethsemane on Maundy Thursday to his death on the cross the following day. (The Latin word *maundy* means "command," referring to Jesus' command "to love one another as I have loved you" in John 15:12-14.) Mark's Gospel, however, is more than a passion narrative; it is a very sophisticated literary composition. In chapter 1, Mark combines several stories together to show a typical day in the life of Jesus. The stories probably occurred over several days or weeks; Mark bunches them together for effect. And he weaves stories together, like the healing of the woman with the hemorrhage and the raising of Jairus's daughter in chapter 5. And he splits stories apart, for instance, mentioning in chapter 1 that John the Baptist was put in prison, but waiting until chapter 6 to tell us that John was beheaded. And he gives us the names of Jesus' brothers—James, Joseph, Judas and Simon—and tells us that he also had sisters (6:3).

Mark lived in Jerusalem and must have witnessed the final days of Jesus' life, including his death on the cross, which is the central focus of his narrative. He wants his readers to know from the beginning that Jesus is going to die. In chapter 3, for instance, we read that the Pharisees and the Herodians plotted together "how to destroy [Jesus]" after he healed a man on the Sabbath (3:6). This is followed by hints and statements in almost every chapter of Jesus' coming death. The Gospels have huge gaps in the Jesus story, but when they come to the last week in his life they give us a day-by-day account of his activities; and when they reach their climax on Good Friday, almost an hour-by-hour account.

A key Markan verse leading up to Jesus' passion is 10:45, in which Jesus says, "The Son of Man came not to be served but to serve, and to give his life as a 'ransom' for many." In the first century, the Greek word *lutron* was money paid to purchase a slave in the marketplace. Jesus uses the word *lutron* to describe his purchasing, through his death on the cross, our acquittal from sin to reconcile us with God.

As mentioned, the Gospels have a two-part structure. The hinge verse in Mark's Gospel is Peter's confession of Jesus as "the Messiah" (8:29), following which Jesus tells the disciples that he "must undergo great suffering, and be rejected by the elders, the chief priests and the scribes, and be killed, and after three days rise again" (8:31). Given Jesus' statement that he would be raised on the third day, it is strange that there are no post-resurrection stories in Mark's Gospel, at least in the shorter ending of his Gospel, which ends at 16:8. Some believe the beginning and ending verses of Mark's Gospel were broken off from the continued rolling and unrolling of the original scroll, with verses 16:9–20 added later to complete Mark's narrative. Markan scholars are on both sides of this issue.

Mark's readers appear to be Gentiles because there is no Jewish genealogy in his narrative; there are very few Old Testament references; some Jewish words and customs are explained (see 7:3–4); and it is a Roman centurion, the commander of a century (one hundred) foot-soldiers, who declared at the foot of the cross: "Truly this man was God's Son" (15:39).

Mark's Message

Nero is believed to have set fire to a residential section of Rome in July 64, on which he later built himself a large, luxurious palace. To counter cries that he was responsible for the fire, he blamed and persecuted the Christians. Some were covered with pitch and burned alive as torches in his gardens; others were dressed in animal skins and torn apart by wild dogs; some were sewn in sacks with rocks and thrown in the Tiber River; others were killed by wild beasts in the Colosseum.

Mark's Gospel is a "tract for hard times." His readers were probably wondering if Jesus was good news or a false hope: Jesus' forerunner, John the Baptist, was beheaded; Jesus himself was crucified; two of the church's greatest heroes, Peter and Paul, had just been martyred; and the persecution of Christians in Rome was on the rise. Mark writes about the crucified-risen Christ to strengthen the faith and courage of his readers, telling them that hoping in Jesus is a real hope—Mark's good news for the Romans—just as it was for his disciples and followers when he told them: "Those who lose their life for my sake and for the sake of the Gospel will [be saved]" (8:35).

Jesus' Miracles

A unique feature of Mark's Gospel is his use of miracle stories: one-third of his narrative is comprised of miracles, compared with only 20 percent in the other three. The miracles attributed to Jesus are not called "miracles"; they are signs of his divinity. The vast majority are *healing* miracles: exorcising demons, curing lepers and giving sight to the blind. The others are *nature* miracles: stilling the wind, feeding the multitudes and raising people from the dead (Jairus's daughter in all three Synoptics, the son of the widow of Nain in Luke, and Lazarus in John).

The miracles point to Jesus' true identity. When the disciples of John the Baptist ask Jesus, "Are you the one who is to come, or are we to wait for another?" Jesus says, "Go and tell John what you have seen and heard: the blind receive their sight, the lame walk, the lepers are cleansed, the deaf hear, the dead are raised [and] the poor have good news brought to them" (Luke 7:18–23).

The Gospels record that Jesus performed some thirty-five "miracles." For those who believe that Jesus was and is the Son of the one who created "the heavens and the earth," there is no reason to question his miracles. For those who don't believe this, there is nothing that will convince them that miracles are even possible. The twentieth-century apologist C. S. Lewis (1898-1963), in his book *Christian Reflections,* said, "Who, after swallowing the camel of the Resurrection, can strain at such gnats as the feeding of the multitudes?"

Matthew: The Jewish-Christian Gospel

Matthew was the most popular Gospel in the early church because its author was believed to have been one of Jesus' disciples, which Mark was not; it has both infancy and resurrection narratives (Mark has neither); and its organized teachings, like the Sermon on the Mount, made it ideal for instructing new believers.

If Mark was the first Gospel, why does Matthew have pride of place? Because it was once believed that Matthew *was* the first Gospel and because it is a more complete narrative. Also, it is the best bridge between the two testaments: the last book in the Protestant Old Testament has Israel waiting for "the Lord whom you seek," the long-awaited Messiah (Malachi 3:1). Matthew begins his Gospel with Jesus, "who is called the Messiah" (1:16).

Some commentators refer to Matthew as the Catholic Gospel. At Caesarea Philippi, Peter confesses Jesus to be "the Messiah, the Son of the Living God." Jesus answers, saying, "You are Peter, and on this rock I will build my church" (16:16-18). Rome understands this verse to mean that Jesus gave Peter the authority to be his vicar or representative on earth, and that Peter passed this authority on in a continuous line of "apostolic succession" from one pope to the next (the current pope, Francis, is the 266th successor of Peter). Protestant scholars say there is nothing in the passage to suggest that Peter's leadership was meant to be passed on in perpetuity to his successors. They read "on this rock" as referring to Peter's rock-like confession of Jesus as the Messiah or Christ, not to Peter per se.

Matthew, the Tax Collector

Matthew's Gospel is attributed to "Matthew the tax collector" (10:3), one of Jesus' twelve disciples. In Mark and Luke, he is called Levi, one of several people in the New Testament with two names, among them Simon Peter, John Mark and Saul who became Paul. Tax collectors were despised because they collaborated with the Romans, levied taxes on fellow Jews, and allegedly had no principles (Matthew's "secret autograph"?). Many commentators believe that Matthew worked for Herod Antipas near Capernaum, collecting custom taxes from traders carrying merchandise on the road from Damascus (Syria) to Acre, a city on the Mediterranean Sea. If so, Matthew would have known how to write and keep orderly records and could have written down many of Jesus' teachings, which are a central feature of his Gospel.

Matthew's Authorship

The Gospels, as mentioned, are anonymous: the authors did not sign their names to their writings. There is a good deal of skepticism regarding Matthew's authorship of the Gospel that bears his name. One reason is because it includes 90 percent of Mark's Gospel. Critics ask, "Why would someone who was with Jesus borrow so heavily from someone who was not, including the account of his own call?" Some believe that Matthew's Gospel was written by his disciples, which is why they had to rely so heavily on Mark. It is supposed that they took Mark's Gospel, the Q materials, Matthew's written remembrances of Jesus' teachings like the Sermon on the Mount and special materials like his birth narrative, and wrote an expanded Gospel which they attributed to their teacher, a practice that honored the one for whom the book was named. Today we might call this plagiarism. In the ancient world, where there were no copyright laws or rules, the use of other people's writings was a normal, accepted practice. Perhaps this is the meaning of "according to," that is, Matthew's Gospel was written according to Matthew (the source) rather than by Matthew (the author).

Structure and Audience

Matthew begins his Gospel with Jesus' genealogy (1:1-17), which may seem strange to us, but would have been very meaningful to his readers: Jesus descending from Father Abraham, through King David, down the Judean line from which the Messiah was to come, to Joseph, his "legal" father. Luke also has a genealogy (3:23-38), which is different from that of Matthew—different numbers of persons (41 in Matthew, 78 in Luke), different names of persons, and a different order of persons: Matthew starts with Abraham and ends with Joseph; Luke begins with Jesus and ends with Adam.

Matthew follows Mark's narrative, into which he inserts five discourses. Many commentators see this as Matthew's attempt to portray Jesus as the new Moses (Moses' five books of the Torah and Jesus' five discourses). The discourses have to do with discipleship (the Sermon on the Mount in chapters 5-7), mission (sending out the Twelve in 10), the kingdom of God (the growth and end-time parables in 13), community life (humbleness and forgiveness in 18) and the coming judgment (signs of the end of the age in 23-25). The discourses usually end with the words, "When Jesus had finished saying these things . . ."

Matthew's readers appear to be Jewish Christians because Jewish words and customs are not explained (his readers know what he was talking about). Matthew is seen by some as the most anti-Jewish of the Gospels, as in his seven woes against "the scribes and the Pharisees" in chapter 23. Some believe that Matthew has been responsible for Christian anti-Semitism because of Pilate saying, regarding Jesus, "I am innocent of this man's blood," and the Jews saying, "[Then let] his blood be on us and our children" (27: 24-25).

Matthew's Message

In Matthew, Jesus is the long-awaited Messiah, the One promised in the scriptures. Matthew sets forth Jesus' messiahship in two ways. First, in his genealogy from Abraham to David to Joseph to show that Jesus was from the house or line or lineage of David, from which the Messiah was to come (2 Samuel 7). Second, in his references to the prophecies of Isaiah, Micah, Hosea, Jeremiah and others, including eleven "fulfillment citations" (proof texts) to show that Jesus fulfilled what had been prophesied about the Messiah.

Jesus' Sermon on the Mount

Jesus' Sermon on the Mount—the most famous sermon of all time, though it takes only ten minutes to read—is Matthew's masterpiece. It is not called a sermon in Matthew; the term comes from Augustine. The "sermon" summarizes Jesus' teachings about how Christians are to live and act in the world, which even non-Christians like Gandhi have acclaimed. The sermon is presented as one long, continuous teaching, but many believe it is a collection of teachings Matthew heard from the lips of Jesus during his Galilean ministry, which he pieced together as a "sermon." We will look at the Sermon on the Mount in chapter 10.

Luke: The Universal Gospel

Luke's Gospel is the longest book in the New Testament, and Luke-Acts (as mentioned, Luke also wrote The Acts of the Apostles) comprises 25 percent of the New Testament. For many people, Luke's Gospel is their favorite Life of Christ. Someone once asked the late Scottish theologian James Denney to recommend a good book on Jesus. Denney said, "Have you read the one that Luke wrote?"

Luke was a second-generation Christian, that is, he did not know Jesus during his lifetime. He based his Gospel on the writings and eyewitness accounts of others (see 1:1-3). Luke is careful to name people and date events as though he is writing history (see 3:1-2), which he continues in his second volume, the outward movement of the good news. This allowed his two works to be taken seriously by readers in the Greco-Roman world. His intent, however, is theological: to show God working out his plan of salvation on the plane of history.

Luke addresses his "orderly account" to Theophilus, "so that [he] may know the truth concerning the things about which [he has] been instructed" (1:3-4). We don't know who Theophilus was. Luke calls him "most excellent," so he may have been a man of some importance. Many commentators think he was Luke's patron, who saw to the publication of his two writings (if so, Luke may have been the first Gospel to go public). Some, however, think that Luke was writing to all who love God—all of the Theophiluses of the world (including us)—because the word *theophilus* is the conjunction of *theo* (God) and *philia* (a Greek word for love).

Luke, the Physician

From the beginning, tradition has assigned the authorship of the third Gospel to Luke. There must have been compelling reasons for doing so because he was not one of Jesus' disciples. It is believed that Luke was a Gentile, though some dispute this because of his knowledge of things Jewish, which could easily have come from the apostle Paul, with whom he traveled. And he seems to have been a doctor, given his use of precise medical language and terms and Paul's reference to him as "the beloved physician" (Colossians 4:14).

It is believed that Luke met Paul at Troas on Paul's second journey in the early 50s; that he helped Paul start a church at Philippi, which he may have pastored for a time; that he later rejoined Paul and accompanied him to Jerusalem at the end of Paul's third journey, and then to Caesarea when Paul was imprisoned there; and that he sailed with Paul to Rome at the end of Paul's life. Some think the first person plural "we" passages in the book of Acts (16:9–17, 21:1–17 and 27:1–28:16) are Luke's "secret autograph." According to an ancient prologue to the Gospel, "Luke was a disciple of the apostles. He accompanied Paul until the latter's martyrdom, serving the Lord without distraction, for he had neither a wife nor children. He died at the age of eighty-four, full of the Holy Spirit."

Structure and Audience

Lukan scholar Darrell Bock (Dallas Theological Seminary) said Luke tells the story of Jesus from the ground up, beginning with his birth. John tells the story of Jesus from heaven down (there is nothing in John about Jesus' birth). We learn about Jesus, Bock says, in the Synoptics—who he was and what he said and did.

Luke also follows Mark's storyline, but he is more ambitious, polished, systematic and expansive in telling his story. The centerpiece of Luke's Gospel is Jesus' ten-chapter journey from Samaria to Jerusalem (9:51 to 19:27). A journey of this length would have taken only three or four days. In Luke's narrative it takes several months.

Luke seems to be writing to a Greco-Roman audience, which can be seen in his dedication to Theophilus, his literary style and vocabulary, his frequent use of Greek words like master rather than rabbi, his general avoidance of Semitisms like Messiah and Son of David, and his limited reference to Jewish customs.

Luke's Message

Matthew wrote that Jesus was the promised Messiah; Luke writes that Jesus was and is the universal Savior. His genealogy, for instance, goes beyond Abraham to Adam—to the beginning of life on earth: Jesus did not come to save only Israel; he came "to seek out and to save [all who are] lost" (19:10). Some call Jesus' homily in the synagogue at Nazareth Luke's "Gospel in a Nutshell" (4:16–21). Jesus understands himself to be anointed by the Spirit to bring the good news of salvation to the poor, the sick, the demon-possessed and the lost; to women as well as men (Luke names thirteen women not mentioned elsewhere); to lepers, tax collectors (Matthew and Zacchaeus), adulterers and adulteresses; and to the hated Samaritans and other despised members of society, even Roman soldiers (7:1–10).

Luke is not as terse and hurried as Mark, who can't wait to get on with his story; or as somber and harsh as Matthew ("Woe to you . . . "); or as otherworldly as John ("In the beginning was the Word . . . and the Word was God"). Luke is hopeful, optimistic and encouraging. Jesus' message is that salvation is here and now, saying (italics added), "*Today* [in the synagogue in Nazareth] this scripture has been fulfilled in your hearing" (4:21); "*Today* salvation has come to this [Zacchaeus's] house" (19:9); "*Today* you [the so-called penitent thief who was crucified with Jesus] will be with me in Paradise" (23:43).

Jesus' Parables

A special feature of Luke's Gospel is Jesus' parables. Luke has the most parables and the best-loved parables, which he skillfully weaves into his narrative, whereas Matthew (as in chapter 13) and Mark (in chapter 4) bunch them together. In chapter 10 we will we look at Jesus' parable of the sower, one of only a handful of parables found in all three synoptic Gospels, and four that are unique to Luke: the good Samaritan and the prodigal son, two of Jesus' best loved and most memorable parables, and two dealing with wealth and possessions, the rich farmer and the rich man and Lazarus.

John: The Fourth Gospel

I have spent most of my Gospel reading time in the three Synoptics, principally Mark and Luke. I have never spent much time in John until I took a class from pastor-author-teacher Darrell Johnson at Regent College in Vancouver, British Columbia. Johnson began each class by quoting from memory John's prologue (1:1-18), which begins with the logos—the Word of God, the self-expression of God—which became incarnate in Jesus and "lived among us."

John's Gospel stands apart from Matthew, Mark and Luke in terms of structure, style and content; the overlap is only 10 percent. Differences can be seen in John's omissions: he has no birth narrative, no baptism, no temptations, no exorcisms, no parables or Beatitudes, no Mount of Transfiguration, and no agony in the garden or on the cross. Differences can also be seen in John's additions: the wedding at Cana, Jesus and Nicodemus, the Samaritan woman at the well, healing the cripple at the pool and the man born blind, raising Lazarus from the dead, and washing the disciples' feet on the night before he was crucified. There are also geographical and chronological differences: in John, Jesus' ministry is primarily in Judea (John's focus is on Jerusalem, not Nazareth, Capernaum and villages in Galilee); and it extends over three years, rather than what appears to be only one year in the Synoptics (John's three years seems more accurate).

Why is John so different? Some believe John based his Gospel on his years with Jesus and chose to highlight different events than those recorded by Matthew, Mark and Luke. Others say John's intention was not to write a fourth synoptic Gospel but, instead, to supplement the other three with a personal reflection on the living, speaking, incarnate Word of God. Because John's Gospel is so different from the other three, it is often referred to, simply, as the Fourth Gospel.

John, the Disciple

John was the younger brother of James (the "Sons of Thunder," Mark 3:17) and, many think, the youngest of Jesus' twelve disciples. Many identify him as "the disciple whom [Jesus] loved" (John 19:26), who isn't named, perhaps out of modesty. Could this be John's "secret autograph"? While many think so, there are serious scholars who do not believe the apostle John and the "beloved disciple" are the same person. Then who was the disciple whom Jesus loved? Some think it was Lazarus. After he died, "Jesus wept" (11:35, the shortest verse in the Bible). The Jews said, "See how [Jesus] loved him." Lazarus, may have been *beloved* but he was not one of Jesus' disciples. Others think it was Simon Peter, to whom Jesus showed his love by redeeming him after Peter had denied him three times during his "trial" by the Sanhedrin.

There are five books in the New Testament that bear John's name: the Fourth Gospel, the three letters of John, and the book of Revelation, though some scholars doubt that John wrote the book of Revelation.

In the Synoptics, Jesus frequently ordered his followers "not to make him known" (Mark 3:12), referred to by some as the Messianic Secret. (If Jesus intended his messsiahship to be a secret, it was a poorly kept secret because people kept referring to him as the Messiah; and the more he told them not to make him known, the more they seemed to do so.) The reason that Jesus did not want to announce his messiahship before he was finished with his mission was that to do so may have resulted in his arrest and crucifixion as an enemy of Rome. With regard to the Gospel, the early church held that John, the son of Zebedee, is "the disciple who is testifying to these things and has written them, and we know that his testimony is true" (21:24).

Structure and Audience

As mentioned above, John does not follow the Synoptists' story line, nor is it clear to whom his Gospel is addressed, but he structures his narrative like the other three—a public ministry and a private ministry. The first half (chapters 1–12) has been called the Book of Signs—six public signs that point to Jesus' divinity: turning water into wine, feeding the multitudes, healing the official's son, the cripple and the man born blind, and the raising of Lazarus.

Darrell Johnson calls chapter 11 the center of John's Gospel. The resuscitation (not resurrection) of Lazarus demonstrated Jesus' power over death, which is one reason why passages from this chapter are often read at funerals and memorial services. Some ask why the raising of Lazarus, Jesus most stunning 'miracle,' does not appear in the other three Gospels. One reason may be that much of the material in the Synoptics is based on the remembrances and words of the apostle Peter, who is not mentioned as being present at the raising of Lazarus.

The second half of John's Gospel (13-21) has been called the Book of Glory—Jesus' hour, his glorification, his resurrection (Jesus' seventh and final sign). Many believe that John wrote his Gospel in Ephesus (western Turkey), the fourth largest city in the Roman Empire, where he lived out the final years of his life at the end of the first century.

Alan Culpepper, in his commentary on John's Gospel, says that John's readers are Greek-speaking Jews because some Jewish terms have to be translated (see 1:41); they have a general knowledge of the Jewish Scriptures and Jewish beliefs and practices; they have some familiarity with Jesus' public life, ministry, death and resurrection, perhaps from reading or hearing one of the Synoptic Gospels; and though they do not live in Palestine, they seem to have some familiarity with the geography of the Gospel story.

John's Message

John begins his narrative with the claim that Jesus is the one in whom "the Word became flesh and lived among us" (1:14). William Barclay (1907-1978), the popular Scottish Bible expositor, said, "This might well be the single greatest verse in the New Testament." Jesus' self-identification is much clearer in John than in the other three Gospels. In John, Jesus says, "I am in the Father and the Father is in me" (14:10). Jesus did not come to bring the message of eternal life; he *is* the message, the very incarnation of the message (see his "I ams" below); nor did he come to speak God's word, as the prophets did: he *was* and *is* the very Word itself.

The spiritual center of John's Gospel are chapters 14-17, in which Jesus sends his Spirit upon his followers. In chapter 15 Jesus said, "I am the true vine ... Abide [or remain] in me as I abide in you." I once heard a sermon in which the preacher said the word Christian is made up of two syllables, *Christ* and *ian*. He said "ian" means "I am nothing." To be *something*—to be reconciled with God—we need to be connected to and abide in Christ.

John tells us that he wrote his Gospel "so that you may come to believe that Jesus is the Messiah, the Son of God, and that through believing you may have life in his name" (20:31).

Jesus and Nicodemus

One of the most familiar stories in the New Testament is the meeting of Jesus and Nicodemus in chapter 3. (Nicodemus appears three times in John's Gospel, but nowhere in the Synoptics.) Nicodemus, who is called "a leader of the Jews" (3:1), comes to visit with Jesus at night, perhaps because he did not want to be seen with Jesus in the daylight or because he wanted an opportunity to visit with Jesus alone, without the crowds. He wants to talk about the kingdom of God. Jesus tells Nicodemus that to enter the kingdom he must be "born again." Our first birth is our biological birth: our birth from "below." Our second birth is our spiritual birth: our birth from "above." When we are born again we become a new creation, with a new purpose and a new will.

John's "I Ams"

A unique feature of John's Gospel is Jesus' seven "I am" statements, which appear in the center chapters (6–15). The "I ams" are metaphors Jesus uses to describe himself as "the way of salvation." He says, "Whoever comes to me . . . follows me . . . enters by me. . . believes in me . . . abides in me . . . will be saved." The Greek words *ego eimi*—"I am"—in John are the same words that appear in the Greek Septuagint when God says to Moses, "I Am Who I Am" (Exodus 3:14). In these passages Jesus says: "I am" the bread of life, the light of the world, the gate, the good shepherd, the resurrection and the life, the way, the truth and the life, and the true vine. We will look at Jesus' "I ams" in chapter 10.

The Gospels: Four Stories, One Jesus

Some say the Gospels are fiction because they have different portraits of Jesus. Not at all. When we read multiple biographies of a famous person like Abraham Lincoln, Winston Churchill or FDR, we find they often differ from one another in emphasis and detail, but each helps us to better understand the person than if we had only one biography. The same is true of the Gospels. The reason they seem different is because each author chose, in shaping his narrative, to emphasize different aspects of the Jesus story for his readers.

Mark wrote to those suffering persecution under Nero; Matthew to Jewish readers that the long-awaited Messiah has come; Luke to communities in the Greco-Roman world that Jesus is Lord, not Caesar; John to his community and the world at large that Jesus is the One in whom "[God] became flesh." Four testimonies, written from four different perspectives, about Jesus the Christ, who lived and died and rose again.

Discussion Questions

1. Which Gospel is your favorite? Have you ever shared one of the Gospels with a seeker or new believer?

2. Summarize the good news of and about Jesus as an outline or model for you and others to use in sharing Jesus' life, message and teachings with others.

3. A unique feature of the Gospels is Jesus' miracles. Have you ever experienced a miracle in your life, or known someone who has? If so, describe what happened?

5

Paul and the Outward Movement

Jesus' final charge to his disciples in Matthew's Gospel—the Great Commission—was to take the gospel to "all nations" (28:19), meaning to all peoples; and in the book of Acts to "the ends of the earth" (1:8), meaning throughout the Roman Empire. The Acts of the Apostles tells how this was done by Paul, Barnabas and others who took the gospel from Jerusalem, the center of the Judeo-Christian world, to Rome, the center of the socio-political world. The time frame of Acts is the first thirty years of the church, from Jesus' death, resurrection and ascension in the year 30 to the arrival of Paul in Rome around the year 60.

The Outward Movement

Howard Clark Kee, in his book *Understanding the New Testament,* said, "No one observing itinerant fisherman and village craftsmen trying to launch an apocalyptic movement in Palestine in the name of an executed Galilean troublemaker would ever have supposed that by the end of the first century there would be flourishing communities of Gentile adherents in the major Mediterranean cities and in Rome itself. The author's detailed and accurate knowledge of the Roman world—including names, titles and functions of the colonial administration of the empire—lend to his work an air of authority and learning."

The Acts of Peter and the Travels of Paul

The book of Acts is the second half of Luke's two-volume work on the origins of Christianity, the story of how the good news spread throughout the Roman Empire in the decades following Jesus' death. Tom Wright calls Luke-Acts the books of two journeys: Jesus' final journey to Jerusalem to die a sacrificial death to reconcile us with God, and Paul's final journey to Rome to preach the gospel in the pagan capital of the Roman Empire.

Although the book is called The Acts of the Apostles, so named by Irenaeus, the bishop of Lyons (France) in the latter half of the second century, only three disciples who were with Jesus are mentioned by name: Peter, James and John. The two books were separated in the second century to combine the four Gospels into one collection and to give Acts a place of its own as the story of the outward movement of the good news.

The book of Acts concentrates on urban centers in the northern Mediterranean world, rather than on small towns in the countryside. And it says nothing about the gospel in North Africa, which had a growing Christian presence, or in the East, India for instance, where it is claimed the apostle Thomas brought the gospel in the year 52. Luke's purpose is to show the movement of the good news from Palestine, a second-rate province at the back end of the empire, to Rome, the very capital of the empire (the last chapter in Acts).

Luke's Authorship of Acts

Luke's authorship of the book of Acts has been challenged by those who ask why, if Luke was Paul's traveling companion, he never mentions that Paul wrote letters. Perhaps because he chose to emphasize Paul's preaching—there are nine (condensed) Pauline speeches in Acts—which is how history was often recorded in antiquity, that is, through the spoken words of the principal characters in a narrative. Others wonder why Luke reintroduces Theophilus at the beginning of Acts and repeats the story of Jesus' ascension, both of which appear in his Gospel. Perhaps because the two books were separate scrolls and this was Luke's way of tying them together.

The Importance of Acts

The book of Acts was initially considered to be of minor importance because it was written by a second-generation Christian and because it was seen primarily as history rather than gospel or good news. But what history! Bruce Metzger, in his book *The New Testament*, mentioned in chapter 3, says the author of Acts cites thirty-two countries, fifty-four cities, nine Mediterranean islands and ninety-five persons, sixty-two of whom are not mentioned elsewhere.

Some think the only reason the book of Acts—the history book of the New Testament—was received into the canon is because its author wrote the third canonical Gospel. Without it, we would not know about Pentecost or the call of Paul on the road to Damascus or the details of Paul's missionary travels in Asia Minor and Europe. And we wouldn't know about the Jewish persecution of the early Christians who, following Jesus' death, "were continually in the temple blessing God" (Luke 24:53), but then were forced out; and some, like Stephen, the first Christian *martyr* (a Greek word meaning "witness") were put to death. This did not enfeeble or destroy the church; rather, it dispersed it far and wide, resulting in the good news being proclaimed throughout the empire.

The book of Acts also gives credibility to Jesus' resurrection. When he was arrested in the Garden of Gethsemane, his disciples, fearing for their lives, went into hiding. They thought Jesus' mission had failed and that his fate would also be theirs. They were too afraid even to bury Jesus, so Joseph of Arimathea (a town northwest of Jerusalem) had to do so. But a few weeks later, on the first Pentecost after Jesus' death, they began preaching the good news on the streets of Jerusalem.

The Structure and Story of Acts

Structurally, the book of Acts has two easily divisible sections. The first half (chapters 1–12) is the Petrine section, the story of Peter and the disciples in Jerusalem; it ends with the death of Herod Agrippa I in 44. The second half (chapters 13–28) is the Pauline section, the story, after Paul's call and conversion on the road to Damascus in Acts 9, of his missionary travels and church-planting work in Galatia, Philippi, Corinth, Ephesus and other cities in the Roman Empire.

Pentecost: The Church's Birthday

The book of Acts opens with Jesus and the eleven disciples in Jerusalem. He spoke with them for "forty days . . . about the kingdom of God" (1:3). He told the disciples, "You will receive power when the Holy Spirit has come upon you; and you will be my witnesses in Jerusalem, in all Judea and Samaria, and to the ends of the earth" (1:8), an important verse in understanding the outline and message of Acts.

Following Jesus' ascension, the disciples met to choose a replacement for Judas, with the "lot" (God's choice) falling to Matthias, who had been with Jesus during his public ministry. Matthias brought the number of Jesus' disciples, again, to twelve (1:21-26), the "new" Israel of God. Ten days later, on Pentecost, from a Greek word meaning "fiftieth"—the fiftieth day after Passover, which commemorated the giving of God's law to Moses on Mount Sinai—the Holy Spirit came upon the disciples and others who began to speak in "other tongues" (fifteen are mentioned). Luke tells us that "Jews from every nation under heaven living in Jerusalem [heard the good news] in the native language of each" (2:5-6). The Holy Spirit, which descended on Jesus at his baptism, launched him on his ministry to Israel; the same Spirit came upon his followers at Pentecost and launched them on their ministry to "the ends of the earth."

The Deaths of Peter and Paul

Many think the book of Acts was written sometime in the eighties, after Luke's Gospel, which scholars also date in the eighties. If so, it was written after Peter and Paul had been martyred during the Neronian persecution in the mid-sixties. Why is there no account of their deaths in Acts? Some think Luke wrote the book of Acts in the early sixties, before Peter and Paul were martyred, which seems unlikely because of Luke's partial dependence on Mark's Gospel, which is dated 65–70. Others think that Luke did not want to offend Rome, whose favor Christians were trying to win. Still others think Luke wanted to end his story of the movement of the good news from Jerusalem to Rome, with Paul teaching about Christ "with all boldness and without hindrance" to show that Jesus' charge to his followers to be his witnesses "to the ends of the earth" had been fulfilled (28:31). There is more on the deaths of Peter and Paul—Peter's crucifixion and Paul's beheading—in the next chapter.

The Apostle Paul: Life, Travels, Writings and Theology

The second half of Acts has to do with the travels and preaching of Paul, the most important, though not the first or only of the early church's missionaries. Well before Paul's first journey in the year 46, churches had been established in Damascus, where Ananias and others were active, and in Antioch (Syria), which had a large Christian community and became Paul's mission base. There were also churches on the island of Cyprus, Barnabas's native land; in Rome, which had a thriving church years before Paul arrived there; and in Alexandria, the home of Apollos, whom we meet in Acts 18 and in Paul's first letter to the Corinthians.

Saul of Tarsus

We know quite a bit about Paul from the book of Acts and from Galatians 1:13-24 and Philippians 3:4-6—much more than we know about the authors of the Gospels. Paul's family was from the tribe of Benjamin; they named him after King Saul, a Benjaminite military leader who was Israel's first king. When Saul and Barnabas were in Cyprus on their first journey, Saul's name changes to the Greco-Roman Paulus or Paul (13:9).

Paul was born in the first decade of the first century in Tarsus, a busy Mediterranean port city and trade center in southeastern Turkey. Paul's parents were Roman citizens, though it is not known how they obtained their citizenship (perhaps for some service to Rome); Paul says that he inherited his citizenship. His father was a leather worker and tent maker, as was Paul. He had a sister whose son warned Paul of a plot against him following his arrest in Jerusalem at the end of his third journey (23:16).

When Paul was old enough, he went to Jerusalem to study under Gamaliel (22:3), a highly respected rabbinic teacher (5:34–39). Paul became a strict, zealous, Pharisaic Jew who persecuted Christians whom he thought were undermining Judaism.

Paul's Conversion

The story of Paul begins with the stoning of Stephen in Jerusalem. Because Jewish execution was forbidden by Rome, scholars think Stephen may have been stoned during a period when there was no Roman governor stationed in Palestine; others think that Jews were sometimes allowed to execute Jews who had violated Jewish law.

The call of Paul is the most dramatic conversion story in the Bible (Acts 9:1-19). In the year 33 or so, when Paul was in his late twenties, he went to Damascus, the current-day capital of Syria, to hunt for "any there who belonged to the Way" (the way of Jesus). As he approached the city, "a light from heaven flashed around him [and he heard] a voice say to him, 'Saul, Saul, why do you persecute me?'" (Paul was persecuting Jesus' followers). Paul was told to go into the city, where he was met by Ananias, who told Paul that he had been chosen "to bring [Jesus'] name before the Gentiles." The story of Paul's call and conversion in Acts 9 is followed by two similar accounts, one in Jerusalem following Paul's arrest at the end of his third journey (22:3-21); the other during his imprisonment in Caesarea (26:9-18).

Paul's Missionary Journeys

Paul's missionary strategy was to establish churches in important cities from Jerusalem to Rome, and for these churches to plant churches of their own, as the Christians in Ephesus did in establishing a church in Colossae. Paul shepherded these and other churches by sending letters and personal envoys like Timothy.

It is not known how many missionary journeys Paul undertook, but three are well-documented in the book of Acts. The first journey (ca. 46-48) team included Paul, Barnabas and Mark (for part of the way); they traveled from Antioch to Cyprus, and then to Galatia (present-day Turkey). The second journey (ca. 49-53) had a new team, with Silas replacing Barnabas and Timothy replacing Mark; they went to cities in Asia Minor that Paul visited on his first journey, and then to Europe, ending in Corinth (Greece), where Paul stayed for eighteen months (it was on this journey that Luke met Paul). On the third journey (ca. 54-58), Paul and his team revisited churches they had established in Asia Minor and Europe, and then settled in Ephesus, where Paul stayed for two years.

Paul's Writings

We know a lot about Paul from his writings. The American New Testament scholar Robert Gundry, in his book *A Survey of the New Testament*, said Paul's letters "are several times longer than the average letter of ancient times, so to a certain extent Paul

invented a new literary form, the epistle—new in its prolonga-
tion as a letter, in the theological character of its contents, and
usually in the communal nature of its address." Paul's letters
follow the Greco-Roman form, with the writer's name at the
beginning, followed by a formal greeting; then the body of the
letter or epistle, which usually included both doctrinal teachings and ethical instructions (exposition and exhortation); and
some greetings at the end.

Paul wrote nine letters to churches in the northern Mediterranean world and four pastoral letters. They were written over
a period of some fifteen years, from 1 Thessalonians (ca. 50) to
the pastoral letters when Paul was imprisoned in Rome in the
mid-60s. We have only one letter from the "hand" of Paul (Philemon). The others are copies of copies so that his letters could be
read by Christians everywhere. Disputes have arisen regarding
the authenticity of some of Paul's letters because, among other
things, there are differences in phraseology, which could easily
have come from his use of different secretaries to whom he
dictated his letters, one of whom even added his name to one
of Paul's letters: "I, Tertius, the writer of this letter, greet you in
the Lord" (Romans 16:22). Though his letters were dictated, Paul
sometimes added a greeting at the end in his own hand, as in
Galatians 6:11 and 2 Thessalonians 3:17.

Paul's letters were occasional, meaning some occasion or
situation prompted their writing, like the Judaizers' disruption
in Galatia. They were carefully written, though some may have
been edited and combined, as perhaps with the Corinthian
correspondence. And there were more letters than the thirteen
we have in the New Testament: the letters referred to in 1 Corinthians 5:9, 2 Corinthians 2:4 and Colossians 4:16 have never
been found.

Some think that Luke assembled Paul's writings from copies
Paul made of his letters. Others think they were gathered together

by Onesimus, the slave mentioned in Paul's letter to Philemon, who became the bishop of Ephesus. Paul's writings were highly valued by the early church because he had "met" the risen Christ on the road to Damascus.

Paul's Theology

Paul grew up believing that the Torah was God's ultimate revelation—and then Jesus "appeared" to him on the road to Damascus and everything changed. Jewish law made one aware of sin, but it had no power over sin. Only by faith, only by believing in and becoming one with Jesus, who was sent to redeem us from our sins, can we be justified—"justification by faith," Paul's doctrinal center—and rightly related to God. The bottom line of Paul's theology is the cross: "We proclaim Christ crucified [for our sins]" (1 Corinthians 1:23).

Paul: The Ideal Man

Paul was the ideal man in the ideal place at the ideal time to launch God's mission to the Gentiles. He was a Pharisaic Jew who was firmly grounded in the Hebrew Scriptures; a non-Palestinian Jew who was able to translate the good news into the language and thought forms of the Greco-Roman world; a Roman citizen who was protected by his rights of citizenship; and a religious zealot, first on behalf of Judaism and then Christianity. During his dozen years on the mission field—from his first journey with Barnabas in 46 to his arrest in Jerusalem in 58—Paul established churches throughout Asia Minor and Europe.

We don't know anything about Paul's physical stature or appearance. A second-century writer said: "He was small in stature, bald, bowlegged, of vigorous physique, heavy eyebrows, a slightly hooked nose, and full of grace."

Galatians:
The Epistle of Christian Freedom

Paul visited several cities in Galatia (modern-day Turkey) on his first journey. After he left, some Judaizers (hard-line Jewish Christians) arrived. They told the Galatians that Paul's preaching of salvation by grace through faith was not enough: it needed to be more firmly grounded in the law of Moses, because the Jews were God's chosen people, from whom Jesus himself came.

Some scholars believe that Galatians was Paul's first letter (ca. 49); it is clearly his most abrupt letter. Paul is angry with the Galatians because they are turning away from the gospel he had just preached and taught them. He writes that a person is not justified by works of the law (Jewish rules, rituals and customs) but through faith in Jesus Christ (2:15-16). He cites the example of Abraham, who believed God's promise that he would have an heir (Isaac)—who was born several hundred years before Moses received the law on Mount Sinai—and "The Lord reckoned it to him as righteousness" (Genesis 15:6). Abraham, thus, was justified by faith, not by Jewish laws and rules. Paul said that if justification comes through the law, "then Christ died for nothing" (2:21). Then why did God give Israel the law? Paul said it was meant to be a custodian, like a trustee for someone under age. But Christ has now come: we are no longer under the law.

The Judaizers were a headache for Paul, but good came from their troublemaking: they forced Paul to articulate the distinguishing differences between Christianity and Judaism, which made Christianity separate, distinct and free from, rather than an extension of, Judaism. The letter to the Galatians contains Paul's fruit of the Spirit, which should be seen in the lives of those who profess to be Christian: love, joy, peace, patience, kindness, generosity, faithfulness, gentleness and self-control (5:22-23). There is more on the fruit of the Spirit in chapter 10.

The Corinthian Correspondence

Paul and his team visited Corinth on their second journey (ca. 50) and stayed for eighteen months. Corinth was a large, industrious city; the capital of the Roman province of Achaia; the second wealthiest city in the empire, after Rome; and terribly immoral (calling someone a Corinthian implied that he or she was immoral). The church at Corinth seems to have been as lusty and ill-behaved as the city itself. Paul's first letter to the Corinthians is an answer to a number of problems that surfaced in the church after Paul left. Those who say, "I wish we could get back to the simplicity of the early church" should read First Corinthians.

In the letter, Paul addresses issues that were brought to him in person and in writing (thus Paul also *received* letters)—by some counts, twelve different issues. Space does not allow for their discussion, but some involve problems the church struggles with even today: cliques and factions, lawsuits against fellow believers, tolerance of promiscuous sexual behavior, issues of marriage and divorce, sensitivity toward new believers, propriety in worship, and the proper exercise of spiritual gifts.

Chapter 13 is Paul's great hymn of love, which he says is patient and kind; not envious, boastful, arrogant or rude; rejoices in the truth; bears, hopes and endures all things; and never ends. We often hear these verses read at weddings, but the love Paul is talking about is not romantic love; it is self-giving acts of love that believers are called to show as a witness to their faith.

1 Corinthians 15:3–8 is the earliest written outline of the preaching of the good news. Paul says that Jesus died for our sins in accordance with the scriptures; that he was buried (he really died); that he was raised on the third day in accordance with the scriptures; and that he appeared to many people to confirm his resurrection, including "more than five hundred

brothers and sisters at one time" (15:7), referring, perhaps, to the many who heard and followed Jesus during his three-year Galilean ministry. When Paul says, "in accordance with the scriptures," he means in accordance with God's plan of salvation revealed in the Jewish scriptures. There were no Christian "scriptures" until the church closed the New Testament canon in the fourth century.

Paul goes on to talk about the future resurrection of all who "belong" to Christ; he explains the nature of our to-be-resurrected bodies, which will be as different from our earthly bodies as a plant is from its seed; and he tells the Corinthians they should be about doing the work of the Lord (15:58).

Paul's second letter to the Corinthians is the most autobiographical of his letters. He tells his readers about his beatings and sufferings "for Christ's sake" and tells about his "thorn in the flesh" (12:7), which has puzzled scholars down through the centuries. God did not remove the thorn; instead, he tells Paul that his grace is sufficient to sustain him in his labors for the gospel. In chapters 8 and 9, Paul appeals to the Corinthians to help destitute Christians in Jerusalem—the first Christian fundraising letter—telling them that doing so will be a blessing to both God and their brothers and sisters in Jerusalem. The letter ends with the popular benediction: "May the grace of the Lord Jesus Christ, the love of God, and the communion of the Holy Spirit be with all of you" (13:13).

Romans: Paul's Magnum Opus

Paul wrote to "all God's beloved in Rome" to prepare for his hoped-for visit to the church in Rome. Paul's letter to the Romans is considered to be his most important writing: the culmination of his thinking after many years on the mission field; the most mature, thoughtful and carefully written statement of his belief in Jesus' salvific death; his last will and testament to the church. Martin Luther called Romans "the purest gospel."

No one knows who founded the church in Rome. It may have been "visitors from Rome" who were in Jerusalem on the first Pentecost (see Acts 2:10). The Roman church was much admired because it was located in the capital of the empire. It must have been a good-sized church—Nero could not have blamed the Christians for burning Rome if they had been a small, insignificant minority—whose members included both Jewish and Gentile Christians.

Romans 1:16–17 has been called "The Gospel According to Saint Paul." Paul writes that the gospel "is the power of God for salvation to everyone who has faith [in Jesus Christ]. For in it the righteousness of God is revealed through faith for faith." The gospel is the good news about how we can be rightly related to God, and this news is for everyone: the only condition is faith. Paul goes on to say that God has been revealed "ever since the creation of the world . . . through the things that he has made" (1:20), but "all have sinned and fallen short of the glory of God" (3:23). The bad news is that "the wages of sin [the payment for sin] is death." The good news is that God has sent one to redeem us from our sins, namely, "Christ Jesus our Lord" (6:23). Romans 8:35–39 is one of the most beloved passages in the New Testament: neither death nor life, neither angels nor demons, neither things present nor things to come "will be able to separate us from the love of God in Christ Jesus our Lord."

Romans 12:1–15:13 has been called "Paul's Sermon on the Mount." He begins by telling the Romans to present themselves "as a living sacrifice" to God, in contrast to Israel's dead animal sacrifices, and to "be transformed by the renewing of your minds" (12:1–2). He goes on to tell the Romans that they are to love one another with mutual affection, live in peace and harmony with others, be patient in suffering, contribute to the needs of the saints, extend hospitality to strangers, rejoice with those who rejoice and weep with those who weep, remember the commandments, welcome those who are weak in faith, and never put a stumbling block in the way of another.

Paul's Other Letters

Paul's most important letters are Galatians, Romans and 1 and 2 Corinthians. These four underlie his theology. Paul's other letters are the following.

First and Second Thessalonians

Paul's first letter to the Thessalonians may have been his first letter or epistle (the other candidate, as mentioned, is Galatians). If true, it would be the first or earliest New Testament book. The Thessalonian letters address questions that arose in Thessalonica after Jews there forced Paul to leave (Acts 17). Some Thessalonians were concerned about the timing of Jesus' return, specifically, what happens to those who die before he returns? Would they miss out when he comes to gather up those who have believed in him? Paul's answer is set out in 1 Thessalonians 4:13–18. When Jesus returns, he will gather up both the living and the dead; neither will have any advantage over the other. In the meantime, Paul tells the Thessalonians to "do good to all . . . rejoice always . . . pray without ceasing . . . and give thanks in all circumstances" (5:12–22).

The Prison Epistles

Paul wrote four letters while he was incarcerated in various prisons—in Philippi (Acts 16), in Caesarea (Acts 23–26) and in Rome (Philemon 23). These letters are referred to as the Prison Epistles. *Philippians* is Paul's letter of great joy to his favorite church. It contains the still popular Christological hymn or creed: "At the name of Jesus every knee should bend . . . and every tongue should confess that Jesus Christ is Lord" (2:10–11). *Colossians* is a letter written to a church that Paul had neither founded nor visited concerning certain heresies that had arisen in the church in Colossae. *Philemon* is a letter Paul wrote in his own hand to Philemon about his runaway slave, Onesimus, who had wronged Philemon in some way. Paul intercedes on behalf of Onesimus, asking Philemon to accept him as a brother in Christ. The letter was preserved, so Philemon must have forgiven Onesimus. *Ephesians* is a circular letter written to a group of churches, one of which was the church at Ephesus. It is one of Paul's most important letters, called by some the Queen of the Epistles. In contrast with Paul's other letters, there is no identifiable "occasion" that prompted Paul to write to the Ephesians. The readers are addressed as Gentiles, but are told not to live as Gentiles because they are now co-heirs with the Jews, God's chosen people. The letter contains a theme central to the Reformation and to Protestant theology: we are saved by grace through faith, not by works (2:8), evangelicalism's DNA.

The Pastoral Letters

The remaining three Pauline letters are called the Pastoral Letters. They contain instructions from the pastor Paul to two young pastors, Timothy in Ephesus, who was Paul's constant companion (Timothy is mentioned in six of Paul's nine church letters), and Titus in Crete. They are told to maintain orthodoxy, to rebuke false teachings that were creeping into the church, to be models of Christian conduct, and are given characteristics to look for in choosing church leaders (1 Timothy 3:1–13).

Hebrews and the Seven General Letters

There are eight letters that follow Paul's letters. Hebrews is first in line because it is the longest non-Pauline letter. It is the only New Testament book that is clearly anonymous; it is more like an essay than a letter (there are no addressees); and it is one of the riddles of the New Testament: it is not known who wrote the letter, or to whom (given its title, many think it was written to Jewish Christians who were considering returning to Judaism), or where it was written (probably Rome, according to 13:24). The letter sets forth the once-for-all-time perfect sacrifice of Jesus for our sins, in contrast to Israel's animal sacrifices at the temple (see 10:1–18). Chapter 11, which highlights the faith of Abraham, Joseph, Moses, Gideon and others, has been called the Bible's "Faith Hall of Fame."

The seven short letters between Hebrews and the book of Revelation are, said one commentator, "miscellaneous mail." They are known by the names of their authors rather than their addressees. The most important of the letters are James, First Peter and First John.

James

The early church believed that the letter of James was written by the oldest of Jesus' four brothers, who became the leader of the church in Jerusalem after Peter left for the mission field. According to Josephus, James was stoned to death in the year 62. James tells his readers to be quick to listen and slow to answer; to be doers of the word, not merely hearers of the word; to bridle their tongues; not to speak evil against another; and to be patient in suffering. Some have called James the "faith plus works" letter. Paul said that we are saved by faith, not by works. James, writing several years later, says, "faith by itself, if it has no works, is dead" (2:17).

First Peter

First Peter was written by the "chief of the apostles," who wrote from Rome. He tells his readers to accept their suffering (under Nero) with cheerfulness, looking to Jesus, who suffered for us, and follow "in his steps" (2:21). Verse 3:15 calls Christians to give an answer, with gentleness and reverence, to anyone who asks about the hope they have in Jesus, a key verse in Christian apologetics. The letter ends with Peter's mention of Mark, "my son [in the faith]," who was with Peter at the end of his life and who, according to tradition, recorded Peter's remembrances of Jesus.

First John

First John is the first of three letters the church has long attributed to John the disciple, though the author of 2 and 3 John calls himself the "elder." John writes against those who denied Jesus' true humanity, saying, "We have heard . . . we have seen . . . and touched with our hands" the risen Christ (1:1). John tells his readers that Jesus is our advocate, one who speaks for us, as in a court of law, with God the Father (2:1–2). In his epilogue, John says those "who believe in the name of the Son of God [know that they have] eternal life" (5:13).

The Book of Revelation

The last book in the Bible—the book of Revelation—is one of the most difficult books in the New Testament, and also one of the most controversial. Many Christians don't know what to make of the book, while others make of it entirely too much. The book is filled with symbolic language—numbers, colors and strange phenomena like a bottomless pit, a lake of fire and bowls of wrath. The author's symbols, however strange to us, would have been understood by those to whom he was writing, much like the number *thirteen* might be today, or referring to the federal government as the White House, or using a donkey and an elephant to symbolize our two political parties. In ancient Israel, horns (of animals) were a symbol of power and the number seven symbolized fullness or completeness. Thus seven horns meant all-powerful and seven eyes meant all-seeing.

It has long been held that the apostle John wrote the book of Revelation, but the author makes no claim to being a disciple or an apostle (he calls himself a "servant"). His book was written from the Isle of Patmos, located in the Aegean Sea some fifty miles southwest of Ephesus in present-day Turkey, where John was incarcerated in a Roman prison. The book was written, during the reign of Emperor Domitian (AD 81-96), a despotic ruler who demanded that public worship be given to him.

Structure and Message

The book of Revelation has two parts. First, John is told by an angel to write what is revealed to him to seven churches (there were more than seven churches in Asia Minor in the first century, so "seven churches" may mean the universal church). The members of some of the churches were guilty of compromise and apostasy (abandoning their beliefs). Second, John is shown visions of plagues, famine, wars and death, each described in vivid language, and is told there will be a final battle—the Battle of Armageddon—following which Satan will be bound and there will be "a new heaven and a new earth" (21:1).

The message of apocalyptic literature like Revelation is that God will save his people, as he did when the Pharaoh was oppressing the Israelites in Egypt. Until God intervenes, however, things will likely get even worse. But God will prevail and reward those who have been steadfast and faithful.

Millennialism

The term "a thousand years" occurs four times in chapter 20. It refers to the return of Christ and his thousand-year (millennial) reign. There are three different understandings of the term *millennialism,* from the word *mille,* the Latin word for "thousand."

Premillennialism teaches that Christ will return before the start of the millennium to defeat the forces of evil in the Battle of Armageddon, after which he will reign for a thousand years. This is the oldest of the millennial views, dating back to the second century. It is also the most literal of the views, with an elaborate theology concerning the final tribulation and the rapture of believers before, during and after the tribulation.

Postmillennialism teaches that Christ will return after a thousand-year period of peace and righteousness to rule over a Christianized world. Postmillennialism was very popular in the nineteenth century. With two world wars in the twentieth century and on-going conflicts in the Middle East and elsewhere in the twenty-first century, few believe that things are getting so much better that Christ is likely to return at any moment.

Amillennialism goes back to Augustine in the fourth century. It does not regard the millennium as a literal one-thousand-year period (a-millennialism means "no millennium"). Augustine said the term "a thousand years" should be interpreted symbolically or figuratively, like other words in the book of Revelation, meaning, in this case, the period between Jesus' first coming and his promised return.

The book of Revelation declares that Jesus is the key to the future, to the coming victory and triumph of God, for he alone holds the "book of life" (21:27). Those who are faithful and stand against the world and its ways will partake in the glory of God's kingdom on earth.

Was Jesus the Hoped-for Messiah?

We are now finished with the Old and New Testaments. Israel's hope then, and that of Orthodox Jews today, is for the coming of the Messiah. Was Jesus God's promised Messiah? His disciples believed him to be the Messiah (Mark 8:29); he claimed to be the Messiah in his "trial" before the Sanhedrin (Mark 14:61–62); and many accepted him as the Messiah, as reported in the book of Acts (2:41, 2:47 and 4:4). The majority of Jews, however, did not think that Jesus was the Messiah. They believed the Messiah would be a royal figure from Jerusalem, not a peasant from an insignificant village in Galilee; that he would embody the highest ideals and purity of Judaism, not someone who ate with tax collectors, healed the unclean and was said to have broken the Sabbath; and that he would lead Israel in the overthrow of Rome, not someone who said, "Love your enemies and pray for those who persecute you" (Matthew 5:44). And almost no Jew believed the Messiah would personally bear the sins of Israel, as prophesied by Isaiah (chapter 53); or that his death would "save" Israel; and they believed the dead would be raised at the end of time, not, as Jesus was, in the middle of time (see John 11:23–24).

God's desire is for the whole world to be saved, not just Israel. The centerpiece of his plan of salvation is Jesus Christ, who Paul said was "a stumbling block to Jews," who were looking for a kingly figure, not a suffering servant; and "foolishness to Gentiles," who wondered how one crucified as a common criminal could be the world's Savior (1 Corinthians 1:23). Paul writes that Jesus died and was raised from the dead to give hope to "everyone who has faith" (Romans 1:16).

Discussion Questions

1. Many of Paul's letters have to do with issues he had to deal with because of his faith. What are some issues you've had to deal with because of your faith?

2. Christians are called to share the good news. Have you ever initiated a verbal or written "This is why I am a Christian" conversation with a non-believing friend?

3. Paul, Barnabas, Luke, Timothy and Titus mentored and discipled others in the faith. Who mentored or discipled you? Who have you mentored?

6

A Brief History of Christianity

In the last chapter we saw how Christianity moved from Jerusalem to Rome in the middle of the first century. This chapter brings the history of Christianity up-to-date—up to the twenty-first century. During the first thousand years there was one church. In 1054, a controversy between Rome and Constantinople resulted in a schism or separation, which divided the church into Roman Catholic and Eastern Orthodox. Five centuries later, in 1517, the writings of a German Augustinian monk named Martin Luther (pictured above) ignited a second schism, which split the Western church into Catholic and Protestant.

The Patristic Period:
Creeds, Constantine and Augustine

The centuries following the death and resurrection of Jesus
are called the Patristic Period—the period of the early Church
Fathers—the period of the formation of the church, the collection
of Christian writings and the church's agreement on the books
to be included in the New Testament canon; the "conversion"
of Emperor Constantine in 312, which led to the establishment
of Christianity as the official religion of the Roman Empire in
380; and the councils of Nicaea (325), Constantinople (381)
and Chalcedon (451), which hammered out the basic tenets
of Christianity, most importantly, the nature of Christ and his
relationship to the Father and the Holy Spirit, the other two
members of the Trinity (there is more on the Trinity in the next
chapter).

The Apostles' Creed

The early church developed creeds—from the Latin *credo*, meaning "I believe"—that summarized essential Christian beliefs.
The Apostles' Creed (page 145) derives its name from a legend
that each of the apostles contributed a clause to the creed (the
original creed had twelve clauses). The creed, though not written
by the apostles, sets forth the bottom-line beliefs of Christianity. It is thought to be the product of prior creeds, including a
baptismal creed dating from about 200. In the ninth century,
during the reign of Charlemagne (742-814), the king of the Franks
and the Holy Roman Emperor, the Apostles' Creed became the
official creed of the Western church. The official creed of the
Eastern church is the Nicene Creed, which sets forth more fully
and clearly the nature of Christ.

Constantine the Great (ca. 280–337)

In the year 312, after a vision of the cross of Christ and the words: "By this sign you will conquer," Constantine defeated his rival, Maxentius, at the Milvian Bridge outside Rome, following which he embraced Christianity. In 313, he issued the Edict of Milan, which gave Christianity legal status in the empire. In 321, he declared Sunday to be a public holiday because it was the day of the week on which Christ was raised from the dead. He later endowed Christian shrines in Rome (Saint Peter's and Saint Paul's Basilicas) and with his mother, Helena, a devout Christian, in the Holy Land (the Church of the Nativity and the Church of the Holy Sepulcher). In 324, he moved his capital to Byzantium, which he renamed Constantinople—"Constantine's City"—which in 1930 was renamed Istanbul, now Turkey's largest city. In 325, Constantine convened a council of 318 bishops at Nicaea, where he lived during the construction of Constantinople, which formulated the Nicene Creed, the confession par excellence of Christian orthodoxy, which was finalized at the Council of Constantinople in 381.

Augustine (354–430)

The most important church father in the West was Augustine, a hinge figure between the end of the early church and the beginning of the Middle Ages, much as Martin Luther stands between the end of the Middle Ages and early modern times. Augustine was born in a small village not far from Carthage in Roman North Africa. His mother, Monica, was a Christian. Augustine was a Manichaean—Mani said there were two deities, one good and one evil—believing that it offered a better answer to the problem of evil than his mother's Christianity.

Augustine had a common-law wife for several years, whom he later painfully abandoned, who bore him a son. At the age of thirty-two, Augustine was convicted while reading a passage in Paul's letter to the Romans in a garden in Milan, Italy, where he was a teacher of rhetoric. Paul told the Romans to live lives pleasing to God, free of lewdness, lust, strife and envy (Romans 13:13-14).

Augustine came under the influence of Ambrose (339–397), the bishop of Milan, one of the great "doctors" of the church, whose clear, reasoned teaching convinced Augustine of the truth of Christianity. Ambrose baptized Augustine and his son on Easter Eve in 387. The following year Augustine returned to Africa. In 395, at the age of forty-two, he became the bishop of Hippo, the modern city of Annaba in Algeria, where he remained for the next thirty-five years.

Augustine's extensive writings left an indelible mark on Christian theology, especially the doctrines of God's grace and the church as the channel of grace; original sin, based on Paul's letter to the Romans (5:12-21); God's election of some and not others for salvation (his most controversial teaching); the equality of the persons (essences) in the Trinity; and free will, the sacraments, war, ethics and spirituality. Next to Paul, Augustine did more to shape the thinking and theology of the Western church than any other person.

The Middle Ages:
Papacy, Schism and Crusades

The Roman Empire lasted for more than twelve hundred years— from the founding of Rome in 753 BC to its fall in AD 476. During the first centuries of the Christian Era, Rome ruled all the lands bordering the Mediterranean Sea. At the height of its power, under Emperor Trajan (AD 98 to 117), the Roman Empire embraced some two million miles and had an estimated population of fifty million people, only a small minority of whom, however, were Roman citizens. In 410, after a long period of steady decline, the Visigoths entered and sacked the city of Rome, and then left. Rome fell in the year 476. The Eastern or Byzantine Empire in Constantinople continued for another thousand years, eventually falling to the Ottoman Turks in 1453.

Among the reasons for the fall of Rome were weak leadership, moral decay, and Rome's inability to finance and maintain an army sufficient to protect it from aggressive, warring neighbors. The thousand years following the fall of Rome—roughly, 500 to 1500—is referred to as the Middle Ages. The late Middle Ages was one of the most creative and fruitful periods in the history of Christianity, with the church leading the way in theology, philosophy, ethics, art, architecture, music and literature.

Rome and the Papacy

During the Patristic Period, the church in Rome became the most important church in Christendom: it was situated in the ancient, imperial capital of the empire; it had the largest congregation of Christians; and its roots went back to Peter and Paul, whose martyred remains were buried there. According to Dionysius of Corinth, Peter was crucified upside down in Rome, claiming that he was not worthy to be crucified in the same manner as Christ. It is said that his bones lie beneath the altar in Saint Peter's Basilica. Paul, being a Roman citizen, could not be crucified; he was beheaded at *Tre Fontaine* (Three Fountains) outside the city. His bones are buried in another basilica, Saint Paul's Outside-the-Walls.

When Rome fell, the Roman church was the most important institution left standing. It claimed that Peter, the first bishop of Rome (not quite true), passed on to his successors the authority to act as Christ's representative on earth, a claim disputed by Eastern Orthodoxy and later by Protestantism. In the fifth century the church began calling the bishop of Rome the pope, from the Latin *papa*, meaning "father."

The Catholic-Orthodox Schism (1054)

The formal schism between the Western church in Rome and the Eastern church in Constantinople occurred in 1054. The Western and Eastern churches were separated by distance: Rome and Constantinople were 1,000 miles apart and had very little contact with one another; by language: the West spoke Latin and the East spoke Greek; and by authority: the West followed the pope and the East followed the first seven ecumenical (church-wide) councils. In addition, the Eastern church venerated icons—paintings of Jesus, Mary and the saints that were used for teaching and devotions—which some in the West viewed as graven images; the East used unleavened bread for the Eucharist; and Eastern clergy persons could marry before ordination, but not after.

In the year 1054, Pope Leo IX excommunicated Cerularius, the Patriarch of Constantinople, for allegedly overstepping his authority. Cerularius returned the favor and the Christian church split in two. In the West it was called Roman Catholic, meaning allegiance to Rome and that it was catholic, from a Latin word meaning "universal." In the East it was called Orthodox (or Eastern Orthodox or Greek Orthodox), meaning true or correct belief, as defined by the ecumenical councils.

The Eastern church did not accept the bishop of Rome as the head of the church. He was recognized as the "first among equals" because of Rome's leadership of the early church, but not the supreme, sovereign head of the church. Also—and the real reason for the split—was that the Eastern church believed the Holy Spirit proceeded from God the Father, based on the Nicene

Creed. The Western church taught that the Spirit proceeded from both the Father *and* the Son, a clause the West added to the Nicene Creed at the non-ecumenical Council of Toledo in 589. The East viewed the "and the Son" language as changing the relationship between the persons in the Trinity.

Eastern Orthodoxy is a federation of self-governing national churches. It is close to Roman Catholicism in its acceptance of the teachings of the church fathers (no *Sola Scriptura*); its observance of seven sacraments, which it calls Holy Mysteries; and its reverence for Mary as *Theotokos* (the God-bearer), who remained forever a virgin. The baptism of adults is by immersion; its eschatology (last things) is amillennial; and there is no belief in purgatory. The Orthodox Old Testament is the Greek Septuagint and its primary confession is the Nicene Creed, without the "and the son" clause. The vast majority of Orthodox Christians live in the former Soviet Union. The Orthodox Church came to the United States in 1794; today there are an estimated 2 million Greek, Russian and other Orthodox Christians in America.

The Crusades (1095–1291)

Islam took control of Christian territories in the Middle East and North Africa in the seventh and eighth centuries, leaving churches in these areas alone and vulnerable. This led to the Crusades, a 200-year series of major and minor military campaigns to expel Muslims from the Holy Land, which had been under Muslim control since 638.

Pope Urban II launched the first crusade in 1095, promising a pardon for past sins to those who responded. The first crusade recaptured Jerusalem in 1099, only to lose it again in 1187. There were several other crusades—Richard the Lionheart led the third crusade in 1190—none of which were successful. In fact, many ended in dishonor as the crusaders turned their attention from reclaiming the holy places of Christendom to pillaging and rape. Sociologist Rodney Stark, in his book *The Triumph of Christianity*, said that pre-Crusade Muslims were guilty of far worse crimes and atrocities against Christians than the other way around, something the West rarely mentions.

Thomas Aquinas (1225–1274)

Thomas Aquinas was the youngest son of Count Lundulf of Aquino, near Naples, Italy. A brilliant, deeply religious man, Thomas entered the Dominican order at the age of seventeen, to the great displeasure of his noble family, and became the Catholic Church's greatest medieval philosopher and theologian. (In 1880, Pope Leo XIII made Aquinas the patron saint of Catholic universities.) Aquinas attempted to construct a synthesis between biblical theology (faith) and natural theology (reason), believing that it was possible, through the use of reason, to come to the knowledge of God. One example was his Five Ways (or arguments) for the existence of God: movement, causation, perfection, contingency and design. Aquinas's crowning achievement was his *Summa Theologica* (Summary of Theology), which underlies present-day Roman Catholic theology.

Monasticism

One response to the church's institutionalization and need for renewal was monasticism, a way of showing one's devotion to Jesus by living a life of prayer, study, meditation and fasting, and also celibacy, which the Second Lateran Council declared, in 1139, to be the rule or norm for priests and others called to the religious life. Communal monasticism began in Egypt in the 300s. It blossomed in the West under Benedict of Nursia (Italy), the Father of Western Monasticism, whose famous rule—The

Rule of Saint Benedict—regarding community life, prayer, study and daily manual labor set the pattern for Benedictine and other monks to this day (the word "monk" comes from the Greek *monachos*, meaning "one who lives alone").

Some of the Catholic Church's most important religious orders were formed during the Middle Ages, among them the Franciscans, founded by Francis of Assisi (Italy) in 1209. Francis gave what he had to the poor (and was disowned by his father for doing so) and became a mendicant—dependent upon alms for living—and ministered to the sick, the poor and the destitute. The Dominican Order of Preachers was founded by Dominic of Castile (Spain) in 1216. It was the first order to establish universities and seminaries to educate the clergy. The Society of Jesus (the Jesuits), now Catholicism's largest order, was founded by Ignatius of Loyola (Spain) in 1540. The Jesuits led the counterattack against the Protestant Reformation.

The Protestant Reformation: Wycliffe, Luther and Calvin

The Reformation—the effort to reform the church—split the Western church into Roman Catholic and Protestant traditions or branches. The Reformers "protested" the papal system, which concentrated power in the pope and the curia, the agencies used by the Vatican to administer the church. They opposed the immorality and corruption of the clergy, some of whom had mistresses and others of whom used their positions for personal gain. They stood against the church's oppression of alleged heretics, the most violent example being the Spanish Inquisition. And they fought to stop the church's sale of indulgences to finance the building of Saint Peter's Basilica in Rome. (Indulgences were written pardons that, it was argued, would shorten one's time in purgatory, the place where souls are said to be purified of unforgiven venial sins so they may enter heaven.) Another factor underlying the Reformation was a growth in nationalism that challenged the authority of Rome, led by princes in Germany and elsewhere in Europe and by monarchs such as Henry VIII in England.

Wycliffe, Hus and Savonarola

Martin Luther is given credit for igniting the Reformation, but the unrest that gave rise to the revolt against Rome began long before Luther appeared on the scene. John Wycliffe, an Oxford professor, is called the Morning Star of the Reformation. He was the first to assert that the Bible was the only authoritative guide for faith and practice, and the first to translate the Bible from Latin, the language of the educated, into English so that it could be read by the people. He also wrote and spoke out against the papacy, apostolic succession, indulgences, transubstantiation (the teaching that during the celebration of the Eucharist the "elements," the bread and wine, are changed into the body and blood of Christ) and the veneration of saints. Jan Hus (1370–1415) was a Bohemian religious reformer who was influenced by Wycliffe; he said the papacy had only human, not divine, authority. The Italian Dominican Girolamo Savonarola (1452–1498) also denounced the papacy. Hus was declared a heretic and burned at the stake in 1415; Savonarola was convicted of heresy and hanged in the public square in Florence in 1498; and forty-four years after his death in 1384, Wycliffe's body was exhumed and burned and his ashes thrown into a nearby river.

Martin Luther (1483–1546)

Martin Luther was born and died in Eisleben, in eastern Germany, the son of a successful copper smelter. On October 31, 1517, at the age of thirty-three, while professor of biblical theology at the University of Wittenberg, Luther posted his Ninety-five Theses (Propositions) Against Indulgences on the door of the Castle Church in Wittenberg. Luther's propositions were not written to launch a new movement (Luther never intended to leave the Catholic Church). They were an invitation to discuss abuses related to the sale of indulgences. (German Christians resented sending money over the Alps to build Saint Peter's Basilica in Rome.)

Luther believed in the forgiveness of sins by and through Christ, which required no payments to the church. In 1521, the Vatican asked Luther to renounce his views. He refused, saying, in his famous rebuttal: "Unless I am convinced of error by the testimony of Scripture, or—since I put no trust in the unsupported authority of popes and councils, for it is plain that they have often erred and contradicted themselves—by manifest reasoning, I cannot and will not recant anything. On this I take my stand." Luther was charged with heresy and excommunicated, that is, denied the sacraments, which the Catholic Church held were necessary for salvation.

Luther's preaching and writings stressed the sole sufficiency of God's grace; faith as the only means for its reception; scripture as the sole authority for faith and life; and Christ as the world's only Savior—summarized as "grace alone, faith alone, the word alone and Christ alone."

Luther was a man of boundless energy and passion. In the 1520s he translated the Hebrew and Greek scriptures into German so they could be read by the people (the *Luther Bible*). In 1525, he married a former Cistercian nun, Katharina von Bora (Martin was 42, Katie was 26), whom he playfully referred to as My Rib, and raised a large and happy family. Luther has been one of Christendom's most prolific writers, with more than 500 published works, many being small pamphlets, but also a number of major works, and also catechisms (instructions) on the Ten Commandments, the Apostles' Creed, the Lord's Prayer and the sacraments for heads of households to teach their children. Luther also loved music and wrote several hymns, including *A Mighty Fortress Is Our God*, called by some The Battle Hymn of the Reformation. Polls and surveys consistently rank Luther as one of the ten most important figures in the history of Western civilization.

John Calvin (1509–1564)

The other giant figure of the Reformation was the Frenchman John Calvin, a second-generation reformer who was twenty-five years Luther's junior. Calvin was born in Noyon, France, northeast of Paris, and raised Catholic. In his early thirties he left the Catholic Church (some say because the church excommunicated his father), following which he devoted his full attention to the cause of Protestantism. Calvin was a first-class intellectual, with a Renaissance education in law, humanities, philosophy, classical literature and the arts, and he was fluent in Hebrew, Greek and Latin. Calvin spent the last twenty years of his life in French-speaking Geneva, Switzerland, where he preached several times a week, wrote widely on Christian theology, and produced commentaries on more than fifty books of the Bible.

Calvin's great contribution to the Reformation was the *Institutes of the Christian Religion*, a systematic statement of Reformation theology, which he wrote, revised and expanded four times over the years 1536 to 1559. Calvin was a more rigorous and systematic thinker than Luther. Also, he was not as Catholic as Luther and went beyond Luther's more conservative reforms regarding church polity and other matters. During and after Calvin's lifetime, Geneva became the center of the non-Germanic Protestant world. Calvinists who came to the

New World called themselves Reformed if they came from the Continent (Dutch Reformed and German Reformed) and Presbyterian if they came from the British Isles.

The Catholic-Protestant Controversy

The following are important differences in beliefs and practices that set Protestantism apart from Catholicism.

- The Reformers rejected the Roman Catholic hierarchical system, with the pope and the curia having total authority over the Church.

- The Reformers taught that salvation is "by grace, through faith" (Ephesians 2:8). The Catholic Church held itself to be the exclusive channel by and through which salvation is made available, through the sacraments, to the people.

- Reformation theology was based on Sacred Scripture (*Sola Scriptura*). Catholic theology gave equal weight to the writings and teachings of the early church fathers.

- The Reformers rejected the Catholic sacramental system. They said there are only two sacraments, Baptism and Holy Communion, not seven; and they rejected the Catholic doctrine of transubstantiation.

- The Reformers believed in the "priesthood of all believers," which eliminated divisions between the clergy and laity. The Reformers said that all believers are called to ministry, not just the ordained clergy.

- The Reformers translated the Bible into the vernacular so that it could be read by the people in their own language. The Catholic Bible was the Latin Vulgate and the church, through the *Magisterium*, the teaching office of the church, was the sole and final interpreter of the Bible.

- The Reformers saw no scriptural warrant for a priest to dispense God's grace. They emphasized, instead, each person's direct access to God through Jesus, the "one mediator between God and humankind" (1 Timothy 2:5).

The Fourfold Reformation:
Lutheran, Reformed, Anglican and Radical

The Reformation was not a single reformation; it was several reformations, which expressed themselves in different forms throughout Europe.

Lutheranism was based on the teachings of Martin Luther.

The *Reformed Church* was based on the theology and teachings of John Calvin, which differed from those of Luther regarding church polity (presbyteries rather than bishops), the Lord's Supper (Calvin saw the supper in more symbolic terms than Luther) and issues of church and state.

The third reformation was the *English Reformation*, which was more political than theological, at least at the outset. King Henry VIII, who reigned from 1509 to 1547, desperately wanted a male heir to continue the Tudor dynasty. His wife, Catherine of Aragon (a region in northeast Spain), was in her forties and the prospects for a son were not promising. He asked Pope Clement VII to annul their marriage—Catherine had been married to Henry's older brother, who died shortly after they were married (Catherine claimed their marriage was never consummated)—which, for complex political reasons, the pope refused to do. Henry divorced Catherine on his own authority as the King of England and married his then-pregnant mistress, Anne Boleyn (their daughter, Elizabeth I, was one of England's greatest monarchs). Henry was excommunicated

(Charles V, the Holy Roman Emperor, was Catherine's nephew and supported her cause with the pope).

In 1534, the British Parliament passed the Supremacy Act, which made the king the head of the Church of England, also known as the Anglican Church, from the Latin *Anglicanus*, the "Land of the Angles" or Angleland (England). Today there are Anglican churches in more than 150 countries of the world, making Anglicanism second only to Catholicism as the most widespread Christian communion. In the United States the Anglican Church is called the Episcopal Church.

The fourth reformation was the so-called *Radical Reformation*, which began with the Anabaptists (Re-baptists), who required baptismal candidates to make a formal profession of faith before being baptized. Churches in the fourth strand or branch of the Reformation went beyond Luther and Calvin. They wanted a simple, less liturgical form of worship—no vestments, stained glass windows, candles, crucifixes or stone altars—and a congregational rather than bishopric form of government. Historians argue about who should be included in the fourth reformation (some of the following were not "radicals"). The *Puritans* wanted to "purify" the Church of England of its Romanism. The *Separatists* "separated" from the Church of England and came to America, where they founded Congregational churches in New England. The *Baptists* "baptized" by immersion after a believer's public profession of faith. The Society of Friends or *Quakers* declared that all should "quake" before the word of God. The *Methodists* believed that all should observe "the method of life" set forth in the Bible.

The Spread of Reformation Thinking

The Reformation was aided by the Renaissance (French for "rebirth") in the fifteenth and sixteenth centuries, a period of intense study of the classics, even the Bible, and achievements in science and the arts, led by Leonardo da Vinci, Raphael, Michelangelo, Erasmus and others. It was also aided by Gutenberg's invention of the printing press in 1456. The sixteenth century was the first "information age," with new ideas going forth into every corner of Europe, feeding a growing sense of nationalism, individualism and democracy. The Reformation set in motion a new age, though those living at the time could scarcely have imagined the consequences of the movement they had set afoot.

The Catholic Counter-Reformation

When the Reformation began to take root and spread, the Catholic Church was forced to meet it head on. One response was the Council of Trent (a city in northern Italy), which met in three long sessions over the years 1545–1563. Trent is considered the most important Catholic gathering or assembly between the Council of Nicaea in 325 and Vatican II in 1962–65. It affirmed the authority of the pope and the teachings of the church fathers; received several Septuagintal books into its Old Testament canon; and affirmed Catholic doctrines rejected by the Reformers, among them the belief in transubstantiation, Mary's immaculate (sin-free) conception, perpetual virginity and assumption into heaven, priestly celibacy, invoking the names of saints in prayers, the belief in purgatory, the use of the Latin Vulgate, and the use of Latin in celebrating the Mass. It also condemned and abolished abuses, including the sale of indulgences. Thomas Bokenkotter, in his book *Dynamic Catholicism,* said that when the Council of Trent finished its work, "even critics had to admit that the job was well done. Trent defined the Catholic position in such clear and trenchant language that henceforth everyone knew exactly where the Catholic Church stood."

Catholics and Protestants agree on the triune nature of God, humankind's fallen nature and separation from God, the full humanity and divinity of Jesus, and Christ's death, resurrection and promised return. Though there are differences in authority, beliefs and the sacraments, the two traditions are much more alike than different.

The Enlightenment

A post-Reformation development that seriously impacted Christianity was the Enlightenment, a European intellectual movement that elevated reason above revelation. Historians argue about the dates of the Enlightenment; the bookends are the mid-1600s to the late-1700s. Enlightenment religious thinking arose alongside the rise in science and philosophy, led by men like Isaac Newton (1642–1727) and Immanuel Kant (1724-1804). They believed in reason as the way we come to know something. The Enlightenment had a high degree of optimism about humankind's ability to understand and control the natural world, which caused a division between science and religion.

Enlightenment theology only mildly embraced, and more often outright rejected, original sin, Jesus' virginal conception, salvific death and bodily resurrection, the Trinity, and the divine inspiration of the scriptures, because they could not be proven or verified by observation or experiment. For the Enlightenment, the essence of Christianity was not about God and things supernatural; it was the Bible's teachings about ethics, morals, and justice. The Enlightenment's optimism about the upward march of human progress suffered in the twentieth century from the first and second world wars and genocides like the Holocaust (more people died in genocides in the twentieth century than in all previous centuries combined).

The American philosopher Thelma Lavine, in her book *From Socrates to Sartre*, tells a story about James Boswell, the famous biographer, who visited David Hume (1711–1776), the great Scottish skeptic and critic of Christianity, when Hume was on his deathbed. Boswell wanted to know if Hume had changed his mind regarding the possibility of life after death. Hume said, "Yes, it's possible. It is also possible that if I throw this piece of coal into that fire that it will not burn. Possible, but there is no basis for believing it—not by reason, not by sense perception, not by experience." For Hume and other rationalists, the way we know something is by scientific testing and observation, which permeates current thinking. John Walton, Wheaton College professor of Old Testament, in his book *The Lost World of Genesis One*, said, "[Because] science can offer explanations for so much of what we see and experience, it is easy for our awareness of God's role [in the world] to drift to the periphery." The result has been a watering down of the authority of the Bible and the teaching of the church as guidelines for Christian belief and living.

Two outgrowths of the Enlightenment were the belief that humankind is the center and measure of all things, which in Europe and North America is gaining strength with each passing year; and Deism, from *Deus*, the Latin word for God. Deists believe in God the Creator, but not in the Triune God of the Bible. They believe that God created the universe and then stepped aside and allowed the universe to operate by natural laws that he had put in place. A reaction to the reason-only belief of the Enlightenment and the Creator-only God of Deism was Pietism, which emphasized a deep, personal faith in Jesus; living a holy, Christ-centered life; and a passion for evangelism and missions.

One of the children of the Enlightenment was Modernism, which held sway in the eighteenth and nineteenth centuries. Modernism believed that it was possible to make and prove absolute truth claims. It was replaced in the 1970s by Postmodernism, which denied Christianity's belief in a true, historical biblical metanarrative. Postmoderns believe that we are shaped by culture and experience, not by revelation or science, and are just as negative regarding Christianity—many think even more so—than Modernists.

Christian Missions

There have been four important periods of mission activity in the church. The first occurred during the years between the death of Jesus in the year 30 and the conversion of Constantine in 312, when Christianity was transformed from a small Palestinian sect into a community of believers representing, perhaps, ten percent of the inhabitants of the Roman Empire. The second took place in the first half of the Middle Ages with the expansion of Christianity throughout Europe. The third took place in the 1500s with the discovery of the Americas and the Far East. The fourth took place in the 1800s with missions into the interiors of India, Africa and China.

In the years following the Reformation, Catholicism won more converts outside Europe than it lost to Protestantism within Europe. The reasons for Catholicism's success were, first, naval powers Spain and Portugal, whose ships sailed the world looking for silk, spices, tea, coffee, tobacco and precious metals, were strongly Catholic; and, second, the Catholic Church had a trained "army" of missionaries—Jesuits (Ignatius considered foreign missions the highest form of Christian service), Franciscans, Dominicans and others—who traveled with sea captains like Columbus on their overseas voyages. The following are some missionary efforts over the last 500 years.

Latin America

The introduction of Christianity to the Americas followed Columbus's first voyage to the New World in 1492, with Spain gaining control of the Aztec empire in Mexico and the Inca empire in Peru in the early 1500s. The most prominent missionary in the early years of Latin America was the Spanish Dominican, Bartolomé de Las Casas (1474–1566), the first priest ordained in the New World. Las Casas opposed the exploitation of the Indians, pleading their case, with little success, in both Spanish America and Spain.

Today South America is the largest Christian continent and Brazil is the largest Catholic country. Two significant developments in twentieth-century South America were, first, the growth of Protestantism from the influx of Protestant mission organizations (in 1900, Latin America was 98 percent Catholic; today it is 15–20 percent Protestant); and, second, liberation theology, which arose in the 1960s as a protest against oppressive government regimes and exploitative capitalists.

India

The first effort to establish churches in India was made by the Jesuit Francis Xavier (1506–1552), who went to Goa, a port city in southwestern India, in 1542. (Xavier is the Catholic Church's "patron" of foreign missions.) German and Dutch Lutheran missionaries went to India in the early 1700s, and the great English Baptist missionary, William Carey (1761–1834), in 1793. Anglican Bishop Stephen Neill, in his book *A History of Christian Missions*, said Carey "marks the entry of the English-speaking world on a large scale into the missionary enterprise—and it has been the English-speaking world which has provided four-fifths of the non-Roman missionaries from the days of Carey to the present time."

Carey's motto was: "Attempt great things for God. Expect great things from God." Carey co-founded Serampore College, the first Christian college in Asia; published the first newspaper in India; translated the Bible, with help from Indian nationals, into several Indian languages and dialects; and founded the Horticultural Society of India to promote advances in agriculture. Church historian Ruth Tucker said, "More than any other individual in modern history, Carey stirred the imagination of the Christian world and showed by his own humble example what could and should be done to bring a lost world to Christ." Although missionaries have been active in India for 500 years, Indian Christians represent only 3 percent of the population.

Africa

The name most often associated with Christianity in sub-Saharan Africa is David Livingstone (1813–1873), a Scottish missionary who was sent by the London Missionary Society to Southern Africa in 1841. Livingstone is perhaps best remembered today by four words spoken to him by Henry Morton Stanley (1841–1904), a reporter for the *New York Herald* newspaper, who was sent to Africa to find Livingstone. Stanley's words, when he found him in Tanzania in 1871, were, simply, "Doctor Livingstone, I presume." Stanley was converted by Livingstone and stayed on in Africa to do missionary work of his own.

Livingstone worked as a missionary under Robert Moffat, the partriarch of Africa missions, and also married his daughter. He was an avid explorer—he discovered Victoria Falls in 1855, naming it for England's Queen Victoria—and pushed further and further into the interior of the continent where, Moffat said, "There are a thousand villages where a missionary has never been seen and the name of Christ has never been heard." Livingstone's writings and lectures on return trips to England opened Africa to the world. When Livingstone died (in Zambia), his heart was cut out and buried in Africa and his body sent to England, where he was given a state funeral and buried in Westminster Abbey. Today Christianity is growing faster in Africa than on any other continent.

China and the Orient

Serious Christian work in China was begun in the sixteenth century by Roman Catholic missionaries. The most prominent Protestant name in China missions is J. Hudson Taylor (1832–1905), a British medical missionary who went to China in 1854. Taylor's emphasis was on evangelism: "Every hour thousands of souls are passing away into death and darkness." Taylor founded the China Inland Mission, the first of many "faith" missions that depended on God to provide for the mission's financial needs. During his years in China, Taylor established a Christian presence in fifteen of China's eighteen provinces.

Over the years Christianity suffered many setbacks in China, most notably under the Communists, but like the first-century church, repression fostered rather than retarded its growth. Philip Jenkins, a distinguished senior fellow at Baylor University's Institute for Studies of Religion, in his book *The Next Christendom: The Coming of Global Christianity* (third edition, 2011), said, "we can reasonably place the number of Chinese Christians [today] at between 65 and 70 million."

According to the British *Daily Telegraph*, "If China continues its current rate of [Christian] conversions, it is on course to become the most Christian nation in the world." The numbers in the *Telegraph* article, and similar estimates by Professor Guang-Zhong Yang, a leading expert on religion in China, are off-the-wall higher than others I have seen. But if they turn out to be anywhere near correct, the growth of Christianity in

China, coupled with the decline of Christianity in America (see page 166 in the next chapter), may result in China having more Christians than the United States by the middle of the century.

Three other Asian countries worthy of mention are the Philippines, the only Christian country in Asia; South Korea, the most Protestant country in Asia; and Japan, a secular country in which Christians comprise less than 2 percent of the population.

An obstacle that Christianity faces in expanding its presence lies in a simple statistic: half of the world's population live in countries that are not open to the gospel. Well over a billion live in Communist countries like Russia and China; a billion and a half live in Islamic countries in the Middle East and Asia; and a billion or more live in countries with entrenched religions like Hinduism, Buddhism and Shintoism.

Christianity in the World

There are 2.3 billion Christians in the world (33 percent of the world's 7 billion population). Philip Jenkins, in *The Next Christendom*, mentioned above, said, "We are going through one of the transforming moments in the history of religion worldwide." He believes that by the year 2050, 72 percent of the world's Christians will live in Africa, Asia and Latin America and that Africa, with a projected one billion Christians, will be the largest Christian continent. Jenkins said the Anglican Church appears to be separating along North-South lines; that there will soon be more Catholics in Africa than in Europe; and that Pentecostal and charismatic believers will exceed one billion by the year 2050. Christianity's soft spot is the Middle East, where Christianity may one day become extinct. In the United States, the decline in Christianity is coming from churches that have chosen to identify with today's secular beliefs and values rather than the saving death and resurrection of Jesus.

Jenkins said, "Many of the fastest growing countries in the world are either predominantly Christian or have very sizable Christian minorities." He believes that conversions and continued high African and Latino fertility rates (the average Kenya family has six children) bode well for Christianity in the years ahead. Three differences between churches in the South and those in the North are that African, Asian and Latin churches, despite their different histories and cultures, believe in the authority of the Bible, are theologically conservative, and are more open to the supernatural than churches in the North.

Christianity in America

Christianity was brought to the New World by Spanish Franciscans, who traveled with Columbus in the 1490s, and by French Franciscans who came to Canada in 1610. They were followed by English Puritans and Separatists, who came to Massachusetts in 1620 and to other cities on the east coast, and by Spanish and Italian Jesuits, who came to Arizona and California in the mid-1600s.

The Coming of Protestant Christianity to America

Protestantism was brought to America by those who tried, unsuccessfully, to reform the theology, worship and polity of the state-controlled Church of England—and were persecuted for trying to do so. In 1620, one hundred and two pilgrims, sponsored by London merchants, set sail on the *Mayflower* for North America, a voyage that took sixty-six days. They arrived at Plymouth, Massachusetts—named for Plymouth, England, from which they had sailed—and established Plymouth Colony. Over the first winter, half of the settlers died of disease and exposure. The rest adapted themselves to their new environment, began repaying their backers, and in November 1621 celebrated "a day of thanksgiving."

America's Pilgrim fathers, and the Puritans who followed them, led the way in establishing Protestant Christianity in the New World. As time went on, dreams of America becoming the "new people of God" began to fade. One reason was the apathy of the original settlers' descendants, who were more interested in establishing themselves and their families than in religion. Another reason was that many of the second-wave settlers came to America to start a new life, rather than for religious reasons.

Surprisingly, those who came to America to escape religious persecution made no provision for the religious freedom of those who came after them. This changed with the First Amendment to the Constitution, which read: "Congress shall make no law respecting an establishment of religion or restricting the free exercise thereof." Church and state were to exist as separate institutions, neither united nor integrated as in England and elsewhere in Europe.

Pentecostalism

The most important religious movement in the last hundred years has been the birth and growth of Pentecostalism, which originated in the United States in the early 1900s. (The Assemblies of God, the largest Pentecostal denomination, was founded in 1914.) Pentecostalism is expanding rapidly throughout the world; in Africa and Latin America it is the largest Protestant movement. One reason for Pentecostalism's growth is the desire for a more experiential faith, one that goes beyond church tradition, liturgy (the order and form of worship), the sacraments and matters of doctrine. Pentecostals—so-called because the first outward sign of the Spirit came on the first Pentecost after Jesus' death—believe that speaking in tongues (other languages) is a manifestation of the Holy Spirit in their lives. Closely aligned with the Pentecostals are the charismatics (from *charisma*, the Greek word for "gift"), who belong to mainline, evangelical and independent churches. Charismatics also believe in the gifts of the Spirit, but are not insistent that speaking in tongues is the only or most important evidence of the Spirit. According to church demographer David Barrett, Pentecostals and charismatics combined, in the year 2000, represented 25 percent of Christians worldwide. Studies show that both groups have continued their growth in the twenty-first century.

Modernism and Fundamentalism

The twentieth century witnessed an American schism between Protestant liberals, who wanted to modernize Christianity—that is, reconcile Christianity with advances in science and biblical scholarship—and conservatives, who argued for the fundamentals of the faith. The term *fundamentalism* comes from a series of ninety or so essays—"The Fundamentals: A Testimony to the Truth"—that were written between 1910 and 1915, funded by Lyman and Milton Stewart, co-founders of Union Oil Company in California. The essays defended Protestant beliefs that biblical critics, liberal theologians, Darwinian evolutionists and secular philosophers were openly attacking. They affirmed conservative teachings regarding the verbal inspiration, inerrancy and authority of the Bible; sin, judgment and salvation; the deity of Christ and his virgin birth, substitutionary atonement, bodily resurrection and imminent personal return; and a wide range of other matters, including biblical criticism, Christian sects and cults, worship, evangelism and missions.

The liberal-fundamentalist conflict culminated in the Scopes Trial in Dayton, Tennessee, in 1925. The American Civil Liberties Union persuaded John Scopes, a high school biology teacher, to teach evolution to test the constitutionality of Tennessee's antievolution law. The fundamentalists were represented by William Jennings Bryan, thrice an unsuccessful Democratic candidate for the presidency, who believed in the literal interpretation of the Bible. The liberals were represented by Clarence Darrow, the celebrated trial lawyer, who was an outspoken agnostic. Bryan agreed to testify as an expert on the Bible; he was brutally cross-examined by Darrow on the early chapters in Genesis. Bryan's statements were sometimes poetic—"It is better to know the Rock of Ages than the age of the rocks"—but rarely convincing. The liberals or modernists won the debate, at least in the eyes of the public. The fundamentalists suffered ridicule and adopted a defensive, Bible-centered, separatist philosophy, which split many denominations in two. Some Americans came to view the term fundamentalism as disparaging or belittling; many within the movement considered it a badge of pride.

Evangelicalism

The early 1940s saw the emergence of a new group, called evangelicals, conservative Christians who wanted to distance themselves from fundamentalism's narrowness and extreme literalism; its social taboos against smoking, dancing and movies; and its distrust of biblical scholarship and science. Fundamentalism's disengagement with the world has led to its declining importance and relevance.

Evangelicalism is a generic term that embraces historic, creedal Christianity. Evangelicals are found in both mainline and independent Protestant churches, and also in Catholic churches, and play an active role in society. A central premise of evangelicalism is having a personal relationship with Jesus Christ.

Some well-known evangelical organizations are the Navigators (1933), the Wycliffe Bible Translators (1934), Young Life (1938), Inter-Varsity Christian Fellowship (1941), Youth for Christ (1945), the Billy Graham Evangelistic Association (1950), World Vision (1950), Campus Crusade for Christ, now called Cru (1951), Youth With A Mission (1960), Langham Partnership, formerly John Stott Ministries (1974), and Prison Fellowship (1976).

According to the Pew Forum, the division between Protestant, Catholic and Orthodox Christians in the United States is 67-32-1 percent, respectively.

Discussion Questions

1. Many people are baptized, confirmed, on church membership rosters, but not active in their church. Are you involved in your church's ministries and outreach programs?

2. Christianity has had many heroes through the ages, among them Francis of Assisi, Luther and Calvin, John Wesley, William Booth (when Booth died, 40,000 people attended his funeral), Dietrich Bonhoeffer, C.S. Lewis, Martin Luther King, Mother Teresa, Billy Graham and John Stott. Who are some of your heroes?

3. What can be done to make Christianity relevant to millennials, selfies and others who have left the church—and also those who have never been part of a church?

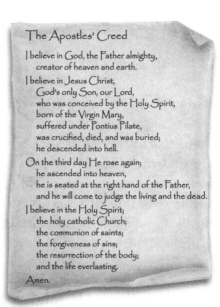

7

Christian Theology and Beliefs

The classic definition of theology, dating back to Anselm (1033-1109), the archbishop of Canterbury in the eleventh century, is "faith seeking understanding"—faith asking questions, faith probing for answers. Does God exist or do we just hope that he does? Are the scriptures the word of God or the words of those who wrote them? What is sin and where did it come from? How does Jesus save us from our sins? Who is the Holy Spirit? What happens when we die? The task of theology is to ask such questions and to answer them in a biblically-based, systematic way.

Christian Theism

Christian theism is the belief that there is one supreme, sovereign God, not many gods, as in some Eastern religions; that God has revealed his love for us and his will for our lives, which are set forth in the Old and New Testaments; that it is possible for fallen, finite human beings to have a personal relationship with the triune God through Jesus Christ; and that there is a further, fuller life beyond this life, in contrast to those who believe that this life is all there is or who believe in reincarnation.

God Our Father: All-Mighty and All-Loving

The ultimate question of life is not capitalism versus communism, or Christianity versus Islam, or health care, illegal immigration or global warming. The ultimate question is: "Does God exist?" The Christian answer, which is a statement of faith, is a resounding YES.

The Knowledge of God

Christians believe there are strong, compelling reasons for believing that God exists.

First, God is made known in creation. The so-called Big Bang, which set everything in motion 13.7 billion years ago, could not have been a random event. There had to have been a supernatural force that brought the universe, the planet Earth and the heavenly bodies into being.

Second, God is made known in his providence—his "provide-ence" and sovereign care of his creation—as in Karl Barth's story of Frederick the Great on page 40, which cannot be seen in the history of any other people.

Third, God is made known in the moral law, the innate law or conscience that distinguishes humans from all other creatures, the "law" that enables us to know right from wrong and urges us to do the right and not the wrong. Immanuel Kant, the foremost philosopher of the Enlightenment, said, "Two things fill my mind with ever-increasing wonder and awe: the starry skies above me and the moral law within me."

Lastly, God is made known on the plane of history—in his rescue of the Israelites, who were living as slaves in Egypt, and in Jesus of Nazareth, the one whom the writer of the letter to the Hebrews said was "the exact imprint of God's very being" (1:3), the one about whom Søren Kierkegaard said, "the infinite became finite."

Belief in God does not prove that God exists. His existence is something that cannot be proven—or disproven, despite the claims of atheists and others. Looking at theism versus atheism, the case for theism is much stronger than the belief that everything came into being by chance, that is, that the universe and life just happened (chance is more like luck; on its own it cannot produce anything).

Some say, "If there is a God, why doesn't he do a better job of convincing us?" God did not create robotic beings; he created free-will human beings with the capacity to make choices. He beckons and draws us, hoping that we will come to him and acknowledge him and love and serve him.

God the Creator

How can we know and visualize God? One way would be to think of God in anthropomorphic (human) terms, as in Michelangelo's painting of God and Adam on the ceiling of the Sistine Chapel in Rome. Another would be to reflect on God's nature and attributes. The late American theologian Langdon

Gilkey, in his book *Maker of Heaven and Earth*, said the most important thing that Christians believe about God is that he "created the heavens and the earth." Christian belief in God's creation comes, first, from our observation of the universe and the wonders of nature; and, second, from the book of Genesis (1:1), the prophets (Isaiah 44:24), the Psalms (90:2), the Gospels (John 1:3), the apostle Paul (Colossians 1:16) and the book of Hebrews (1:2). How did God create? Out of nothing (*ex nihilo*) rather than forming what already was. Before God created, there was nothing but God.

God's Divine Nature and Attributes

- Christians believe that God is a *spirit-being*, not a physical-being with arms and legs.

- Christians believe the essence of God is *love*, a love so great that he gave his Son that we "may not perish but have eternal life." (The word *perish* does not mean physical death. We will all die one day. It means that we will spend an eternity separated from God.)

- Christians believe that God is *eternal*. Everything began with God; there was no time when God "was not"; he is "from everlasting to everlasting" (Psalm 90:2); he is the same yesterday, today and tomorrow; he does not grow older with each passing year.

- Christians believe that God is *omnipotent*, meaning all-mighty and all-powerful, one who is able to do "whatever pleases" him (Psalm 135:6); that he is *omnipresent*, meaning everywhere present at one and the same time (Psalm 139:7–12); and that he is *omniscient*, with perfect knowledge of things past, present and future (Proverbs

5:21 and Hebrews 4:13).

- Christians believe that God is both *transcendent*, meaning outside and beyond all that is, as in the creation of the universe, and also *immanent*, meaning present and active, as in the Exodus and Jesus of Nazareth.

- Finally, Christians believe that God is *personal*, someone who wants to have a relationship with us. Three of God's personal characteristics are love, mercy and compassion.

Nonetheless, some find it incredible to think that an enlightened person could believe in God. Everyone would agree that scientists are enlightened persons. Theoretical physicist Michael Guillen, in his book *Can a Smart Person Believe in God?*, cites an article in the April 1997 issue of *Nature* magazine titled "Scientists Are Still Keeping the Faith." The authors of the article, Edward Larson and Larry Witham, reported on a study they made that revealed "about 40 percent of all American physicists believe in a personal God." Guillen adds to his belief that "smart people" can believe in God by citing a 2003 Harris Poll "that among Americans with post-graduate degrees—in other words, our country's most well-educated men and women—85 percent believe in God." So enlightened persons—in fact, a great many of them—believe in God.

The Triune Nature of God

There are two great mysteries that underlie the Christian faith. The first is the Incarnation—the belief that God entered human history in the person of Jesus of Nazareth. C. S. Lewis, in his book *Miracles,* said, "The central miracle asserted by Christians is the Incarnation. Every other miracle prepares for this or exhibits this or results from this."

The second big mystery is the Trinity—the belief that God comes to us in the person of Jesus of Nazareth through the power of the Holy Spirit. The triune nature of God is succinctly stated in the Apostles' and Nicene Creeds, but God being both one-and-three is impossible for humans to understand or explain. J. I. Packer, in his book *Concise Theology*, says trying to do so "is beyond us."

The word Trinity comes from the Latin *trinitas*, meaning "threeness," which does not mean three separate, independent beings. This would be "tri-theism." It means that the Godhead is comprised of three co-eternal, co-equal, interconnected "persons" or "beings" or "essences." The word Trinity is not found in the Bible (nor is the word Incarnation), but the threeness of God is alluded to in several places—twelve different places, according to Thomas Oden in his book *Classic Christianity*. One place is Matthew 28:19, where Jesus tells the disciples to baptize others "in the name of the Father and of the Son and of the Holy Spirit." Analogies, though imperfect, are sometimes helpful in explaining difficult concepts. An analogy for something that is both one-and-three at the same time is the rainbow: each color is distinct from the others, but all are part of the same "bow."

The following are some non-theistic beliefs. *Atheism* is the belief there is no God (the prefix *a*, as mentioned earlier, means "no," so a-theism means "no god"). *Agnosticism* is the belief that it is not possible to know whether or not God exists (*gnosis* is the Greek word for knowledge, so a-gnosis means "no knowledge"). *Polytheism* (*poly* means many) is the belief that there are many gods or deities, as in Hinduism, which has thousands of gods. *Pantheism* (*pan* means all) is the belief that all is God or that God is in everything, which the New Age Movement calls *monism* (one-ism). *Deism*, from the Latin *Deus* (God), is the belief that God is not involved in life on planet Earth (page 134). *Animism* is the belief that all natural phenomena (humans, animals, plants, stones) have souls.

Angels, Satan and Demons

The modern world dismisses angels, Satan and demons as superstition and views people who believe in them as naïve, but the scriptures have much to say about them.

Angels are mentioned in more than half of the books of the Bible, and two angels are named—Michael, the archangel or highest angel (Daniel 10:13, Jude 9 and Revelation 12:7) and Gabriel (Daniel 8:16 and Luke 1:19 and 1:26). What are angels and what is their function? Angels are spirit beings; and though they are created beings, they are immortal beings (Luke 20:36); and though they are often described in masculine terms, they are not sexual beings. Their function is to act as messengers of God—the word *angel* comes from a Greek word meaning "messenger"—as when the angel Gabriel brought messages to Zechariah about Elizabeth's pregnancy (Luke 1:11-20) and to Mary about the birth of Jesus (Luke 1:26-38); and in dreams to Joseph about Mary's pregnancy and to take his family to Egypt (Matthew 1:20-21 and 2:13); and appearing to and speaking with the women at Jesus' tomb (Matthew 28:2-7 and John 20:12-13).

Angels encourage and minister to God's people and oppose the work of Satan and his demons. Are angels still active? There is no scriptural warrant for believing they were active only in biblical times; and Jesus said, "when [the dead rise they will be] like angels in heaven" (Mark 12:25); and the book of Revelation suggests that they will be active at the end of the age. Are there "guardian angels"? Matthew 18:10 ("their angels") and Acts 12:15 ("his angel") suggest the possibility of an angel for each believer, but there isn't much more than this to go on.

Satan is mentioned in the Old Testament, but he is much more prominent in the New Testament, where he is mentioned by almost every writer. Who is Satan? He is a being whose pride set him against God, becoming the archenemy of God, who was cast out of "heaven" (Luke 10:18). Satan is not the opposite of God; he is a created being who is the opposite of Michael the archangel. He is also called the devil, the translation of Satan in the Septuagint, the one who fell from heaven (Luke above), Beelzebul (Mark 3:22), the evil one (1 John 5:18), the tempter and other names.

Satan is not a thing. He is an active spirit being with an intellect and a will whose mission is to oppose God (the word *satan* comes from a Hebrew word that means "to oppose"), tempting us to follow him and his evil ways, as he tried to do to Jesus in the wilderness (Mark 1:12-13). At the end of the age—at the last battle—Satan will be destroyed for all time (Revelation 20:10). C. S. Lewis said that some people take the devil too seriously, while others don't take him seriously enough.

As angels are God's agents, demons are Satan's agents—evil spirit beings that are hostile to God and the people of God, which is why so much is written about Jesus' exorcizing them. In Jesus' day (and even today) it is evil, demonic spirits that must be defeated, not earthly powers like Rome. Although some scholars and psychologists dismiss the idea of demons and demon possession, the latter is a worldwide phenomenon.

The Doctrine of Creation

Martin Luther said the doctrine of creation "is the foundation of the whole of Scripture." It is one of the pillars on which our faith rests. If we have doubts regarding the Christian view of creation—for instance, if we believe that the universe came into being by chance and produced planets like our own, or that life came into being by chance and evolved upward—our faith, like Jesus' story of the house built on sand in the Sermon on the Mount, rests on a weak foundation.

Science and Religion

Science clearly dominates our way of thinking, not only about the world, but about life in general, including religion. Before looking at the doctrine of creation, we need to understand how science arrives at its conclusions. First, it conducts experiments and records observed facts and occurrences. Second, it hypothesizes about the meaning of its observations and findings. Third, it tests its hypotheses until a particular hypothesis is proven either true or false. There is no conflict here between science and religion. The conflict comes when science postulates about things that cannot be proven, such as the creation of the universe and living beings.

The Creation of the Universe

How did the universe come into being? The most popular theory is the Big Bang, the belief that 13.7 billion years ago a super-stupendous explosion gave birth to the universe, which is expanding today in all directions at tremendous speeds. The expansion of the universe was discovered by the astronomer Edwin Hubble—after whom the Hubble Telescope is named—in 1929, which gave rise to the Big Bang hypothesis.

Every movement has a cause, so there must have been a first or primal cause that gave birth to the universe. This is much easier to believe than to think that the universe, with its billions of stars and planets, and the earth, with its widely-diverse forms of life, just happened. Something or someone had to start everything on its course, someone who existed before and is independent of both time and space.

In his book *Reasonable Faith*, William Lane Craig said, "I was talking with a guy who thought he was very clever. He said, smugly, 'If God created the universe, where did God come from?' I replied, 'God didn't come from anywhere. God is eternal and has always existed.'"

The Creation of Life

How did life on earth come into being? Is there any evidentiary support for the biblical view that God created life on earth? Some say that living matter came into being by chance after the earth cooled down. But how could inanimate matter give birth to animate, purposeful life like human life? Living matter can only come from preexisting living matter. Charles Darwin's theory of natural selection may help explain how life evolved, but not how it came into being in the first place.

The premise that the building blocks of life came into being by chance and evolved into higher forms of life is challenged by scientists like the late British astronomer Sir Frederick Hoyle. In his book *The Intelligent Universe,* Hoyle, who was not a Christian, said the probability of the 2,000 or so enzymes (proteins within cells) required for life coming together in the right sequence would be "the same probability as throwing an uninterrupted sequence of 50,000 'sixes' with unbiased dice."

A stronger case can be made for microevolution, with different varieties of plants, fish and animals, and even humans, which we see everywhere around us. This is referred to as theistic evolution, the belief that God brought everything into being in the beginning, and then let nature take its course. Critics say that theistic evolution is nothing more than Deism in new clothes.

Dr. Francis Collins, who has doctorates in medicine and chemistry, is both a world-class scientist and a believing Christian. Collins directed the recently completed Human Genome Project, which mapped out the DNA code of life. (Collins is now Director of the National Institutes of Health.) As a young man he was an agnostic and then an atheist. In his book *The Language of God: A Scientist Presents Evidence for Belief,* Collins tells how, as a result of his work on the genome project, he came to believe there is a Creator God behind the intricate design of the universe and the DNA of life. "The God of the Bible," Collins said, "is also the God of the genome. He can be worshiped in the cathedral or in the laboratory. His creation is majestic, awesome, intricate and beautiful."

Sin: Origin and Universality

The book of Genesis opens with the story of the first "parents" of the human race, Adam and Eve, who disobeyed God and fell into sin, resulting in their banishment from the Garden of Eden. This is the biblical explanation for the fallenness of the human race—at least the Christian explanation, because there is no concept of innate or indwelt sin in Judaism, Islam and other religions—which Christians see as the core human problem, and Jesus' saving death as the solution to the problem.

The Doctrine of Sin

Sin is a theological concept: it is disobedience to the divine law and will of God. One Greek word for sin is *hamartia,* which means "missing the mark." We miss the mark when we step over the line, and also when we don't step up to the line. What is the mark or line? In a word, it is love. We sin when we do not love God with our whole heart, soul, mind and strength (Mark 12:30), when we disobey his law and commandments (1 John 5:3), when we do not show love and compassion to our neighbors and others (Leviticus 19:18).

Boston College philosopher-theologian Peter Kreeft says that sin is to the soul what disease is to the body. Our indwelt sinfulness—our "sin disease"—gives rise to sinful acts, sometimes called 'actual' sins or 'daily' sins. (See the Seven Deadly Sins in chapter 9.) Christians believe that Christ died to redeem us from our sins so that we may not, as has been said many times already, "perish" in our sins.

Original Sin

The term original sin is not found in the Bible; it comes from Saint Augustine . It refers to Adam and Eve's sin of disobedience in the Garden of Eden in Genesis 3. Some ask, "How could a couple eating an apple condemn the entire human race?" They say original sin refers to the "origin" of sin—our inborn state of sin—not to Adam and Eve eating from a forbidden tree. It is said that "In Adam's fall, we sinned all." I wonder how this applies to peoples who were not Adam's descendants, like those mentioned in Genesis 4:12-16?

The origin of sin and evil is second only to the origin of life as the greatest of all enigmas. Where did sin come from? How is it that human beings become evil people? How is it, asked American theologian Bernard Ramm, that a one-year-old infant is convicted twenty years later of selling drugs or car theft or rape or perhaps even murder?

In an effort to come to grips with evil, most religions have a doctrine of sin. Some believe that sin comes from uncontrollable cravings; others believe that we are born neutral and are pushed one way or the other by good and evil forces. Christianity teaches that sin is part of the human condition and has been since the dawn of history.

Looking at the world around us we see sin and evil everywhere: crime and thuggery on the streets of our cities, terrorism around the world, the use of deadly drugs and other substances, spousal abuse and child molestation, corruption and payoffs in government and business, racial and ethnic conflicts and "cleansings," suicide bombings and school-yard shootings, and on and on. The British writer G. K. Chesterton (1874–1936), in his autobiography *Orthodoxy*, said that original sin is one Christian doctrine that no one can dispute. All you have to do, he said, is read the morning newspaper. Today we might say all you have to do is watch the evening news on television where, it is said, "What bleeds, leads."

Adam and Eve

Those who read the Bible literally read Genesis 3 as the account of sin entering the world through the disobedience of Adam and Eve (they both sinned, but the New Testament talks only about Adam's sin). Paul elaborates on the Genesis story of the fall in the garden in his letter to the church at Rome, saying, "Just as sin came into the world through one man . . . so death has spread to all because all have sinned" (5:12), implying that Adam's sin spread like a virus throughout all of creation.

There are credible commentators, however, who read Genesis 2 and 3 differently. One is the highly-regarded French theologian Henri Blocker. In his book *Original Sin: Illuminating the Riddle,* he carefully exegetes (interprets) Genesis 3 and Romans 5 and summarizes writings on sin by other scholars. Blocher's conclusion is that the origin of humankind's sinfulness and its transmission are a mystery.

Though Adam's sin and its transmission are a mystery, at some point in time, from the earliest hominids to later *homo sapiens* (the species to which human beings belong), God created man and woman in his "image and likeness" (Genesis 1:26), which made human beings different from all other creatures. Augustine said "the image of God" refers to the soul that God implanted in the bodies of humans; others believe the term refers to the whole person, not just the soul.

Though many read Adam eating from the forbidden tree as a story, it is a story that still holds the field: we are sinful and separated from God and have been since the fall of Adam and Eve, though many believe we are not sinful because of their sin but because of our own sins. Nowhere in scripture does Jesus attribute our sinfulness to the first couple eating from the forbidden tree.

Those who read Genesis 3 as a story are less concerned with the question of how sin entered the human race than with our being forgiven for our sins so that we may be deemed righteous in the sight and presence of God on judgment day. Is this even possible? Yes, by believing that Jesus, "the one mediator between God and man" (1 Timothy 2:5), died a sacrificial death to reconcile us with God.

Jesus Christ: Birth, Death and Resurrection

The fundamental question of every religious person is the question of the Philippian jailer in the book of Acts: "What must I do to be saved?" (16:30)—meaning what must I do to be reconciled with God. Paul's answer to the jailer (and to us) is: "Believe on the Lord Jesus and you will be saved."

The Person and Nature of Christ

The early church debated the person of Christ. Was he truly God—the incarnate Son of God—or only the adopted (at his baptism) son of God? The Council of Constantinople (381), in its final wording of the Nicene Creed, said that Jesus was "very God of very God, begotten not made, of one substance with the Father." The early church also debated Jesus' nature. Was he part God and part man? And if there were "parts," were they different or equal, and were they separate or mixed? The Council of Chalcedon, a city on the Bosporus near Constantinople, declared in 451 that Jesus was one person with two natures, one divine ("conceived by the Holy Spirit") and one human ("born of the Virgin Mary"), and these natures were neither separate nor mixed: Jesus was both fully human and fully divine.

As to his *humanity*, Jesus was born of a woman, tested in the wilderness, ate meals with friends and sinners, went to weddings, preached to the crowds, debated the Pharisees, was weary and sometimes sorrowful (as when Lazarus died) and at times even angry, and he died and was buried.

As to his *divinity*, Jesus was conceived by the Holy Spirit, healed the deaf and the blind, stilled the wind and the sea, raised people from the dead, knew what others were thinking (Mark 2:8), knew that he was going to be killed by the authorities in Jerusalem (Mark 10:33–34), claimed oneness with God, and assumed God-only attributes such as forgiving sin.

Jesus' Virginal Conception

The conception of Jesus in the womb of Mary, by the power of the Holy Spirit, underlies the church's teaching that Jesus was God-in-the-flesh. The scriptural basis for this is John 1:14: "And the Word [of God] became flesh and lived among us." We talk about Jesus' *virgin* birth, but he was born the same way all babies are born. The nativity narratives are not about his birth. They are about his conception by the Holy Spirit to become the one in whom God entered human history. Luke, who tells us that he investigated "everything carefully" (1:3), may have learned about Jesus' conception from Mary when he was in Palestine during Paul's imprisonment in Caesarea in the late 50s (Mary is believed to have lived into the 60s).

The Roman Catholic Church teaches that Mary "was preserved immaculate from the stain of original sin by the grace of God." Mary's *immaculate conception* is the Catholic Church's attempt to explain how Jesus was born of a human mother without the taint of original sin. There is no support for this in the scriptures; it comes from the writings of the early church fathers. The Reformers held that Jesus, who was conceived by and filled with the Holy Spirit, was sinless from the very moment of his conception.

Today the virgin birth is a stumbling block in a world in which science holds sway over so much of our thinking. Jesus' virginal conception may seem impossible to believe, but no more so than his resurrection, for which there is substantial, credible evidence.

According to British theologian Keith Ward, the strongest argument for the veracity of the birth narratives is that it is hard to see why they would have been invented when their claim—that a child born out of wedlock was the genetic, messianic descendant of King David—would have been so offensive to Jewish ears.

To deny that Jesus "was conceived by the Holy Spirit and born of the Virgin Mary," as we confess in the Apostles' Creed, is to deny that Jesus was God incarnate, which is to deny his "savior-ness." We are not saved by good works and worthy deeds. We are saved by God—by believing in God-incarnate, God-in-the-flesh, Jesus Christ.

Jesus' Saving Death

Christianity is a religion of salvation, as are many other religions. Jesus' mission was a *rescue* mission—a mission to rescue us from our estrangement from God.

The apostle Paul said we are saved "by grace through faith" (Ephesians 2:8). The first part of the Ephesian equation is God's gift of grace (Jesus' death "for us"), which is totally free. There is nothing that we can do to earn our salvation, nothing that will oblige God to save us. But for God's grace to be *saving* grace, it must be accepted in faith. This is the second part of the equation.

Karl Barth, the most influential Protestant theologian in the twentieth century, said the most important word in the New Testament is the Greek word *hyper*, which means "on behalf of," referring to Jesus' saving death on our behalf to reconcile us with God.

The term theologians use in talking about Jesus' saving death is "atonement." To understand our at-one-ment with God, we have to go back to ancient Israel, where priests sacrificed animals to cover the sins of the people (Leviticus 1–7). Isaiah said that a "suffering servant" is coming who will be "despised . . . rejected . . . wounded . . . crushed . . . [and] stricken" to redeem us from our sinful transgressions (52:13-53:12). Jesus told the disciples that this prophecy "must be fulfilled in me" (Luke 22:37). The great irony is that the one who came to offer new life to others had to give his own life to do so.

People sometimes ask, "What does it mean to be saved?" It means that having confessed our sins, and believing that Jesus died to save us from our sins, they will no longer be held against us. But how does Jesus' death in the first century save us from our sins in the twenty-first century? Paul, in his letter to the Romans, said that we are saved "through faith . . . by faith" (1:17). We are saved through the faithful act of Jesus dying for us on the cross . . . and by our faith that his death was, is today and will be on judgment day, salvific for all who have believed in him. What are we saved from? We are saved from our sins, and our failure to honor God and obey his laws and commandments, and to live under the lordship of Jesus.

How can we be sure of our salvation? The doctrine of Assurance (of salvation) is contained in Jesus' promise that those who believe in him will be "given eternal life" (John 10:27-29). Can we lose our salvation? If we truly believe in the efficacy of Jesus' saving death, our salvation is secure. If we had to work out our salvation, as do adherents of the religions in chapter 8, our salvation would depend on our achievement rather than the finished work of Christ on the cross.

Jesus' Bodily Resurrection

There were many messianic movements before and after Jesus; they all collapsed with the deaths of their founders (see Acts 5:36-38). Why did the "Jesus movement" survive—not only survive, but *flourish*? In a word, it was Jesus' resurrection. Within a generation of his death, countless cities in North Africa, Asia Minor, Greece and Italy had large, thriving, culturally-diverse communities of believers in Jesus' resurrection. What convinced them that Jesus had been raised from the dead?

First, the *empty tomb*. If the Jews had produced Jesus' body, it would have put an end to his followers' claim that he had risen from the dead. The German theologian Paul Althaus said, "The claim that Jesus had been raised could not have been maintained for a single day, for a single hour, if the emptiness of the tomb had not been established as a fact for all concerned."

Second, the *written testimonies* to Jesus' resurrection in the New Testament (there are twelve accounts of the risen Christ in the Gospels, Acts and Paul's letters). No one would have taken the time or gone to the expense of writing about an executed

Jewish preacher-teacher from rural Galilee if he had remained in the grave.

Third, the *witness of the disciples*, who fled when Jesus was arrested, but after Pentecost came out of hiding to preach his resurrection, and many were martyred for doing so, both in Jerusalem (like Stephen) and in Rome (like Peter and Paul)—and no one, Paul Little said earlier, puts his or her life on the line for something they believe to be untrue.

Fourth, the discovery of the empty tomb by *the women,* who along with minors, slaves and convicts were not considered credible witnesses in the first century. (Paul, in writing to a Greco-Roman audience, does not include women in his list of those to whom Jesus appeared in 1 Corinthians 15:5–8.) If the Gospel writers had fabricated their stories to make them more believable, they would have had men, not women, as the first witnesses.

Fifth, the conversion of *Saul of Tarsus*, an early persecutor of Christians who, after "meeting" the risen Christ on the road to Damascus, became Christianity's greatest thinker and church-planting champion.

Jesus' resurrection is the *hinge* between the earthly Jesus, who walked the dusty roads of Galilee and Judea, and the heavenly Jesus, who was raised from the dead and ascended to heaven.

The Holy Spirit: The Third Person of the Trinity

The Holy Spirit, or Holy Ghost, from the English word *gast*, meaning spirit, is the third person of the Trinity. The word *gast* (ghost) comes from the *King James Bible*—an unfortunate word or term because it has led some to think of the Spirit as a ghost-like being. The Spirit is not a ghost. He is a person—and more than a "person": a co-equal, co-eternal member of the Triune Godhead.

Although the Spirit is mentioned throughout the Bible, there is not much written about him in the scriptures or in Christian literature, nor are many sermons preached about him in church, nor have I devoted much space to him in this book—in contrast to several pages devoted to God the Father and two full chapters to Jesus of Nazareth.

The divinity of the Holy Spirit is mentioned many times in the Bible. One important place is Jesus' virginal conception in Luke 1:26-38. The angel Gabriel told Mary that she would have a son. Mary said, "How can this be, since I am a virgin?" Gabriel said, "The Holy Spirit will come upon you [and your child] will be called the Son of God." The Spirit that "comes upon" Mary is the Spirit of God.

The most concentrated teaching about the Holy Spirit—also called the Paraclete, the Advocate, the Counselor and the Comforter—are Jesus' sayings in John chapters 14-16. Jesus tells the disciples that after he leaves them he will send the Holy Spirit to counsel, guide, comfort and support them.

As to the work of the Spirit, one function is to grant gifts to believers, some twenty of which the apostle Paul mentions in 1 Corinthians 12:8-11, Romans 12:6-8 and Ephesians 4:11. (In 1 Corinthians 12:11, Paul says that every believer has at least one gift.) Two other works of the Spirit are the regeneration of believers, enabling them to be born "again" or "anew" (John 3:3-8); and sanctification, the continuing work of the Spirit that enables believers to grow in holiness (2 Thessalonians 2:13-14). Paul tells the Galatians, in verses 5:22-23, about the "fruit" of the Spirit, which we will look at in chapter 10.

How does one receive the Holy Spirit? Most sacramental denominations believe that one receives the Spirit, in all his fullness, at baptism. Others believe that a necessary precedent to receiving the Spirit is a public profession of faith in Jesus as Lord and Savior.

People talk about being "in" the Spirit. Hank Hanegraaff, in *The Bible Answer Book*, says, "What does it mean to say that the Holy Spirit is 'in' [you]? It is not to point out where the Holy Spirit is physically located, but rather to acknowledge that you have come into an intimate, personal relationship with him through faith and repentance. The preposition 'in' is not locational but relational."

The Church: Marks, Sacraments and Polity

The Nicene Creed confesses four "marks" of the church, namely, that it is *one* (one body under the lordship of Christ), *holy* (set apart for Christian ministry), *catholic* (universal) and *apostolic* (called to proclaim Jesus).

The Protestant Church

There are thousands of Protestant denominations, some as small as a single church. Denominationalism in America is on the decline. Some think that Christianity is on the decline as well, as seen in polls and reports of dramatic declines in church attendance. Diana Butler Bass, in her book *Christianity After Religion*, using a stock market term, says the church is in a bear market, quoting two scientifically grounded polls showing the number of self-identified Christians has fallen by 10 percent over the past twenty years. People are bored with churches that are same-old, same-old. They are spending their Sundays going to sporting events, shopping and on family outings. Others are turned off by churches that preach only politically-correct sermons and focus more on membership numbers and fundraising than on the Bible, spiritual formation, evangelism, missions, and caring for the least, the last and the lost.

In 2014, the Pew Research Center surveyed 35,000 adults regarding their church affiliation. Twenty-nine percent said they were not affiliated with any religious institution. They are referred to by the media as Nones because, when they were asked by Pew demographers what church they belonged to, they said "None." The tipping point came in the 1990s, when the number of nones grew from 8 percent of the adult population to almost 30 percent today (the increase in nones has been greatest among mainline Protestants and Roman Catholics). Alan Cooperman, Pew's director of religious research, said the rise of the nones "is big, it's broad and it's everywhere." The Pew survey disclosed that, "Whether nearing retirement or just entering adulthood, married or single, living in the West or the Bible Belt, Americans in virtually all demographic groups are less likely to describe themselves today as Christians."

The nones are the third largest "religion" in the world, after Christianity and Islam, with an estimated 56 million in the United States and more than one billion worldwide. The largest cohort of nones is the under-30 group, many of whom were raised in the church, but no longer consider Christianity relevant. A challenge to the church today is to discover ways to preach and teach the truth, believability and importance of Jesus' salvific death.

The Emerging Church

A new movement is the emerging church, which takes its name from the belief that as culture changes—we now live in the postmodern world—a new way of doing church needs to emerge as well. The movement began to blossom in the

1990s. Organizationally, it is a loose association of independent "churches," with no agreed-upon statement of belief, no centralized leadership, and no institutional structure. Its appeal is to young adults, the age group the traditional church is losing.

Some say the emerging church is a passing fad that will burn out and disappear (the same thing was said about Pentecostalism a hundred years ago); others call it the new Christian left because it waters down biblical Christianity. Those within the movement say that it is a more authentic way of living for Christ in and for the world.

Emergent theologian Tony Jones, in his book *The New Christians: Dispatches From The Emergent Frontier,* says, "The hope of emergents is [for the] reinvigoration of Christian theology ... not in the ivy towers or in the pulpits and pews but on the street." Some wonder if the emerging church will live beyond the lives of its founders and leaders—as the Reformation did beyond the lives of Luther and Calvin—or if it is just another in a long line of attempts to rewrite historic Christianity.

The Church's Sacraments

The word *sacrament* comes from *sacramentum,* a Latin word meaning "sacred oath," referring to oaths that Roman soldiers took in which they pledged their lives to the emperor. Most sacramental churches believe that sacraments bestow grace or are channels of grace. The Belgian Dominican theologian Edward Schillebeeckx said, "Just as we encounter God in the tangible Jesus, so we encounter Jesus in the tangible sacraments."

The church has long recognized two sacraments instituted by Jesus, called the Gospel Sacraments: *Baptism* (Matthew 28:19), the sealing of God's new covenant and Jesus' promises; and the *Lord's Supper* (Luke 22:19-20), also called the *Eucharist,* from the Greek word *eucharistia,* meaning "to give thanks," or

Holy Communion, meaning "common union." Non-sacramental churches (Baptist, Brethren, Pentecostal and others) prefer the word *ordinance* to sacrament, meaning that Christ ordained these acts.

Baptism has been practiced by the majority of Christians since the first Pentecost following Jesus' death (Acts 2:38). Though baptism has a long history, there are widespread differences in its understanding and practice, prompting one writer to refer to baptism as "the water that divides." Two examples are infant baptism versus youth dedication and baptismal immersion—going down into the water and coming up, dying to sin and rising to new life—versus affusion (pouring) and aspersion (sprinkling). Some, particularly Catholics, believe that baptism washes away original sin; for others it is a sign of inclusion in God's covenant of grace.

There are also differences in the sacrament of Eucharist or Communion. At one end are Roman Catholics, who believe the eucharistic elements (the wafers and wine) are changed into and become the body and blood of Christ. At the other end are those who believe that Christ is (only) symbolically present in the partaking of the sacrament. In the middle are those who believe that Christ is mystically present in the celebration of the sacrament. There are also differences in its practice. Most sacramental churches observe the Lord's Supper at every service; those who see the sacrament in symbolic terms observe it less frequently.

In addition to the two Gospel sacraments, Catholic and Orthodox churches recognize five other sacraments: *Confirmation*, the confirming of vows made by one's parents and sponsors at baptism; *Reconciliation*, previously called Confession, the forgiveness of post-baptismal sins; *Matrimony*, the covenanting together of a man and woman in the sight of God; *Ordination* or Holy Orders, the consecration of those set apart for Christian ministry; and *Anointing the Sick*, the sacrament of healing, formerly called Last Rites.

Church Polity

There are three forms of church governance or polity: Episcopal, Presbyterian and Free or Independent. *Episcopal*, from a Greek word meaning "overseer," has bishops with authority over ecclesiastical districts, synods and conferences. This is top-down authority and the earliest form of church polity. It is found today in Catholic and Orthodox churches, and within Protestantism in Episcopal, Lutheran and Methodist churches. *Presbyterian* comes from a Greek word meaning "elder." This is a representative form of government, with power and authority vested in presbyteries comprised of clergy persons and governing elders in churches within a district or region, as in Presbyterian and Reformed churches. *Independent* churches operate without bishops or presbyteries. They have a bottom-up form of authority, as seen in Baptist, Brethren, Evangelical Free, Congregational, Covenant, Nazarene and Pentecostal churches.

The End Times: Heaven, Hell and the Hereafter

Where is history headed? The Greek view was that history is cyclical, like the seasons of the year. The Eastern view is that history is an illusion. The secular view is that history is a series of unconnected events without meaning or, as Henry Ford once said, "Just one thing after another going nowhere." The Christian view is that history is headed toward an end time when Jesus will return and raise to everlasting life all who have believed in him. His return is something he promised (John 14:3), that others prophesied (Hebrews 9:28), and that all the creeds confess. When is Jesus coming back? Jesus said, "only the Father" knows (Mark 13:32). Paul says that his return will come as a surprise—"like a thief in the night" (1 Thessalonians 5:2)—so we should, as the Boy Scouts say, "Always be prepared."

Resurrection and Judgment

According to the Bible, at the end of the age there will be a general resurrection of all who have ever lived, and then a final judgment. What will the judgment be? For those who have believed in Jesus, it will be eternal life; for those who have not, it will be everlasting punishment, as in Matthew's story of the sheep and the goats (25:32-46). Some argue, however, that God must have a Plan B for godly people who died before Christ was born, and for those since his death who have never heard the gospel—children who die in infancy, those who are mentally disabled, those raised in other faiths, those who live in closed societies or remote areas of the world. They say punishing people for not responding to a message they have never heard is inconsistent with God's love and mercy. They believe that God will judge people on the light they have received. Another view is annihilationism, the belief that God knows those who love him and those who don't (Hebrews 4:13), and those who don't will simply perish (John 3:16).

The Intermediate State

The playwright George Bernard Shaw said, "Death is the ultimate statistic: one out of one dies." What happens at death, and between death and the general resurrection? Regarding death, Christians hold different views. Some believe that both the body and the soul go to paradise, based on Jesus' statement to the thief who was crucified with him on the cross: "Today you will be with me in Paradise" (Luke 23:43), which does not appear to be heaven but an intermediate venue. (Jesus said the thief would be with him *today* in paradise, then Jesus died and was in a tomb for three days, so paradise sounds like a place other than heaven.) Others believe that the soul—the nonphysical spiritual entity that indwells those "in Christ"—separates from the body and lives on until the body is resurrected. Still others believe that we perish completely (as in cremation) and are later resurrected. Catholics believe that those who die with unforgiven venial (minor or pardonable) sins go to purgatory to have their souls purified; those who die with unforgiven mortal (grave or deadly) sins may, depending on the severity of their sins, lose their salvation.

The period between death and final resurrection is called the Intermediate State, about which the Bible tells us, one writer said, "little more than a whisper." Theologians who hold that the soul continues to live on say that it goes to a place that is permanent and eternal, but incomplete until Jesus returns and gathers up all who have believed. Then, so the argument continues, the soul takes up residence in a new, resurrected body.

Heaven and Hell

What do we know about heaven and hell? Not much. Some think that heaven is a physical place in outer space where we go when we die—a place with streets of gold, white robes and halos and harps. The Old and New Testaments say something different: there will be a "new heaven and a new earth" (Isaiah 65:17 and Revelation 21:1-2), which Jesus affirms in the Lord's Prayer when he tells the disciples to pray for God's kingdom to come "on earth as it is in heaven." The view that Jesus will return to rule over a redeemed heaven-on-earth comes from the writings of Tom Wright and others. Rob Bell, in his book

Love Wins, says that when God's kingdom comes, "earth and heaven will be the same place." So we won't go to a retirement home in the sky when we are resurrected. We will take up residence in a new, transformed heaven on earth, an active, busy place with meaningful, fulfilling, joyful God-given work to do. What about hell? Is it a subterranean pit at the bottom of the earth? A place of fire, the gnashing of teeth and eternal suffering, as in Matthew's story of the end of the age (25:41)? C. S. Lewis, in a 1961 preface to *The Screwtape Letters,* the book that earlier established his fame as a Christian apologist, said, "My symbol for hell is something like the bureaucracy of a police state," perhaps like Stalinist Russia, with its drabness, shortages of everything from food to electricity, and Gulag labor camps and prisons. Hell is the dwelling place of those who rebel against and reject God. They are not sent to hell; they get there, Lewis said elsewhere, "by their own steam."

The Life Hereafter

Our heavenly bodies will be a continuation of our earthly bodies; if not, we would not be "resurrected." Tom Wright refers to our to-be-resurrected bodies as "transformed physicality." He says that we often say about a person who is sick or dying that he or she is but a shadow of their former self. In thinking about our lives beyond the grave, Wright said that our earthly bodies are but a shadow of our future selves—our "imperishable" bodies, which will be free of disease and decay (1 Corinthians 15:35–44). How old will we be when we are resurrected? Thomas Aquinas said that we will be the same age as Jesus when he was resurrected (thirty-five). An interesting thought, but what about those who die in infancy or in their teens or twenties? When Jesus returns, where will he "land"? According to the prophet Zechariah, when the Lord comes "his feet shall stand on the

Mount of Olives" (14:4).

Will we know those whom we love? The Apostles' Creed confesses the belief in "the communion of saints," the common bond of believers in and through the Holy Spirit. The American theologian R.C. Sproul, in his book *Now, That's a Good Question!*, understands this to mean that we will be in fellowship with everyone who is "in Christ." Will there be marriage in heaven? It is popular to think so, and there is no reason to believe that married couples will not be reunited, but Jesus said to the Sadducees, in response to a question about marriage in heaven: "When [the dead rise] they neither marry nor are given in marriage" (Mark 12:25). God told the first humans to "multiply and fill the earth" (Genesis 1:28); this will not be necessary in the next life.

What else can be said about our hereafter? Only that, "No eye has seen, nor ear heard, nor the human heart conceived, what God has prepared for those who love him" (1 Corinthians. 2:9). To say more is impossible because, as Rabbi Louis Jacobs observed, "For human beings in this world to try to grasp the nature of the hereafter is like a man born blind trying to grasp the nature of color."

Discussion Questions

1. How can God be both three persons and one? Who is the Holy Spirit? Are we sinful because of Adam and Eve's disobedience?

2. Jesus' resurrection is the cornerstone of Christianity. What are the most compelling/convincing arguments that Jesus rose from the dead and is alive today?

3. When a conversation turns to religion, are you nervous around people who believe differently than you do? Or excited for an opportunity to share your faith and beliefs?

8

Other Religions and Beliefs

Today there is a great movement of people to the West, especially to America. Some come to start a new life, others to be reunited with relatives who came before, others to study in our colleges and universities. When they come, they bring with them religious beliefs that most Christians know little or nothing about. In this chapter we will look at other world religions and belief systems and compare them with Christianity. Some may wonder why this book bothers with other religions. The reason is to show the unique, distinctive beliefs of Christianity compared with those of other religions.

Eastern Religions

The two principal Eastern religions are Hinduism and Buddhism (the principal Western religions are Judaism, Christianity and Islam, though the majority of Muslims live in the Middle East and Asia). Millions of Americans are involved in some form of Eastern mysticism. According to a Pew Report, 24 percent believe in reincarnation. The following are important differences between Christianity and Eastern religions.

First, Christians believe in a God who made himself known in Jesus Christ; Hindus believe in a pantheon of gods, who are impersonal and unknowable. Second, Christians believe in humankind's sinfulness and separation from God; there is no sense of indwelt sin or fallenness in Eastern religions. Third, Christians believe in the forgiveness of sins so that we may be "at one" with God; Hindus and Buddhists believe in a continuous cycle of reincarnations until one's soul is released from his or her body. Lastly, Christians believe that salvation comes from above (God's grace) rather than below (liberating oneself from the cycle of birth, life, death and rebirth).

Hinduism: The Religion of India

Hinduism dates back to the second millennium before Christ. It is the religion of India (85 percent of all Indians are Hindus). The word *Hindu* comes from the Sanskrit word *Indus*—"people of the land of Indus"—referring to those who lived in the Indus Valley (now Pakistan). The Joshua project, which tracks world religions, estimates there are 1.1 billion Hindus (15 percent of the world's population), which makes Hinduism the third largest religion behind Christianity and Islam.

Origins and Practices

Hinduism had no founding father, has no institutional form, has temples but no corporate or formal day of worship, and believes in a multiplicity of gods. A dark side of Hinduism is the caste system of social stratification, which dates back to the 1500s BC. Hindus believe the caste system is part of the cosmic law of cause and effect, part of the explanation of why things are the way they are. There are four primary castes and thousands of subcastes, which are hereditary and for life: one cannot move from one caste to another. Those who have been expelled from or have abandoned their caste are called "outcastes." Those considered ritually unclean are called "untouchables," of which there are several million in India. Untouchability was declared illegal in 1950, but still persists in employment, village life, table fellowship and marriage.

Something that is little understood in the West is Hinduism's reverence for the cow, which cannot be killed and consumes grain needed to feed India's masses. Hindus believe the cow is the living symbol of mother earth and the divine blessings she showers upon humankind. Reverence for the cow symbolizes reverence for all animals, which is one reason most Hindus are vegetarians; another reason is the belief that animals contain reincarnated souls.

Brahman, Atman and Reincarnation

Hindus believe that the human soul, called *atman*, is linked with the universal soul, called *Brahman*. One's state in life is determined by one's *karma*, a Sanskrit word meaning actions or deeds. Bad karma leads to the reincarnation of the soul into lower orders (animals, plants and insects); good karma into higher orders (higher castes). The goal of Hindus is to secure the release of their atman from the endless repetition of births, deaths and rebirths and merge with and dissolve into Brahman, at which point the soul enters a state of supreme blessedness.

How does one break free of the wheel of reincarnation? The four paths are, first, reading the scriptures—the *Vedas* (wise sayings), the *Upanishads* (sitting near one's teacher) and the *Bhagavad Gita* (the Song of the Lord, Hinduism's favorite Bible)—and studying with gurus. Second, practicing disciplines and psychophysical exercises that concentrate one's attention on the atman. Third, offering sacrifices and making pilgrimages to sacred places such as Varanasi, Hinduism's holiest city, located on the banks of the Ganges River (Hindus bathe in Mother Ganges to wash away bad karma). Fourth, doing works of charity.

A Western form of Hinduism is Hare Krishna—*Hare* means Lord and *Krishna* is the avatar (divine manifestation) of Vishnu, one of the three principal deities in Hinduism. Hare Krishnas believe in karma and reincarnation, but not in a plurality of gods or the caste system.

Hinduism versus Christianity

Three differences between Christianity and Hinduism are as follows: First, Christianity believes in a single, sovereign, personal God; Hinduism believes there are thousands of gods. Second, Christianity believes that salvation comes "by grace through faith"; Hinduism believes that salvation from *samsara*, the cycle of ongoing reincarnations, comes from knowledge, devotion, sacrifices and good works. Third, Christianity believes that Christ's saving death is offered to everyone, no matter what caste he or she is born into; and it is offered in this life and with assurance, not in some future reincarnated life.

Buddhism: The Middle Way

Buddhism is the other major eastern religion. It differs from Hinduism in three regards. First, it does not believe in a God or gods; second, it believes there is a way—the Noble Eightfold Path—to lessen the time one spends on the wheel of reincarnation; third, it has no caste system. Buddhism is coming to the West, with immigrants from Cambodia, Thailand, Vietnam and other Southeast Asian countries. There are an estimated 500 million Buddhists in the world, making Buddhism the fourth largest world religion.

Origins and Practices

Buddhism was founded by Siddhartha Gautama, who was born in 566 BC in what is now Nepal. Gautama's father was a tribal chieftain who shielded him from the cruelties and sufferings of life. According to legend, when Gautama finally ventured out into the world, the only happy man he saw was a serene and peaceful hermit. At the age of twenty-two he left his wife and child and embarked on a quest for peace and serenity, which came to him six years later.

According to Gautama, the cause of suffering is craving things that are worldly and temporal. The way to peace and serenity is the Middle Way of moderation between pleasure and denial, between indulgence and asceticism. Gautama became known as *Buddha*, a Sanskrit word meaning one who has attained enlightenment (Buddha is a title, like Christ, not Gautama's name). He gathered around him disciples, founded monasteries and began teaching his newfound enlightenment. Over time he came to be venerated and statues and temples were built in his honor.

Buddhism, like Christianity, Islam and other religions, has various streams or branches. In Buddhism, there are three "vehicles," as they are called. Theravada is the oldest and most orthodox of the three. Mahayana is a somewhat softer path and the most popular of the three. Vajrayana is a middle path between the other two. It is prominent in Tibet and is often referred to as Tibetan Buddhism.

A popular form of Buddhism in the West is Zen Buddhism, which came to the fore after the Second World War. Zen adherents practice meditation according to strict rules (the word *zen* means "meditation"), hoping they will achieve enlightenment more quickly, thereby shortening their time on the wheel of reincarnation.

The best known Buddhist in the world is Tenzin Gyatso, the fourteenth Dalai Lama, who was born in 1935. *Dalai* means "ocean" and *Lama* means "guru," so the Dalai Lama is the "ocean teacher," one whose spirituality and wisdom are as great as the ocean. The current Dalai Lama has been living in exile in India since China assumed control of Tibet in 1959. Tibetans believe that Gyatso is the reincarnation of the thirteenth Dalai Lama (each Dalai Lama is thought to be the reincarnation of previous Dalai Lamas and personages going back to Buddha). Tibetans regard the Dalai Lama as the spiritual and political leader of their country.

The Noble Eightfold Path

Buddha (or "the Buddha") taught that there is something one can do to escape the misery of this life, rather than suffering until one's soul is released from his or her body. What can one do? Adopt wisdom, morality and meditation as the essence of life and follow the Noble Eightfold Path of right views, aspirations, behavior, speech, livelihood, effort, mindfulness and contemplation. In Mahayana Buddhism, elders called *bodhisattvas* take a vow to help others achieve *nirvana*, a Sanskrit word meaning to "blow out" the flame of desire, the cause of suffering.

Christianity versus Buddhism

Three differences between Christianity and Buddhism are as follows: First, that Christianity believes in a Creator who revealed himself in his incarnate Son; Buddhism does not believe in a Creator God or higher being (in this sense, Buddhism is more like a philosophy than a religion). Second, Christianity believes the human race is fallen and in need of a savior; Buddhism does not believe that humans are fallen, so there is no need of a savior-redeemer. Third, Christians look forward to a resurrected life with the Triune God and all other believers; Buddhists look forward to escaping the on-going bondage of *samsara* (rebirths) and to the absorption of the finite self into the infinite, like a drop of water falling into an ocean.

Shintoism, Sikhism and Other Religions

The following are a number of other Eastern religions. The largest is *Confucianism*, a system of ethics based on the teachings of Confucius (551–479 BC), considered by many to be China's greatest teacher. Confucianism is concerned with right relationships, especially within the family, and the virtues of respect, compassion, benevolence, wisdom, trustworthiness and propriety. Confucianism was the official "religion" of China until the revolution of Sun Yat-sen, the father of modern China, in 1911.

Taoism (pronounced Dowism) is another ancient, atheistic Chinese belief system, founded by Lao Tzu or Lao Tse (604–517 BC). The three "jewels" of Taoism are compassion, moderation and humility. When there is equilibrium between the *yang* (positive, active, masculine and warm) and the *yin* (negative, passive, feminine and cold), there is harmony between humankind and the universe, which in Taoism is the goal of life. Taoism is not a major religion, but there is a growing interest in its writings.

Shintoism is the "way of the gods," the ancient (sixth century AD) religion of Japan. It has to do with nature, family, personal purity and, religiously, with the worship of spirits called *kami*, of which there are some 300 different varieties. Shintoism had no founder, does not believe in a sovereign, supreme God, has no religious texts or scriptures or institutional form of worship, and does not believe in the need of salvation. Many kami are considered ancestors of ancient clans and are worshiped at both public and in-home shrines.

Sikhism was founded by Guru Nanak (1470–1540) around the year 1500 in Punjab in northwest India. It is a middle way or path between Hinduism and Islam, being monotheistic on the one hand but believing in reincarnation on the other, but not in the caste system. The term *sikh* comes from a Sanskrit word meaning "disciple," one who studies with gurus and follows their teachings. The goal of Sikhism is to be absorbed into *Sat Nam*, the true, eternal guru. Sikhism is a small but influential religion that has found its way to North America.

Baha'ism is a recent world religion. It was founded in 1844 in Iran by Bahu'u'llah (1817–1892). Baha'ism teaches the oneness and equality of all people; that truth is relative, not absolute; and that Baha'ism is the fulfillment of all other religions.

Islam: Submission to Allah

The third great monotheistic religion, along with Judaism and Christianity, is Islam, an Arabic word meaning "submission" to the will of Allah, the Arabic name for God (Allah comes from the Arabic words *al*, meaning "the," and *ilah*, meaning "deity"). Islam is a large (1.7 billion), worldwide, rapidly growing, well-funded missionary faith. It is the dominant religion and way of life in some 60 countries of the world. (Christianity is the major religion in some 120 countries.) There are an estimated 8 million Muslims in the United States.

We think of Muslims as Arabs, but among the ten largest Islamic countries, only one, Egypt, is Arabic. The largest Muslim country is Indonesia (60-plus percent of the world's Muslims live in Southeast Asia). Muslims worship in mosques ("place of prostration") where the faithful—usually only men, at least in the main hall—gather together to pray as a group. The prayers are led by an Imam ("he who stands before others"), a person with religious training who delivers a sermon on Friday, Islam's day of formal worship. Most mosques have a minaret to call Muslims to worship, a fountain for ceremonial washing and, if large enough, education rooms for teaching the Koran and Islamic law.

After the collapse of the Ottoman Empire in 1923, many Muslim countries became secular, believing it was the way to modernity, growth and prosperity, as in the West. Serious Muslims discovered that secularism made it difficult for them to live pious lives and pushed for Sharia, the strict, demanding legal and moral code or law of Islam (food laws, the role and status of women, prayer, punishments for speaking ill of Muhammad or the Koran), resulting in the birth of Islamism, a modern, increasingly radical form of Islam. In many Muslim-majority countries, surveys reveal that 90 percent of the population want Sharia to be the law of the land.

History shows that religious conflicts are often resolved by the conversion of one side to the other. It will be difficult for the West to convert fervently believing Muslims, for whom Islam is a way of life, to Christianity, which has led commentators to observe that the conflict between Islam and Christianity will be with us for a very long time.

The Prophet Muhammad

The founder of Islam was Ubu'l Kassim, who became known as Muhammad, the "Praised One." Muhammad is so revered that when Muslims mention his name it is followed by the words, "Peace be upon him." Muhammad was born in 570 in Mecca in Saudi Arabia. He was orphaned at the age of six and raised first by a grandfather and then by an uncle. When he was twenty-five years old he married a wealthy widow, Khadija, some fifteen years his senior, and became a successful merchant. Muhammad and Khadija had two sons, who died in childhood, and four daughters, the youngest of whom and Muhammad's favorite was Fatima, who married Muhammad's cousin, Ali.

In the year 610, when Muhammad was forty years of age, he claims to have had several visits or visions of the angel Gabriel while meditating in a cave on Mount Hira, north of Mecca. Gabriel told Muhammad that he was Allah's messenger and promised to dictate to him the word of God. Muhammad did not consider himself to be divine, but the one chosen by God to be his final prophet—the "seal" of the prophets (twenty-five prophets are mentioned in the Koran, among them both Jesus, who is mentioned often than Muhammad, and John the Baptist).

Community leaders in Mecca rejected Muhammad's monotheism and opposed his preaching against the worship of idols. In the year 622, Muhammad fled to Medina, 250 miles north of Mecca, referred to by Muslims as the *Hijra*—"the emigration." Medina was inhabited by both Christians and Jews, who undoubtedly influenced Muhammad's thinking and theology. In the year 630, Muhammad and his followers invaded and took control of Mecca, now Islam's holiest city. Muhammad died unexpectedly in 632 at the age of sixty-one. He is buried in Medina, the City of the Prophet. Following his death, Islam, aided by the sword, spread across North Africa and into Spain, challenging Christianity on its own soil.

Sunnis and Shi'ites

Muhammad died without appointing a successor and Islam divided into two major groups, the Sunnis and the Shi'ites. The Sunnis, with 85 percent of Islam's adherents, are the mainstream. They follow the *sunna* (way or custom) of Muhammad and are led by caliphs (successors or representatives) from the Kuraish tribe, to which Muhammad belonged. Adherents of al-Qaeda, ISIS, Boko Haram and other militant groups are Sunnis.

The Shi'ites—from *Shia Ali*, the "Party of Ali," Muhammad's cousin and son-in-law—believe they are the true successors of Muhammad, whose legacy continues today in spiritual leaders like the Ayatollahs (Sign of God) in Iran and elsewhere. Shi'ites say the sunna is good, but it needs to be continually reinterpreted by Ali's descendants and successors.

The Koran

In Islamic theology, God did not reveal himself in the form of a person, Jesus, but in words, which are recorded in the *Qur'an* (English: Koran), a word meaning "recitation." According to Islam, the recitations were revealed to Muhammad over a twenty-three-year period (from 610 to 632) in Mecca and Medina, the two cities where Muhammad lived. The recitations were given in manageable segments so they could be memorized. A major difference between the Koran and the New Testament is that no one was in the cave with Muhammad to hear Gabriel's words, in contrast to the multiple attestations of Jesus' words and acts in the Gospels. Muslims believe that Muhammad passed his revelations on to his secretary, Zayd, which were later organized into a book by Uthman, the third caliph, around the year 650. Others believe that Muhammad wrote, edited and arranged the revelations while in Medina.

The Koran has 114 suras or chapters, ordered by length rather than chronologically, which makes the Koranic narrative hard to follow. The Koran is filled with stories about Adam, Abraham, Jacob, Moses, David, Mary, Jesus, John the Baptist and others who appear in the Old and New Testaments. The Koran is slightly smaller than the New Testament.

Judaism, Christianity and Islam

Judaism, Christianity and Islam are monotheistic religions, though they see themselves differently. Tom Wright, in his "Living Faith" DVD series, said Jews say, "There is one God and Israel is his chosen people." Christians say, "There is one God and Jesus is his only begotten Son." Muslims say, "There is one God and Muhammad is his final prophet." One difference between the three religions is that Jesus ascended to heaven, whereas Abraham is buried in Hebron in Israel and Muhammad in Medina in Saudi Arabia.

There are three areas where Jews, Christians and Muslims share common beliefs. First, all three religions look back to Abraham as their founding father. Islam believes that Abraham was a Muslim because Muslims submit to the will of God and Abraham was the first person to do so (leaving Haran to go to Canaan). Muslims also believe that Ishmael, who was born fourteen years before Isaac, was the "promised son" and that it was he, not Isaac, whom God commanded Abraham to sacrifice on Mount Moriah.

Second, all three revere Jerusalem as a holy city, but for different reasons. In the case of Islam, because it was from Jerusalem that Muhammad made his famous "night journey" (in 620) to the seventh heaven where, Muslims believe, Allah resides. (Some Muslims believe this to be an actual journey; others a dream or vision.) The golden Dome of the Rock in Jerusalem was later built over the rock from which Muhammad allegedly ascended to memorialize the event.

Third, all three are "Religions of the Book." Islam reveres the Torah, the book of Moses; the Psalms, the book of David; the Gospels, which it reads as biographies of Jesus, not the way of salvation, and in places has even rewritten (in the Koran, Jesus was born under a palm tree, not in a manger); and most important, the Koran, Islam's holy book. Muslims believe there is an exact copy of the Koran in Arabic in heaven.

Jesus

Islam reveres Jesus (*Isa* in Arabic). It believes in his virgin birth and miracles and that before he died he was "assumed" into heaven, where he now resides with Allah. But Islam does not consider Jesus to be divine, because it would be unfitting for the sovereign God of the universe to become incarnate in a human being (in the Koran, Jesus is called the Son of Mary, not the Son of God). Nor does Islam believe that Jesus was crucified, because Allah would not allow one of his prophets to die such a disgraceful, humiliating death. Islam believes that someone was crucified in Jesus' place, most likely Simon of Cyrene, who carried Jesus' cross to Golgatha. Because Muslims believe that Jesus did not die, he was not, of course, raised from the dead.

Sin and Salvation

Islam teaches that men and women are fundamentally good, not fallen. The fall in the Garden of Eden was caused by Satan, who tempted Adam (not Eve), who repented and was forgiven by Allah. Because Muslims do not believe that humankind is fallen, there is no need for a savior. On the other side of the coin, there is no assurance of salvation. Everything is on hold until the Day of Reckoning, when each person appears before Allah (not Jesus) to be judged by his or her deeds (salvation by works). Those judged to have been faithful go to a paradise of unbelievable sensual pleasure; sinners go to a hell of indescribable punishment.

The two principal differences between Christianity and Islam are Jesus' salvific death and bodily resurrection, which are bottom-line, non-negotiable Christian beliefs. Another difference is that in Islamic countries the religious law is supreme. There is no division between secular and sacred, between state and church. Sharia is the law of the land.

The Five Pillars

There are five pillars that undergird life for observant Muslims. They come from the *Hadith*, a collection of Muhammad's sayings that was assembled after his death. The pillars are as follows (surprisingly, Sharia is not one of the pillars).

First, the *profession* that, "There is no God but Allah, and Muhammad is his prophet." Allah is not the personal God of Christianity; he is never described as a God of love ("For God so loved the world"); he is never referred to as Father, as in the Lord's Prayer; his spirit does not indwell his followers; and he is not Triune.

Second, *prayers* to Allah five times a day: upon rising, midday, mid-afternoon, sunset and upon retiring (the afternoon and sunset prayers are often combined in non-Muslim countries). When Muslims pray, they prostrate themselves in a position of humility. In public prayers, the words come from the first chapter of the Koran and follow established formulas.

Third, *almsgiving*, the sharing of one's wealth to support the sick and the needy. The amount varies, but the practice is one-fortieth (2.5 percent) of a person's wealth, which is strictly enforced in some countries (as a tax) and voluntary in others.

Fourth, *abstinence* from food and drink (for those in good health) and sexual intimacy from sunrise to sunset during the month of Ramadan, the month it is claimed the angel Gabriel first appeared to Muhammad on Mount Hira.

Fifth, a *pilgrimage* to Mecca once during one's lifetime, if possible, to worship at the Great Mosque and kiss the Black Stone, the most venerated object in Islam. Muslims believe the stone was given to Adam by the angel Gabriel; that it was placed in the *Kaaba* (cube) inside the Great Mosque by Abraham; and that it was once white but humankind's sin turned it black.

Many Muslims believe in a sixth pillar, *jihad*, meaning "spiritual struggle," one aspect of which involves waging war against enemies of Islam. Muslims believe that suicide bombers and others who give their lives for Islam are assured of a place in paradise.

Black Muslims

A twentieth-century, African-American expression of Islam is the Nation of Islam (NOI), which was founded in 1931 in Detroit by William Fard, who claimed to have been born a Muslim in Mecca. Ward mysteriously disappeared in 1934 and was succeeded by his assistant, the anti-Christian Elijah Muhammad.

NOI adherents are known as Black Muslims (in the beginning, the NOI was more interested in blackness than in religion).

Malcolm X, the son of a radical Baptist minister in Omaha, Nebraska, was the leading spokesperson for the NOI in the 1950s. Malcolm took the surname X, a symbol for something unknown, because he did not know his African surname. Malcolm preached black pride and black power, which led to the change from Negro to Black. In 1963, after visiting Mecca and seeing different races worshiping together, Malcolm left the Nation of Islam and became a Sunni Muslim and publicly espoused orthodox Islam. In 1965, he was assassinated in a public auditorium in New York City. Today there are 2–3 million Black Muslims in the United States. Most belong to orthodox Islamic communities like the Community of Al-Islam in the West.

Mormonism, Jehovah's Witnesses and Other Religious Movements

A challenge to Christianity over the last couple of centuries has been the emergence of religious sects and cults that parade under the banner of Christianity, but deny the central truth claims of Christianity. The word *cult* is a descriptive term, though some find it offensive, preferring, instead, the term *new* or *alternative religious movement,* which I use in the pages that follow. American religious historian Ruth Tucker, in her book *Another Gospel,* defines a new or alternative religious movement as a religious group whose founder claims to have received a special revelation from God to proclaim a message not found in the Bible. Tucker says that most alternative religious movements have authoritarian leadership structures, are legalistic in lifestyle, are exclusivist in outlook, and have a persecution complex.

Common Beliefs

The following are beliefs of alternative religious movements that differ from the truth claims of Christianity. First, they deny the Bible's final authority, claiming it to be faulty and incomplete, which their founders have replaced with their own writings, two examples being Joseph Smith's translation of the *Book of Mormon* and Mary Baker Eddy's *Science and Health*. Second, they worship a god other than the biblical God and do not believe in the Trinity (new religious movements are unitarian rather than trinitarian). Third, they deny the divinity of Jesus, believing him to be human only, and none regard him as a savior. Lastly, new religious movements do not believe in justification by faith; they believe in salvation by works, especially works on behalf of their movement such as proselytization.

The Church of Jesus Christ of Latter-day Saints

Four well-known new religious movements were founded in the nineteenth century. The oldest and largest is the Church of Jesus Christ of Latter-day Saints ("Latter-day" refers to the time before Jesus returns; "Saints" are members of LDS churches). The Latter-day Saints movement is popularly known as Mormonism. It has been called the most distinctive and successful religion ever born on American soil, which is why I am spending more time on the LDS—its founder, history and beliefs—than on other new religious movements.

The name Mormon comes from the *Book of Mormon*, which the LDS claims to be equal to the Bible. It is the story of Lehi and his family, from the tribe of Manasseh, who sailed from Israel to the Americas around 600 BC (2,100 years before Columbus arrived in 1492). Two of Lehi's sons, Nephi and Laman, split the Lehites into rival nations, the Nephites and the Lamanites. In AD 385, they fought a catastrophic war in which 500,000 persons are said to have been killed. Archaeologists have discovered no artifacts to support this story. The Lamanites defeated the Nephites and became the ancestors of the American Indians, which is disputed by anthropologists who believe the ancestors of the North American Indians were Asians who came across the Bering Strait land bridge 25,000 years ago.

The historian-prophet Mormon was the military commander of the Nephites. He is said to have written an abridged history of the two nations on sheets made of gold. The sheets were given to his son, Moroni, who completed the history of the Nephites and buried the plates in a hill near modern-day Rochester, New York. The Book of Mormon, which ends in the year 421, contains thousands of words from the *King James Bible*, many verbatim, which was written twelve hundred years after the Book of Mormon; and it mentions animals, metals, glass, silk, food-plants, grains and other things that came well after—not before—Columbus's arrival in the New World in 1492.

Mormonism stands or falls on Joseph Smith, so we need to start with his story. Smith was born in 1805 in Sharon, Vermont. He claims to have had a vision of God and Jesus appearing to him when he was fourteen years old. They told him to restore the Christianity practiced by Jesus' disciples. A few years later, Smith was told about the golden plates by the angel Moroni. (The LDS is the Church of *Jesus Christ* of Latter-day Saints, but the personage that stands atop Mormon temples is the angel Moroni, not Jesus.) Smith translated the plates from "Reformed Egyptian" (there is no credible evidence that such a language ever existed) into English. The *Book of Mormon,* named for its alleged original author, was published in 1830. After Smith finished his translation, the plates were taken to heaven by Moroni, making any critical study of the plates impossible. Smith claims that John the Baptist came to earth and ordained him to the Aaronic priesthood (Exodus 28-29) and that Peter, James and

John conferred upon him the Melchizedek priesthood (Psalm 110:4). In 1830, Smith founded the LDS Church with six friends at Fayette, New York.

Smith and his followers moved from state to state to avoid persecution, finally settling in Nauvoo ("beautiful place"), Illinois, on the Mississippi River. During this period Smith took to himself some forty wives, following which plural marriage became an accepted Mormon practice. In 1844, Smith was arrested for smashing the printing presses of a newspaper in Carthage, Illinois, that was printing articles denouncing Smith and Mormon polygamy. He and his brother were shot and killed by an angry mob before they could be brought to trial. Following Smith's death, Brigham Young, the American Moses of Mormonism, led thousands of followers on a sixteen-month trek to the Salt Lake Basin in Utah, arriving there in 1847. In 1890, the LDS abandoned polygamy when it became clear that its continued practice would prevent Utah's entry into the union (some fundamentalist Mormon sects continue to practice polygamy).

The LDS has 14 million Saints (adherents) worldwide. It comprises the sixth largest religious body in the United States, after the Catholics, Baptists, Pentecostals, Methodists and Lutherans; and it is larger than two of the oldest churches in America, the Presbyterians and Episcopalians. (Mormons call non-Mormons *Gentiles*.) Mormons are much admired for their family values, chastity, education, industriousness, patriotism, and the care of their members. College-age youth give two years of their lives to mission work around the world. A distinctive Mormon practice is the avoidance of alcohol, tobacco and caffeine. Another practice is tithing, which has made the LDS a multibillion dollar organization.

Mormon beliefs are based on the *Book of Mormon*, the *King James Bible* (as "correctly interpreted" by the LDS Church) and two writings of Joseph Smith, *Doctrine and Covenants* and the *Pearl of Great Price*. These four comprise the Mormon canon, along with the teachings of Smith, Young and other LDS "prophets."

The Church of Jesus Christ of Latter-day Saints considers itself to be a unique, distinct expression of Christianity, but many of its teachings differ significantly from those of historic, orthodox, creedal Christianity.

God. Mormonism is polytheistic, believing in the existence of "gods" other than the monotheistic God confessed in the Apostles' and Nicene Creeds. The Mormon god who rules over planet Earth is Elohim, one of the Old Testament names for God. He was a human on a planet near the star Kolob (?) who was appointed god of planet Earth by "a council of the gods." Elohim is a flesh-and-bones physical being, not a spirit being, as set forth in John 4:24, and he is married—Mormons believe in a Heavenly Father and a Heavenly Mother—and lives with his wife in the "celestial heaven." Mormonism does not believe in the Trinity; it believes that Elohim and Jesus are separate physical beings and the Holy Spirit is an influence and the three are distinct and independent from one another. Lastly, Mormons do not believe that "In the beginning God created the heavens and the earth" (Genesis 1:1). They believe that God organized what already existed, bringing order out of chaos rather than something new out of nothing.

Jesus. Mormons do not believe that Jesus "was conceived by the Holy Spirit," as stated in the Apostles' Creed. They believe he was fathered by Elohim through sexual intercourse with Mary. As such he is not, in the language of the Nicene Creed, "very God of very God." He is, instead, every Mormon's elder brother, with the same nature as other created beings. The LDS teaches that Jesus returned to Earth—to the American continent—in AD 34 and preached the gospel.

Sin and Salvation. Mormons do not believe in original sin or that men and women are fallen. They believe that Adam and Eve's fall in the Garden of Eden, which Joseph Smith said was located in Jackson County, Missouri, was theirs alone. And they do not believe that we are saved by *grace through faith* (Ephesians 2:8). They say faith is not enough. It must be supplemented by observing the ordinances of the LDS Church, among them baptism by immersion, the laying on of hands, marriage-for-all-eternity in sealed temple ceremonies (to get around Jesus' statement in Mark 12:25 that there will be no marriages in heaven), the payment of tithes, and keeping the commandments and doing good works.

Eternal Life. Mormons believe there are three heavens. The highest is the celestial heaven, the home of faithful members of LDS churches, who some believe may one day become gods themselves based on the Mormon doctrine of *eternal progression*—the Mormon teaching that "As man now is, God once was; as God now is, so man can become," called the Snow Couplet (Lorenzo Snow was the fifth president of the LDS Church). Eternal progression means that faithful, observant Mormons may one day become gods of planets elsewhere in the universe. The LDS believes that at the end of the age, Jesus will return and there will be an ingathering in God's New Zion (New Jerusalem) in Missouri.

I shared what I wrote about Joseph Smith and the LDS Church with a Mormon-turned-Evangelical businessman whose great-great-grandfathers came west with Brigham Young in the 1840s. He wrote to me and said, "As a former Mormon, with deep roots in the LDS Church, I must say that your short summary of Mormonism is the best I have ever read."

Jehovah's Witnesses

Jehovah's Witnesses is the second-largest, made-in-America religion, with perhaps 5 or 6 million adherents. It was founded in 1884 by Charles Taze Russell (1852–1916). Jehovah's Witnesses meet in modest Kingdom Halls (Mormons meet in temples and churches); prefer the name Jehovah to God (Jehovah is a late, artificial translation of Yahweh, one of the Hebrew names for God); are millenarian in theology, waiting for the end of the world; and consider Christianity an apostate religion, believing they are the sole bearers of God's truth.

Witnesses, as adherents are called, believe that Jesus was the Archangel Michael, who laid down his spirit nature and became a man. JWs deny the Trinity; deny Jesus' deity, atoning death and physical resurrection; and believe that good works are necessary for salvation. Witnesses do not celebrate Christmas, Good Friday or Easter—believing them to be pagan holidays—or their own or anyone else's birthday. Some consider Jehovah's Witnesses un-American because they do not vote, pledge allegiance to the flag, sing the national anthem, or serve in the Armed Forces. Witnesses, like Mormons, are required to do two-by-two (Mark 6:7), door-by-door (Acts 20:20) proselytizing. To be a member in good standing, Witnesses must devote a certain number of hours each month to proselytization.

Christian Science

Christian Science is another made-in-America religion. It was founded in Boston in 1879 by "Mother Mary" Baker Eddy (1821–1910), the self-proclaimed revealer of God's true word. The movement has Christian in its name, but it does not believe in Jesus' sacrificial death because Scientists, as adherents are called, do not believe in physical death; or in the Trinity or Jesus' virginal conception or bodily resurrection; or in original sin or heaven and hell. Christian Science's denial of important bottom-line Christian beliefs has led some to call the movement "Eddyism."

Scientists believe in the superiority of spirit over matter; that evil, sickness and death are illusions (when people die, they pass on to another form of existence); and that Jesus is the Way-shower who revealed God as a spiritual principle. Christian Science is in serious decline, with an aging membership and only a few hundred churches, each of which is expected to provide a public Reading Room for proselytization purposes, many of which have closed.

The Unity School of Christianity

The Unity School of Christianity was founded by Charles and Myrtle Fillmore in 1889. The term *unity* refers to the oneness or unity of each individual with God (Jesus is the inner Christ who resides in each individual). Though Unity has "school" in its name, its members meet in churches. Unity believes the Bible to be an allegory; that God is a "principle" of love; and that Jesus was human only, not divine. It also believes in reincarnation (Charles Fillmore claimed to be the reincarnation of the apostle Paul) and that salvation comes when one breaks free of the cycle of birth, death and rebirth, at which point one's physical body is replaced by a spiritual body. Unity's popular monthly publication, *Daily Word*, is distributed in more than 100 countries around the world.

New Religious Movements in the Twentieth Century

The second half of the twentieth century saw the rise of a number of new religious movements. One that was popular for many years was the *Unification Church*, which was founded in 1954 in South Korea by Sun Myung Moon (1920-2012). According to Moon, God chose Jesus, the second Adam, to father a pure, sinless race, but Jesus was killed before he could marry the second Eve and begin the process. Moon claimed to be the third Adam, the one called by God to redeem the human race. The Moonies have declined in numbers in North America, but the movement is said to be large and growing in parts of Asia.

The *Church of Scientology* was founded by L. Ron Hubbard in the 1950s. Hubbard was a science-fiction writer and journalist who said, "If a man wants to make a million dollars, the best way would be to start a new religion." Scientology, the religion started by Hubbard, and the two religions below, make no claim to being Christian.

Scientologists believe that humans are imprisoned by past memories and experiences, called *engrams*, that need to be released and cleared so individuals can escape the wheel of reincarnation and realize their inborn divine potential.

Eckankar is a pantheistic religion founded in 1965 by Paul Twitchell, who embraced Eastern religions and was a staff member of the Church of Scientology. Twitchell claims to have learned the principles of Eckankar from a 500-year-old Eck master, who traced his lineage back to the beginning of life on earth. The goal of Eckankar adherents is out-of-body soul travel to Sugmad, the everlasting Eck, at which point one's soul is freed from the cycle of birth, death and rebirth.

Wicca, though small in size, is a fast-growing movement, with the number of Wiccans doubling every year or two. Wicca is a neo-pagan, nature-based religion founded by Gerald Gardner, a retired British civil servant, in the 1950s. Wiccans believe in a duotheistic godhead comprising a god and goddess, sometimes symbolized as sun and moon. A distinctive aspect of Wicca is its belief in witches, witchcraft and sorcery. Wicca denies the biblical God; original sin (right and wrong are relative concepts);

Jesus as God's sinless, virgin-born Son (some view him, instead, as a 'wizard'); and that after repeated reincarnations one is allowed into "summerland."

The New Age Movement

The New Age Movement is not a new or alternative religious movement. It is a worldwide philosophy dating back to the early 1970s that believes the present age is coming to an end, to be replaced by a new age, the mythical Age of Aquarius. New Agers are pantheists (all is God and God is in all) who believe in the interconnectedness of humanity, nature (Mother Earth) and the divine, a belief system called *monism* (one-ism). They also believe in the law of karma and the transmigration of human souls or spirits.

The goal of New Agers is to release their hidden, suppressed, higher selves and merge with the divine force or power of the universe. How is this possible? Through visualization techniques and hypnosis; by getting in touch with spirit entities to receive their wisdom, often aided by psychics and crystals (New Agers believe that God is an energy force that vibrates throughout the universe and use crystals to connect with his energy); and through yoga, meditation and other techniques.

Do All Roads Lead to God?

In today's world of religious pluralism, Christians are in contact with people of other faiths. Some say that all religions are the same, just different paths to the top of the mountain. But the beliefs of the other four major world religions are different from those of Christianity: we are not saved by Moses; Hinduism's gods are not living, active, personal beings; we do not find "enlightenment" by believing in Buddha; and Muhammad was not Allah's son.

Christians don't go up the mountain to be with God; he comes down, as he did in Jesus, to be with us. Karl Barth was once asked if God had revealed himself to peoples of other religions. Barth said, "No, God has revealed himself only in his Son." Christianity teaches that religions and beliefs like those in this chapter may lead to 'a' god, but not to the knowable, loving, triune God of Christianity. The difference between Christianity and Hinduism, Buddhism, Islam, Mormonism and other religions is the difference between doing and done. The religions in this chapter believe that salvation comes by doing something. Christianity believes that everything necessary for salvation has already been done by Jesus on the cross. As Christians, all we need to do is believe in the "done-ness."

Discussion Questions

1. Do you have neighbors, colleagues and friends who are adherents of other religions? Have you ever shared your faith with them? Have they ever shared theirs with you? If so, what happened?

2. Some say that Hinduism, Judaism, Christianity, Islam, Mormonism and the other religions in this chapter are just different ways to connect with God. What are the bottom-line beliefs of Christianity that distinguish it from other religions?

3. Have you ever had a Mormon or Jehovah's Witness knock on your door and ask to talk with you about their religion? If so, what did they say to you and what did you say to them?

9

Prayer, Study, Service and Evangelism

We sail along in life, and then run aground on the rocks of misfortune. We invest our lives in our children, only to see them make bad decisions and destroy the dreams we had for them. We have the perfect job, and then our company downsizes or is acquired by a competitor and our job is eliminated. We eat right and exercise, and then are hit with a debilitating illness. Where do we find solid ground? The refrain in the hymn *My Hope Is Built on Nothing Less* reads: "On Christ the solid rock I stand; all other ground is sinking sand; all other ground is sinking sand."

A Place to Stand

Elton Trueblood, a noted twentieth-century Quaker author, theologian and the director of Religious Information under President Eisenhower, wrote a book called *A Place to Stand* in which he said, "The three areas that must be cultivated [to build a strong faith] are the inner life of devotion, the intellectual life of rational thought, and the outer life of human service." This chapter looks at these three, and the Seven Deadly Sins, apologetics and evangelism.

Growing in Christ through Prayer

Polls indicate that a majority of Christians are dissatisfied with their prayer lives. One reason is that in our busy world we find it difficult to be quiet before the Lord—to sit and "wait upon the Lord." The Westminster Catechism of 1647 asks: "What is the chief end of man [and, today, woman]?" The answer: "To glorify God and enjoy him forever." We glorify God when we come to him in prayer; we enjoy God when we bask in his presence, like a child sitting on the lap of a parent or grandparent. Brother Lawrence, a seventeenth-century French Carmelite lay brother, said we shouldn't come into God's presence only at certain times, for instance, when we pray. We should "practice the presence of God" in everything that we do.

Martin Luther said, "Just as the business of the tailor is to make clothing, and that of the shoemaker is to mend shoes, so the work of the Christian is to pray," which is the highest and holiest "work" that a Christian can do. In its simplest form, prayer is seeking and speaking to God. It is practiced by adherents of all major religions. The primary prayer of Jews is the *Shema,* the Hebrew word for *hear*: "Hear, O, Israel: The Lord is our God, the

Lord alone" (Deuteronomy 6:4). The most common prayer of Christians is the Lord's Prayer (Matthew 6:9-13), which is recited in most churches every Sunday. In Islam, the Salat or Salah, a ritualistic prayer that comes from the first chapter of the Koran, is recited by Muslims five times a day while prostrated in the direction of Mecca.

Christian prayers are both communal (in worship services) and private. Public prayers usually close with the words, "In Jesus' name" or "For Jesus' sake" or "Amen" (truly or verily). Private prayers are said by some upon rising in the morning, by others at bedtime. Many say prayers at meals, either vocally or quietly. Some keep prayer journals to record prayer petitions and responses to their petitions. In worship services, some pray kneeling, others standing; some sit and clasp their hands; Pentecostals often raise their hands while speaking (praying) in tongues, called *glossolalia*, from the Greek words *glossa*, meaning "tongue," and *lalia,* meaning "talk." Some prefer to pray spontaneously, others use fixed formulas like the Lord's Prayer, others read from a prayer book like the Episcopal *Book of Common Prayer.* Catholics use rosaries, from the word *rosarium*, meaning "garden rose," one of the flowers used to symbolize Mary, which begins with the words: "Hail Mary, full of grace, the Lord is with thee." The rosary chain has beads that highlight events in Jesus' life.

Thanking and Listening to God

Prayer is being with God, communing with God, thanking him for his love, blessings and grace and beseeching him to "speak" to us and guide us. Examples of God speaking in the Bible are his words to Moses at the burning bush (Exodus 3), at Jesus' baptism (Mark 1:11) and on the Mount of Transfiguration (Mark 9:7). God also speaks in visions, as in the story of Isaiah hearing God say,

"Whom shall I send?" (Isaiah 6:1–8); in dreams to Joseph about Mary and to "flee" to Egypt (Matthew 1:20 and 2:13); in words of knowledge about people and situations, as in Jesus' words to the woman at the well in Samaria (John 4:16–19); and, most importantly, through his written Word.

Moderns have trouble waiting to *hear* from the Lord. We are in a rush to tell God what's on our mind. Others, who have never experienced God, don't believe that he speaks to us. Some think that God may have spoken to prophets and apostles in biblical times, but not today (there is no scriptural warrant for believing that God spoke only in biblical times).

It is said that "God speaks to those who take the time to listen, and he listens to those who take the time to pray." A book with real-life stories of ways that God speaks in dreams and visions and through people and circumstances is Joyce Huggett's book *Listening to God: Hearing the Many Ways God Speaks to Us.*

Forms of Prayer

Vocal prayers are spoken prayers, either out loud or privately and quietly. A helpful outline for verbal or spoken prayer is the acronym PRAY. The letter **P** stands for praise—praising God for his goodness and for the gift of faith and thanking him for those we love and who love us. **R** stands for reflect—reflecting on the greatness of God and on verses in the scriptures or readings in a devotional as they come into our mind. **A** stands for ask—asking God to forgive us, in the words of the Book of Common Prayer, "for doing those things we should not have done and not doing those things we should have done"; petitioning God for personal needs; and offering intercessory (on behalf of) prayers for those in need of God's ears and presence, perhaps someone who is out of work or whose marriage is in trouble or who has suffered a personal tragedy. **Y** stands for yearn—yearning to be at one with God, for intimacy with God, to be more in love with God, who does not care about the correctness or beauty of our words, only that we come to him with a prayerful heart.

Meditative prayer is praying with the mind, based on a passage of scripture or a reading in a daily devotional. In meditative prayer we reflect on God's words to us. Dietrich Bonhoeffer said, "You do not analyze the words of someone you love, but accept them as they are said to you; so it is with meditation." They become, writes Quaker scholar Richard Foster in his book *Prayer*, "A living word addressed to us. A call to repentance, to change, to obedience. In meditative prayer, God addresses us personally."

Contemplative prayer is the most advanced level of prayer. Vocal prayer is praying with words; meditative prayer is praying with our mind; contemplative prayer is praying with our heart. Contemplative prayer is hungering for a genuine "felt experience" of God, for hearing God's "still small voice," for union and intimacy with God. How do we do this? By quieting down so that we can listen to and connect with God, who is everywhere present, like radio waves everywhere around us, waiting to speak to us.

The Lord's Prayer

Jesus' disciples asked him to teach them how to pray. His response—"Pray then in this way" (Matthew 6:9)—is called the Lord's Prayer, which was not Jesus' personal prayer because it petitions God to "forgive us our sins" (NRSV: "our debts") and Jesus was sinless. The Lord's Prayer is an excellent format for prayer; some use it as an outline for their nightly prayers. It takes only fifteen seconds to *say* the prayer, but several minutes to reflect and meditate on its petitions.

The prayer opens with a short introduction: "Our Father in heaven," which implies that God is a person—a person that loves us in a special way, like the father of the prodigal son who rejoiced when his wayward son came to his senses and returned home.

This is followed by three supplications to God: first, that his name—his very essence—be hallowed and reverenced as the sovereign God of the universe; second, that his rule and reign over the earth will soon come; third, that his will be done—his will that we love him and others and invite non-believers into the kingdom.

The second half of the prayer contains three personal petitions, which William Barclay said can be thought of as present, past and future. We pray for today—for our "daily bread," which includes shelter, medical care and other necessities of life. Next, we pray for yesterday—for thoughts, words, deeds, hurts, debts and trespasses that need to be forgiven. We don't confess these things to tell God something he doesn't already know; we confess them so we may be forgiven. Finally, we pray for tomorrow—for God to be present when we are tempted. Being tempted is not a sin; everyone is tempted. It is yielding to temptation that is sin. How do we avoid yielding to temptation? By avoiding occasions of temptation and by asking God to keep us from falling prey to sin (see 1 Corinthians 10:13).

The Lord's Prayer in Protestant churches ends with the doxology (praise to God): "For thine is the kingdom and the power and the glory, forever and ever."

The Practice of Prayer

We do not learn to pray by reading books on prayer; we learn by engaging in the discipline of prayer. The following are suggestions from people who have an active prayer life.

First, dedicate a certain time each day to being alone with God, perhaps first thing in the morning before our minds begin racing with all the tasks we have to do. Second, find a quiet place to be alone with God, as Jesus often did (early in the morning "he got up and went out to a deserted place and prayed," Mark 1:35). Third, get comfortable, perhaps light a candle, and center your mind on Christ. Fourth, keep a spiritual diary to record thoughts and reflections that come to you during these times.

One way to deepen our prayer life is with a daily devotional. *My Utmost for His Highest* by Oswald Chambers (1874-1917) is the best-selling devotional of all time. *A Guide to Prayer* by Reuben Job and Norman Shawchuck is a book "for every pilgrim who yearns for God." The *Andrew Murray Daily Reader* will help you "experience a deeper fellowship with God." All three are excellent.

Answers to Prayer

What about answers to prayer requests and petitions? Some prayers are answered immediately; others require persistence; and sometimes the answer is no, as in Paul's prayer to God to remove the thorn in his flesh (2 Corinthians 12:7-10). God hears all prayers. We don't know why he seems to answer some (to our satisfaction) and not others. Some say the issue is not too few answers, but too few prayers.

Fasting

Following his teaching on prayer in the Sermon on the Mount, Jesus says, "whenever you fast . . . when you fast . . . your fasting" (Matthew 6:16-18), indicating that he intended his disciples to fast after he left them. Fasting—abstaining from food but not water—was widely practiced in the early church and fast days were obligatory in the Middle Ages. Unfortunately, most Protestants do not fast, perhaps because the Reformers rejected "things Catholic." Fasting is an important spiritual discipline—controlling the carnal side of our nature so that we might "feast" instead on God. Richard Foster's book *Celebration of Discipline* has some helpful guidelines on the practice of fasting.

Growing in Christ through Study and Service

Prayer is the interior life of growth. Next, we need to make the Jesus of our heart the Jesus of our mind, and then let our faith issue forth in works of service. Study will help us give an answer to those who ask about the hope we have in Jesus (1 Peter 3:15). Service will let others see how this hope expresses itself in the good works spoken of by Paul in his letter to the Ephesians (2:10) and by James (2:14-26).

Growing in Christ through Study

God wants us to grow in knowledge—to "be transformed by the renewing of [our] minds" (Romans 12:2). The following are suggestions for studying the Bible.

First, get a study Bible in a modern translation, one that has introductions to the individual books and comments on the text. Start with small, digestible doses of Scripture, reading slowly and carefully, asking what the meaning of the passage was for those to whom it was written (you will need a study Bible or Bible commentary to do this) and what it means to you and for your life.

Second, be consistent. Get in the habit of reading the Bible every day.

Third, be systematic. Stay with something and see it through to the end, rather than jumping from one book of the Bible to another. A good place to begin would be with one of the Gospels, perhaps Luke because of the orderliness and completeness of his narrative. Start by reading the entire Gospel. Then go back to the beginning and read about Jesus' birth, conflicts, healings, miracles, teachings and other *pericopes* (self-contained stories) and his saving death and resurrection. If you read a pericope every day, Doctor Luke will keep you busy for months.

Lastly, find ways to apply the Bible's teachings to your life. The purpose of Bible study is not information but *transformation.*

In addition to studying the Bible, one should read books on the life of Jesus, what Christians believe, and how to live Christianly in the world. Serious students should build a Christian library. Begin with a good introduction to the Bible, like John Drane's *Introducing the Old Testament* and *Introducing the New Testament* (third editions, 2011). Then buy *The Oxford Companion to the Bible* (1993), Tyndale's *Life Application New Testament Commentary* (2001) and Mark Strauss's *Four Portraits, One Jesus* (2007). Then add Zondervan's *Handbook of the History of Christianity* (2006), Millard Erickson's *Introducing Christian Doctrine* (second edition, 2001), the *Penguin Dictionary of the Bible* (2007), and books on Christian living by Tom Wright, John Ortberg, Bill Hybels and others.

Growing in Christ through Service

Christians are the best argument for Christianity—and sometimes the worst. We are at our worst when we fail to reflect in our lives the one we profess as Lord and Savior. If we want others to consider the person, claims and promises of Jesus, we need to be the further incarnation of his message and teachings. How should we do this? Jesus tells us, in the story of the sheep and the goats in Matthew's Gospel (25:31–45), that we are to feed the hungry, clothe the naked, care for the sick and visit the incarcerated. We also need to champion social justice, speak out against immorality, care for the environment, and show Christian kindness to everyone who crosses our path.

One way to be a living witness to the love and message of Christ would be to get involved in your church's outreach program, or go on a mission trip to an impoverished area of the world, or work with a mission agency in your city. Jesus said those who work to advance the kingdom of God will receive, in this age and in the age to come, eternal life (Luke 18:28-30).

Obstacles to Growth: The Seven Deadly Sins

The church in the Middle Ages developed two lists of "sevens," a good biblical number: God rested on the seventh day; seven priests marched around Jericho seven times on the seventh day; Jesus said that we are to forgive seventy times seven; the author of the book of Revelation is told to write to seven churches, after which he has several visions of sevens.

The first list of sevens contained seven virtues, comprising the four cardinal virtues of prudence, justice, temperance and fortitude from Greek philosophy, and the three theological virtues of faith, hope and love from 1 Corinthians 13:13.

The second list contained seven sins. They were originally called "cardinal" sins (like cardinal virtues) or "capital" sins, meaning they were the cause or source of other sins. For instance, avarice is a cardinal or capital sin because it leads to lying, cheating and stealing to achieve its ends. The Seven Deadly Sins, which can weaken and destroy our faith, come from Pope Gregory the Great in the sixth century. They are *pride*, the sin of self-love and self-promotion; *envy* and jealousy, which poisons the soul and spirit, resulting in bitterness and isolation; *anger* that is hurtfully projected on to others; *sloth*, slovenliness, apathy and neglect; *avarice* and greed for power and possessions; *gluttony* and self-indulgence; and *lusting* to satisfy our fleshly desires.

Pride is the first and most important of the seven sins because it is the core or root sin, which issues forth in other sins. C. S. Lewis, in his classic, *Mere Christianity*, said, "Pride is the one sin of which no one in the world is free; which everyone in the world loathes when he or she sees it in someone else; and of which hardly any people, except Christians, ever imagine they are guilty of themselves." Pride is going our own way; it is *my* will be done, not *thy* will be done. How do we overcome pride? By practicing its opposite, which is humility. Rick Warren, in *The Purpose Driven Life*, said, "Humility is not thinking less of yourself; it is thinking of yourself less."

Christian Apologetics: God, Evil and Miracles

The defense of Christianity is called apologetics, from the Greek word *apologia*, which means making a formal defense. The work of apologetics is to answer those who challenge the beliefs of Christianity—those whose naturalist worldviews do not allow for the possibility of a supernatural being; those who ask why an all-powerful, all-loving God allows evil and suffering to exist; those who cannot bring themselves to believe in Jesus' virginal conception, miracles and bodily resurrection.

The Existence of God

There are two "tracks" to God, one by way of nature, the other by way of revelation—the "works" of God in the world and the "words" of God in the scriptures. Natural theology teaches that it is possible to believe in a Creator God by reflecting on "the heavens and the earth." Astronomers tell us there are more than 100 billion galaxies in the visible universe, and that our galaxy, the Milky Way, has approximately 100 billion stars. The origin of the universe—or universes, referred to by scientists as the "multiverse"—cannot be understood as a random accident of physics.

Regarding life on planet Earth, some say that given enough time it's possible that life itself could have formed and evolved without a Creator—like those who say that a group of monkeys with typewriters could, if given enough time, produce a work of literature. Physicist Gerald Schroeder, in his book *God According to God*, tells about a group of British college students who arranged an experiment to test this possibility. In 2003, in a zoo in Devon, England, six monkeys pounded away on a keyboard for a month and failed to produce a single English word.

The second way we know God is by and through the scriptures, which is called revealed theology. If God exists, it seems natural that he would reveal his love for us and his will for our lives. How does God do this? By calling prophets, disciples, apostles, preachers, evangelists and others to speak his word so that one day all the world will know him. It is said that natural theology tells us of God's creating will and revealed theology of his saving will.

There is also a third way that we know God: through the inner witness of the Holy Spirit. There are things that we know are true even though we cannot prove them. Right now, for instance, I am typing these pages on my word processor, and I am hungry and thinking about lunch, but I cannot prove that this is what I am thinking or even that I am hungry—but I know these things are true, and I know in my heart that God created the universe and life and that he loves me.

Evil and Suffering

There are no satisfactory answers to evil and suffering, other than to say that free-will human beings often make decisions that result in their (and often others) personal suffering. Some think that God owes them a pain-free, comfortable life. God is not in the happiness business. He is in the grace business, offering us forgiveness for the sins that separate us from him.

Suffering, though, is not the end of the story. Joni Eareckson Tada was injured in a diving accident in Chesapeake Bay in 1967, when she was a teenager, leaving her paralyzed from the neck down. Joni said she believed that "one day I would have a body that worked, hands that could hug, feet that would run ... that I had not been left alone ... that God would give me a new body beyond the grave." As Paul told the Corinthians, God has prepared something wonderful and beautiful for those who love him (1 Corinthians 2:9).

What about natural disasters—earthquakes, tsunamis, tornadoes and the like? The Oxford theologian Austin Farrer (1904-1968) was asked what God was doing during the Lisbon earthquake in 1755 in which an estimated 50,000 people died. Farrer said, "God was letting nature operate by its own laws. When there is a shift in the earth's tectonic plates, there is an earthquake."

Why do things continue to be so bad, with terrorism and conflicts around the world, hunger, incurable diseases, ignorance and poverty, animosities between people and nations? The reason is that God's plan of restoration is not finished. When Jesus returns he will defeat the powers of sin and evil, he will make all things right, and he will establish God's renewed, redeemed kingdom on earth for all eternity.

Jesus' Conception, Resurrection and Miracles

Non-believers reject the Incarnation, the Resurrection and Jesus' miracles because they cannot be understood in human terms. But many things cannot be understood in human terms. Take the brain, for example. No one can explain how the wiring in the brain allows us to reason, dream, love, remember the past, create works of art and enjoy rippling waves, glorious sunsets and fragrant aromas. Just because we cannot explain how Jesus was virginally conceived, performed miracles and rose from the dead does not mean that these things did not occur.

The Message of Evangelism: Jesus Christ

Songwriter Andrew Lloyd Webber wrote a musical called *Jesus Christ Superstar*. The opening line in the lead song is, "Jesus Christ, superstar, are you who they say you are?" Jesus asked his disciples a similar question: "Who do you say that I am?" (Mark 8:29). What about today? Some say that Jesus was an imposter, claiming to be the divine Son of God, saying, "The Father and I are one." But we do not find a deceitful Jesus on the pages of the New Testament. We find someone who is kind, loving and merciful. Others say that Jesus was a man about whom his followers developed a legend after his death. If Jesus was just a legend, how did Christianity become the official, authorized religion of the pagan Roman Empire? Believers say that Jesus was and is the incarnate, still-living Son of the Creator of the universe—"the Lord of lords and King of kings" (Revelation 17:14)—who one day is coming to raise up all who have believed in him (John 6:40).

The real issue, though, as C. S. Lewis observed in *God in the Dock*, is not "What do we think of Christ?" but "What does Christ think of us?" We have all sinned in thought, word and deed, which no honest person would deny. How can our sins and transgressions be forgiven? By believing in and trusting that Jesus' atoning sacrifice will cleanse us from all unrighteousness.

At the end of the day, though, the story of Jesus always comes back to his resurrection on Easter morning, about which the following can be said.

First, fifty days after Jesus' death, his disciples declared on the streets of Jerusalem that he had been raised from the dead (Acts 2:22–24). If the Jews had wished to dispute this, they would have needed only to go to the tomb of Joseph of Arimathea, a well-known Jewish leader in whose family tomb Jesus was placed, and produce his corpse. This would have ended everything. There is no record of anyone coming forward to say that Jesus' body was still in the tomb or that it had been stolen by the disciples (according to Matthew 27:62–66, the Jews asked that Roman guards be placed at the tomb to prevent this from happening).

Second, as Frederick Buechner said in chapter 3, if Jesus had not been raised there would be no New Testament, no church and no Christianity. Why not? Because a dead, still-in-the-tomb Jesus would not have been "good news."

Third, many who publicly testified to Jesus' resurrection were imprisoned (Acts 5:17–18), stoned to death (Stephen in Acts 7:59–60 and James, the half-brother of Jesus, in the year 62), nailed to crosses (Simon Peter and untold others), beheaded (the apostle Paul and Justin Martyr, who was beheaded for refusing to offer sacrifices to the Roman gods), burned at the stake (Polycarp, the bishop of Smyrna) and those who were, for the public's entertainment, clawed to death by lions and other animals in the Colosseum. What gave them the strength to endure persecution—and for many, sure and certain death—rather than renounce their belief that Jesus had been raised from the dead? The strong, credible, hope-filled testimony of those who had seen the risen Christ.

The Mechanics of Evangelism: Sharing the Gospel

It is said that God has a plan for our lives. It may be more accurate to say that he has a purpose for our lives: to know Jesus Christ and to make him known to others.

In the 1940s there was an outbreak of polio in the United States. In 1952, Dr. Jonas Salk invented a vaccine to prevent polio and there was a widespread program of inoculation. Today polio has been eradicated in the United States and throughout the world (Pakistan and Afghanistan are the only two countries that have any incidence of polio). This would not have happened if the vaccine had remained in Dr. Salk's laboratory. It had to be distributed to areas of need to be effective. The same is true of the gospel: it has life-saving power, but it has to get to the point of need to be effective. Paul said to the church in Rome: "How beautiful are the feet of those who bring good news" (10:13-15). The following are some suggestions for sharing the good news.

First, begin where the other person is and ask, if you are comfortable doing so, about his or her faith and beliefs. This often leads to their asking, in return, "What do you believe?" which opens the door for you to share the unique, distinctive beliefs of Christianity.

Second, focus on the central message, which is having a personal relationship with Jesus Christ. Don't get sidetracked trying to explain the mysteries of the faith, or the lifestyles and acts of other Christians, even church leaders (our trust is in Jesus, not in fallen humanity), or why there is evil and suffering in the world. Keep to your beliefs and what they mean to you and for your life—that Christ has given you something to live for (his promise of eternal life) and something to live by (his sermonic and parabolic teachings).

Third, avoid Christian in-talk about the Bible being "the inspired word of God" or being saved "by the blood (or cross) of Christ" or being "justified by grace through faith" or the need to be "born again." In-talk hinders effective conversation.

Fourth, all religions have some truth. Do not speak ill about or judge other religions as false and avoid making claims about Jesus being superior to the founders of other religions. This allows for open discussion. Dialogue is far more productive than argument.

Lastly, remember that our role as witnesses is to be presenters, not persuaders. We are to present the good news of Jesus as lovingly as possible (1 Peter 3:15), and then let the inner witness of the Holy Spirit work in the lives of those with whom we have shared the gospel.

If someone wants to become a Christian—wants to accept Christ into his or her life—the following three-step **ABC** outline is a good way to do so. First, *admit* and acknowledge your sins, failings and transgressions against God and others; second, *believe* that Jesus died for you and invite him into your life; third, *confess* Jesus as your Lord and Savior.

Making a decision for Jesus is not a one-time decision or transaction. It is the first or beginning step in a life of believing in and following Jesus and sharing him with others. It is like marriage, which is more than a one-time "I do" at the altar. Being saved, or justified to use Paul's term, launches us on a new, forever Christ-centered life.

Christian writer Os Guinness said, "The problem with most Christians is not that they aren't *where* they should be. The problem is that they're not *what* they should be right where they are." What should we be doing "right where we are"? Sharing the good news of and about Jesus Christ.

Pascal's Wager

Blaise Pascal (1623-1662) was a seventeenth-century French mathematician who invented, some believe, the first workable calculating machine to help his father, a tax official, prepare his daily reports; a physicist who invented Pascal's Law, which underlies the principles of hydraulics; and the inventor of the barometer. Pascal died at the young age of thirty-nine. His thoughts on religion were published after his death under the title *Pensées* (French for "thoughts"), which has become a Christian classic. One of the best-known sections in *Pensées* is Pascal's "wager." Pascal said that we all make a bet or wager on God, whether we know it or not. If we bet on God, and there is a God, we win everything. If we bet on God, and there is no God, we lose nothing because there is nothing to lose. If we deny or reject God, and there is a God, we lose everything.

Philosopher-theologian Peter Kreeft, in his book *Christianity for Modern Pagans,* which is based on Pascal's *Pensées,* said "it is eminently reasonable for anyone to 'bet' on God, to hope that God is, to invest our life in God." Pascal's wager comes down to betting that Jesus is who he and the New Testament said he was and is, namely, the life-giving Son of God.

Discussion Questions

1. What is your prayer format? Do you keep a journal to record prayer requests and answers? If you struggle with prayer, what are some of your struggles?

2. Martin Luther said, "God doesn't need our good works. Our neighbors do." What are some good works activities you have been involved in?

3. What is the best Christian book, other than the Bible, that you have read? Have you ever shared or given the book to a non-believer?

10

Biblical Guidelines for Christian Living

Christians struggle with how to live Christianly in a world that makes demands that are contrary to the teachings of Jesus, Paul and others in the New Testament. How are we to live out and give witness to our faith? The best guide or compass would be to have a solid, believable Christian worldview about the origin of the universe and life on planet Earth, about loving and serving God and others, about the purpose and meaning of life, about issues of social justice and caring for the poor, and about what happens when we die.

The Christian Worldview

Religions have different worldviews. Jews, Christians and Muslims believe in a single, sovereign God; Hindus believe there are thousands of gods; Buddhists do not believe in a God or gods. The Big Five and other religions also have different views of creation, salvation and heaven and hell. Christianity's worldview beliefs are expressed in its scriptures, church-wide creeds and doctrinal teachings. Two texts central to Christian beliefs and practices are the Ten Commandments and the Sermon on the Mount, which we will look at in this chapter, along with five of Jesus' parables and his seven "I am" statements. We will close by developing ways to guide us in living Christianly in the world.

The Ten Commandments: Rules for Christian Living

Israel was called to be God's "light to the nations" (Isaiah 42:6). How was Israel to be such a people? By observing the commandments God gave to Moses on Mount Sinai, which are contained in the books of Exodus (20:3-17) and Deuteronomy (5:7-21). Jesus affirms the commandments in his dialogue with the rich young man (Mark 10:19) and the apostle Paul in his letter to the Romans (13:9).

Many people read the Ten Commandments as a series of narrow "shall nots." Pastor James Moore, in his book *When All Else Fails . . . Read the Instructions*, says, "The Ten Commandments tell us how things work, how life holds together, how God meant things to be. Anyone who is awake enough to 'smell the coffee' can easily see that life is better when we love God and other people . . . when we respect our parents and tell the truth . . . when we are honest and faithful in all of our relationships."

The Ten Commandments are numbered differently. Catholics and Lutherans, for instance, combine the first two commandments into one (no other gods and no graven images) and divide the tenth into two (coveting possessions and coveting persons). The first four commandments have to do with our vertical relationship with God; the second six with our horizontal relationship with others. The following are brief comments on each of the commandments.

1. **You shall have no other gods before me.** The word "gods" reflects the fact that there were many gods in the ancient world. For Israel, there was only one God—the 'wholly other' God who called Abraham, led the Israelites out of Egypt, and entered into covenants with the patriarchs and leaders of Israel. The Israelites were to worship this God and no other. Today we do not think in terms of a plurality of gods, but we do elevate many things to the level of worship: reputation, success, wealth, power, pleasure, health, and on and on. After filming *The Ten Commandments* (1956), Cecil B. DeMille was asked which commandment he thought people break the most. DeMille said, "The first one. It is the one that Israel broke first and the one we still break most often." We are called to love God with all of our heart, soul, mind and strength (Mark 12:30), which means giving God first priority in our lives.

2. **You shall not make for yourself an idol.** God told Moses, "I am who I am" (Exodus 3:14). God spoke but was not seen. For this reason, no graven (sculpted, carved or chiseled) image was possible. When the Romans entered Palestine in 63 BC, they were surprised that the Israelites had no image or idols of the God they professed and worshiped, in contrast to the Roman army, which carried flags and standards with

the emperor's image wherever it went. Some claim that paintings, statues and icons of Jesus are "images." They are not images; they are symbolic representations of God's personification of himself in the human Jesus. Today we don't make idols of God, but we do idolize others—royalty, rock musicians, movie and television stars, professional athletes, fashion models—until they fade away. We are called to worship and idolize God and God alone.

3. **You shall not make wrongful use of the name of the Lord your God.** The word God does not denote the name of God—which was so sacred that it was never audibly uttered in ancient Israel—but the *essence* of God. Today this commandment refers to language that profanes God in speech, jokes, writings and graffiti. Christians are called to take God's name in earnest, not in vain—from the Latin *vanus*, which means to empty, diminish or depreciate—as we pray in the Lord's Prayer: "Hallowed be thy name."

4. **Remember the Sabbath day, and keep it holy.** God rested on the seventh day so that he could enjoy his creation (Genesis 2:2); Israel rested on the seventh day so that she could enjoy God. In a mythical conversation between God and the people of Israel, God said, "If you obey my commandments, I will give you a great gift." The people asked, "What is this gift?" God said, "The world to come." They asked, "What will the world to come be like?" God said, "It will be like one continuous, everlasting Sabbath." The word Sabbath comes from the Hebrew word *shabbat*, which means to cease or stop or rest. The Christian Sabbath is different than the Jewish Sabbath: it commemorates the day that Jesus rose from the dead. Unfortunately, Sunday has moved from being a Christian holy day to a secular

holiday. We honor this commandment by worshiping God and being in fellowship with other believers.

5. **Honor your father and your mother.** The fifth commandment is the only one without a "shall not" and the only one with a promise: "So that your days may be long." This and the remaining five commandments have to do with our relationships with others—our parents, our spouse and our neighbors, all six of which Jesus mentions in his conversation with the rich young man (Mark 10:19). This commandment addresses the need to honor and care for our parents, and to be family for those who have no family, showing them the kind of hospitality Jesus referred to when he said, in Matthew's story of the sheep and the goats, "I was a stranger and you welcomed me" (25:35).

6. **You shall not murder.** This commandment has to do with the sanctity of life. It has been broadened to include any form of killing and is the biblical basis for those who oppose capital punishment, war, euthanasia (mercy killing) and recruitment by the government into the armed forces. It is also the basis for those who believe that life begins at conception and that aborting an embryo is killing one made in the image of God.

7. **You shall not commit adultery.** The thrust of this commandment is the fidelity of persons who have been joined together "to become one flesh" (Genesis 2:24 and Mark 10:6-9). Many feel the sexual revolution of the 1960s, which exploited sex throughout society in movies, novels, television, advertising, language and even dress, started a downward spiral in sexual mores. The result has been a breakdown in the family unit. Sex is one of God's

wonderful gifts, but it must be enjoyed within marriage, not promiscuously.

8. **You shall not steal.** This commandment prohibited the stealing of another Israelite's property, particularly those who were poor and powerless. Today the commandment has to do with honesty. In its broadest form it deals with the misappropriation of funds and property, the bribery of government and corporate officials, the manipulation of the economic system for personal gain, and the falsification of records and reports.

9. **You shall not bear false witness against your neighbor.** In ancient Israel, giving false witness against another was a serious offense, because the one accused was guilty until proven innocent, the opposite of our jurisprudence. In capital crimes, the one bringing the charge had to throw the first stone. If the evidence against the accused was shown to be untrue, the accuser was stoned in his or her place. Today this commandment has to do with truthfulness. It includes perjury, slander, libel and gossip—in fact, the protection of another person's reputation against any form of false witness, even remaining silent when a person is being wrongly accused. We need to tell "the whole truth and nothing but the truth."

10. **You shall not covet.** The final commandment is a prohibition against unhealthy lusting after status, success, power, wealth, possessions and, well, what don't we covet these days? Joseph Heller, the author of the anti-war novel *Catch-22*, once had a conversation with a wealth-accumulating multimillionaire, who told Heller that he'd never make any money writing books. Heller said, "You may be right, but

I have something you'll never have." "What's that?" asked the multimillionaire. "I have enough," said Heller. How do we conquer covetousness? By practicing its opposite, which is contentedness.

Are the Ten Commandments applicable today, or are they old, antiquated, out-of-date rules for another society and another time? According to a 1990s Barna Report, 64 percent of Americans strongly agreed and another 15 percent somewhat agreed that the Ten Commandments are "relevant for people living today." Former television journalist Ted Koppel, in a speech to a graduating class at Duke University, said that Moses came down from Mount Sinai with Ten Commandments, not Ten Suggestions. "The sheer beauty of the Commandments," Koppel said, "is that they codify in a handful of words accept-able human behavior, not just for then or now, but for all time."

The Sermon on the Mount: The Christian Manifesto

The two principal teachings in the early church were how to *enter* the kingdom of God and how to *live* in the kingdom. The clearest and fullest teaching about living in the kingdom is the so-called (by Augustine) Sermon on the Mount in Matthew 5:1–7:29. The "sermon" is presented as a single, unified piece, but many believe it is a summary of Jesus' teachings because of its length and complexity and because there is a different order, wording and placement of some of the passages in Luke's Gospel.

In the Bible, mounts and mountains are places where God spoke and revealed himself. Examples include Mount Moriah, where Isaac was taken to be sacrificed; Mount Sinai, where Moses received the Ten Commandments; Mount Carmel, where

Elijah battled the prophets of Baal; the Mount of Transfiguration, where Elijah and Moses appeared with Jesus; and Mount
Zion, where the scriptures say God resides (Psalm 48:1–2). Most
scholars believe that Jesus' sermon was delivered at a site called
Tabgha, near what is now the Church of the Beatitudes on the
western slope of the Sea of Galilee.

Jesus' sermon is addressed to the kingdom community,
not the world at large. It opens with eight beatitudes—eight
qualities that should be seen in the lives of Christians, like
Paul's nine fruits of the Spirit in Galatians 5. Some are dis-
couraged because they are unable to live out Jesus' teachings
in the Beatitudes. This is a wrong reading. The Beatitudes are
not commandments, like the Ten Commandments. They are
statements that say we are blessed—*beatitude* comes from a
Latin word meaning "blessed"—when we mourn and come to
the aid of others, when we hunger and thirst to be right with
God, when we are merciful and kind, when we strive for inner
purity, when we are at peace with those around us.

The eight beatitudes are not one long, continuous sermon (I
have heard many three-point sermons, but never an eight-point
sermon). They are the bottom lines of sermons Jesus preached
time and again throughout Galilee, which Matthew summarized
in a series of eight teachings.

1. **Blessed are the poor in spirit.** Blessed are those who realize
    they are helpless to save themselves, those who put their
    total trust and hope in God, those who bet their lives on
    the grace and mercy of God. Peter said to Jesus: "Lord, you
    [alone] have the words of eternal life" (John 6:68).

2. **Blessed are those who mourn.** Blessed are those who
    grieve over the cruelty and pains of the world, those who are
    moved by the sufferings of others and offer them comfort,

rather than passing by like the priest and the Levite who refused to help the man beaten by robbers on the road to Jericho in the parable of the good Samaritan (Luke 10:25–37).

3. **Blessed are the meek.** Blessed are those who are gentle, loving and compassionate, those who are willing to humble themselves before others, like the father who ran to greet his wasteful younger son and tried to reason with his angry older son in the parable of the prodigal son (Luke 15:11–32).

4. **Blessed are those who hunger and thirst for righteousness.** Blessed are those who hunger to be right with God, those who thirst after his will, those who desire to be upright and righteous in his sight. Amos told the Israelites that God does not want false worship; he wants justice "to roll like the waters and righteousness like an ever-flowing stream" (Amos 5:24).

5. **Blessed are the merciful.** Blessed are those who do not repay evil with evil but with love, those who show kindness and mercy to all, those who are willing to forgive and forget grievances against them, as Jesus did on the cross: "Father, forgive them; for they do not know what they are doing" (Luke 23:34).

6. **Blessed are the pure in heart.** Blessed are those whose motives are true and genuine, those who pray for an inner purity of heart, as David did after his adulterous affair with Bathsheba and the murder of her husband, Uriah, when he prayed: "Create in me a clean heart, O God, and put a new and right spirit within me" (Psalm 51:10).

7. **Blessed are the peacemakers.** Blessed are those who strive for peace and right relationships, those who are active peacemakers between persons at enmity with one another, those like Saint Francis of Assisi, who prayed: "Lord, make me an instrument of your peace."

8. **Blessed are those who are persecuted for righteousness' sake.** Blessed are those who speak out against social and political injustice, those who are willing to defend Christ's name before others. Jesus said that all who stand firm to the end for his sake "will be saved" (Mark 13:13).

Many view the Beatitudes as the preamble to the Sermon on the Mount. Following the Beatitudes, Jesus tells the disciples to be "the salt of the earth" (holy, pure and distinctive, as is salt) and "the light of the world" (an illuminating witness to God's presence in the world). If we are neither salt nor light—if we are indistinguishable from non-Christians—how will others be drawn to consider the person, teachings and promises of Christ? Jesus goes on to say that he came to fulfill the law and the words of the prophets, that is, to bring them to completion. He follows with six antitheses (contrasts of opposites) in which he says, "You have heard that it was said . . . but I say to you . . . control your anger and lust, avoid divorce and the taking of oaths, do not take an eye for an eye (Leviticus 24:20) but turn the other cheek, and love your enemies and pray for those who persecute you," Jesus' most unique and dramatic teaching.

Jesus goes on to talk about prayer and fasting (discussed in chapter 9); the impossibility of serving two masters, God and wealth (Jesus is not condemning wealth; he is talking about the unhealthy pursuit and use of wealth); striving "first for the kingdom of God and his righteousness"; judging others (Jesus' metaphor of the "log in the eye"); "doing to others as you would have them do to you" (the Golden Rule); and the two kinds of gates, trees and house builders. Who are Jesus' true disciples? Jesus said not those who call him Lord but those who do "the will of my Father in heaven."

How can we live out Jesus' sermonic teachings? By keeping our focus on the preacher of the sermon. Charles Blondin, the French tightrope walker, crossed over Niagara Falls twenty-one times in the summer of 1859. When he was asked how he did it, Blondin said, "I keep my eyes on an object on the far side of the falls and never look away." How can we live out the Sermon on the Mount? By keeping our eyes on Jesus.

The Good Samaritan, Prodigal Son and Other Parables

Parables are not unique to the New Testament. The Old Testament also has parables, like the one Nathan told to David about a rich man who took a poor man's one ewe lamb, referring to David's taking of Bathsheba (2 Samuel 12). There are some forty-five parables in the first three Gospels. John has discourses rather than parables, as in Jesus' conversation with the woman at the well.

The parables in the Gospels are summaries of Jesus' teachings. When he wanted his listeners to plant God deep within their hearts, he told the parable of the sower and the seeds. When he wanted to teach them to be merciful to those in need, he told the parable of the good Samaritan. When he wanted to tell them about God's forgiveness, he told the parable of the father who rejoiced when his prodigal son repented and returned home. When he wanted to teach them about the proper use of wealth, he told the parables of the rich farmer and the rich man and Lazarus.

One can read the parable of the good Samaritan in less than two minutes and the parable of the prodigal son in less than three minutes. Jesus must have enlarged these parables when he told them to his listeners, perhaps beginning the story of the good Samaritan with a description of the road to Jericho, a twenty-mile, bandit-infested road between Jerusalem and Jericho; telling his listeners about injuries that would have been sustained by a man who was mugged, robbed and left to die; perhaps telling them why a priest and a Levite might have passed him by (to prevent their defilement under Jewish law if the man was dead); and more about the Samaritan, who felt compassion for the man, treating his wounds and caring for him on their way to the inn. The same would have been true of his story of the prodigal son, Jesus' story about God's forgiveness and joy when we repent and return to him.

There are different kinds of parables. Some are *similitudes* in which Jesus says, "The kingdom of God is like...," as in Mark 4 and Matthew 13; others are *narratives* like the good Samaritan and the prodigal son, many of which have a surprise ending; others are *allegories* in which each detail symbolizes something else, as in the parable of the sower. Up to the end of the nineteenth century, all of Jesus' parables were viewed as allegories. Since the beginning of the last century, scholars have come to believe that most of the parables were meant to convey a single main point.

The German scholar Joachim Jeremias said that all of Jesus' parables are unique. When we read or hear them, Jeremias said, we are listening to *Jesu ipsissima verba*, to "Jesus' very words." The following parables come from Luke, who has the most parables, and some of the best-loved parables, which he weaves into his narrative.

The Sower (Luke 8:4–15)

The parable of the sower is a unique parable: it is one of only five parables found in all three synoptic Gospels; it is one of only a handful of allegorical parables; and it is one of only two parables with an explanation. In Luke's Gospel, the sower is the first parable that Jesus uses to teach those who came to hear and follow him. In the parable, the sower is Jesus, the seed is the gospel, the soil is the hearer of the gospel, and the different soils are the different responses to the gospel.

In its allegorical form, the hard path (walking paths) represents those who shut their minds to God's word, those who see and hear but refuse to believe, like the Pharisees. The thin soil (thin soil over rocks) refers to those who receive God's word and then fall away, those whose faith is shallow and rootless, like the pre-Jesus-resurrection Peter, who confessed Jesus as the Messiah and then denied him. The thorny soil (soil where seeds and weeds grow together) refers to those who believe God's word but never give it first place in their lives, those whose faith is choked by the goods, comforts and pleasures of the world, like the rich young ruler, who when Jesus told him to sell his possessions and give the proceeds to the poor, went away sad, "for he was very rich" (18:18–25). The good soil (deep, fertile, well-prepared soil) refers to those who hear God's word as a saving word, those who believe, like the woman with the hemorrhage and Jairus (8:40–56), and are richly blessed.

Bible scholars understand the parable of the sower in different ways. Some see it as a warning: only those who plant the gospel in their lives (the rich soil) will be saved. Others see it as an encouragement: "For those who have [faith], more will be given," like the hundredfold growth in the parable (8:8).

The Good Samaritan (Luke 10:25–37)

The good Samaritan is perhaps Jesus' best-known parable; others would say the prodigal son. We refer to the Samaritan as *good*, but he is not called good in the parable. This is a later interpretation, one that has made its way into everyday usage, even into the media with reports such as, "Today a good Samaritan rescued . . . . " The parable of the good Samaritan appears at the beginning of Luke's travel narrative when Jesus "set his face to go to Jerusalem" (9:51).

In the parable, a lawyer, an expert in the law of Moses, asked Jesus what he must do to inherit eternal life. The lawyer understood that he was to love God and his neighbor. What he didn't understand was that a neighbor is anyone who is in need.

The priest and the Levite refuse to care for the fallen man because, if he was dead and they touched him, it would have prevented them from exercising their priestly/temple duties. They are more interested in keeping the law than in showing love and mercy to someone who is in need.

The Samaritan—from Samaria, the region between Galilee and Judea (see map on page 243)—was and is the perfect example of loving one's neighbor. He did for a Jew something that no Jew would do for a Samaritan (Jews and Samaritans had no relations with one another, according to John 4:9); he did not worry about what he should do or what others would think of him and he did more than the minimum—he treated the man's wounds, he transported him to the inn, he paid for his care, and he agreed to pay more if more was needed.

The parable of the good Samaritan presents a problem: are we to care for everyone who crosses our path? If not, where do we draw the line? Jesus' command to love one's neighbor is a universal command; it is not limited to those who are easy or convenient to love. Today in Israel it might mean a Jew showing kindness to a Palestinian or vice versa. In the United States it might mean having concern for an American Muslim or someone accused of a crime or someone with a different sexual orientation.

The Rich Farmer (Luke 12:13-21)

Luke has several parables having to do with wealth. The setting of the parable of the rich farmer (or rich fool) is similar to many others: someone asked Jesus to settle a dispute, in this case having to do with inheritance. Jesus refuses to intervene in what is a private matter, but uses the occasion to tell a parable about wealth and the proper use of one's possessions. The farmer in the parable has had a bumper crop. He wants to build bigger barns to store his good fortune, rather than sharing it with those in need. Jesus calls the man a fool because he put his security in his possessions. Our lives will not be measured by our homes, cars, bank accounts and investment portfolios; they will be measured by our relationship with God. In fact, Jesus said on another occasion, "It is easier for a camel to go through the eye of a needle than for someone who is rich [and selfish] to enter the kingdom of God" (Luke 18:25). In this life, faith in Jesus Christ is the only riches we need to store.

An American businessman sold his company for several million dollars. A friend of his knew that he tithed to support various Christian ministries. Realizing how much money the man was now worth, he said, "Do you still intend to tithe ten percent of your income?" The businessman said, "Yes, but to myself. I can live on ten percent" (called reverse tithing, which Rick Warren and others practice). Jesus told his disciples that those to whom much has been given, much will be required; and those to whom much more has been given, even more will be required (Luke 12:48).

The Prodigal Son (Luke 15:11-21)

Some call Jesus' parable of the prodigal son the "pearl among the parables." Others call it the greatest short story ever told. The prodigal son follows two others on lostness: the lost sheep

(15:3-7) and the lost coin (15:8-10). The verse preceding the three lostness parables says that "great multitudes accompanied him," indicating that Jesus is still on his way to celebrate his final Passover in Jerusalem.

The parable has been called the Prodigal (wastefully extravagant) Son, the Lost Son, the Younger Brother, the Two Sons, the Waiting Father, the Forgiving Father, and other names. The parable has a lot of symbolism: the younger brother represents those who fall into sin, repent and are forgiven; the older brother represents the self-righteous Pharisees who refuse to seek the lost and fail to rejoice when any are found; the father represents God, who rejoices when sinners repent and return home.

The father is wealthy, with both flocks and servants. The younger son asks for the inheritance that would one day come to him (under Jewish law, as the second son, he would inherit one-third of his father's estate). Inheritances were usually given upon the death of the estate holder. By returning home and living off his father's estate, the younger brother would deplete the estate that would one day come to the older brother, which is one reason he was angry.

The parable of the prodigal son is the story of a father who lost two sons, one to a foreign country, where he squandered his inheritance, the other who refused to join in the celebration when his profligate brother returned home. The younger brother repented, which caused his father much joy. We are not told what happened to the older brother. Did he finally welcome his brother home, or did he stay outside pouting and feeling wronged? Which brother are we? Do we rejoice when sinners we know repent and come to faith? Do we help them come to faith?

The Rich Man and Lazarus (Luke 16:19–31)

The parable of the rich man and Lazarus is another "odd man out" story of Jesus. It is about the responsibility of those blessed with wealth to care for others. In the parable a rich man feasted "sumptuously every day." A poor man named Lazarus (the only parable of Jesus in which a person is named, though the Lazarus here is not the brother of Mary and Martha), who was covered with sores, hoped for a few crumbs to satisfy his hunger. He died and was carried away by angels. The rich man also died and went to Hades, the netherland between heaven and hell, "where he was tormented." The surprise is that Lazarus went to heaven, but the rich man did not because he ignored the beggar at his gate, and in doing so he ignored God as well. The apostle John echoes this teaching, saying, "How does God's love abide in anyone who has the world's goods and sees a brother or sister in need and yet refuses help? (1 John 3:17).

Pastor Bruce Larson said that Albert Schweitzer was convicted by the parable of the rich man and Lazarus. Schweitzer believed that Africa was the poor man at the gate of Europe. He left the academic world, where he had doctorates in music, theology (his *Quest of the Historical Jesus* is still a Christian classic) and medicine and, in 1913, went to care for the sick "at the gate" in Lambaréné (present-day Gabon in west central Africa). When Schweitzer died in 1965, his hospital and leper colony was caring for 500 patients. One day we will be called to account for the gifts and blessings we have received and the treatment of those at *our gate.*

Jesus' "I Am" Statements

The center chapters in John's Gospel contain seven "I am" sayings of Jesus—seven metaphors from everyday life in which Jesus promises salvation to those "who come to me, who believe in me, who abide in me."

- After feeding the multitudes, Jesus said: "I am the bread of life [the bread that sustains life forever]. Whoever comes to me will never be hungry, and whoever believes in me will never be thirsty" (6:35). Jesus said something similar to the woman at the well in John chapter 4: "the water that I give [will be the water of] eternal life" (4:14).

- Referring to himself as the true, everlasting light, he said: "I am the light of the world. Whoever follows me will never walk in darkness" (8:12). See also John 1:6–9.

- Speaking to the crowds, Jesus said: "I am the gate [to eternal life]. Whoever enters by me will be saved" (10:9). As in the Sermon on the Mount, Jesus is the "narrow" gate (Matthew 7:13–14).

- Using the Old Testament image of God as our shepherd, as in the twenty-third Psalm, Jesus tells his listeners: "I am the good shepherd. The good shepherd lays down his life [to protect and save] his sheep" (10:11).

- After the death of Lazarus, Jesus said to Mary and Martha: "I am the resurrection and the life. Those who believe in me, even though they die, will live [eternally], and everyone who lives and believes in me will never die" (11:25–26). These verses are often read at Christian funerals.

- Speaking to Thomas and the disciples, Jesus said: "I am the way, and the truth, and the life" (14:6), meaning the true and certain way that leads to eternal life.

- Using familiar agricultural imagery, Jesus said to his disciples: "I am the vine [the life-source], you are the branches. Those who abide in me and I in them will bear much fruit" (15:5). How do we grow in faith? By abiding in Christ, the heavenly vine.

William Barclay tells a story about a missionary traveling through an unknown country at night. His guide was up ahead. The missionary, looking down, could not see the road. He said to the guide, "I can't see the way." The guide replied, "I am the way. Follow me and you will reach your destination." The Christian's destination is a more perfect union with God. How is this possible? Through Jesus, our guide. He is "the way"—the way we have access to God, the way we come into the presence of God—and this way is open to all who follow the one whom God sent to lead and guide us, namely, Jesus the Christ.

Habits of Godly Living

The year 1989 saw the publication of Stephen Covey's bestseller, *The Seven Habits of Highly Effective People.* How can we live out and give witness to our Christian faith in today's world? One way would be to develop "Seven Habits of Godly Living" from the Bible's teachings on Christian virtue, character and behavior. Some biblical texts that will help us to do this are the following.

The last *six of the Ten Commandments*: honoring our parents and others, defending the sanctity of life, being faithful in marriage, having honest dealings with others, being truthful at all times and in all things, and not coveting persons and property that don't belong to us (Exodus 20:12-17).

Peter's *seven characteristics* of Christian faith: goodness in all things, knowledge of the truth, self-control, unshakable perseverance and endurance, godliness in thought and deed, warmhearted affection toward others, and selfless love (2 Peter 1:5-7).

Matthew's *eight beatitudes* in the Sermon on the Mount: being God-centered rather than self-centered, having compassion for others, being gentle and humble, seeking after righteousness, being merciful and forgiving, having pure thoughts and motives, being a peacemaker, and standing up for what is right and just (Matthew 5:3-10).

Paul's *nine fruits* of the spirit in his letter to the Galatians: love for others, inner peace, outer joy, patience in difficult circumstances, kindness in dealing with others, generosity toward others, faithfulness in all relationships, gentleness and sensitivity, and self-control of thoughts, words and deeds (Galatians 5:22-23).

Paul's *ten virtues* in his letter to the Colossians: compassion, kindness, humility, meekness, patience, forbearance, forgiveness, love, peace and thankfulness (Colossians 3:12-15).

From these and other texts in the New Testament—Jesus' six antitheses in Matthew's Sermon on the Mount (5:21-48), Paul's teachings on Christian behavior in his letter to the Romans (12:9-21), Paul's attributes of love in 1 Corinthians (13:4-8), the exhortations in the letter to the Hebrews (13:1-5) and the letter of James—we can develop personal, tailor-made Habits of Godly Living to guide us in being Christ-like in our homes, neighborhoods and places of work, and in our recreation and leisure.

A Summary of the Good News

What I have tried to say in this book is summarized by Paul in his letter to Titus, a book that is rarely read and hardly ever preached. Paul tells Titus, in verses 2:11-14, "For the grace of God has appeared, bringing salvation to all, training us to renounce impiety and worldly passions, and in the present age to live lives that are self-controlled, upright and godly, while we wait for the blessed hope and the manifestation of the glory of our great God and Savior, Jesus Christ. He it is who gave himself for us that he might redeem us from all iniquity and purify for himself a people of his own."

Discussion Questions

1. In the Sermon on the Mount, Jesus said, "You have heard that it was said ... but I say to you ..." When Jesus returns, what do you think he will say to us?

2. Jesus talks about wealth and possessions in his parables of the Rich Farmer and the Rich Man and Lazarus. How should we share our wealth with the poor, the needy and the disadvantaged? What are some guidelines to help us know how much to give or share?

3. The parable of the good Samaritan implies that we are to care for all in need who cross our path. Are we to care for "everyone" who crosses our path? Where do we draw the line?

Epilogue:
What's Christianity All About?

I once asked John Stott, the English preacher, scholar, evangelist and expositor of the Bible, what he thought was the bottom-line essence of Christianity. Stott, who died in 2011, wrote some fifty books. He is best known for *Basic Christianity*, which has sold 2.5 million copies, has been translated into languages around the world, and was called by *Christianity Today* one of the top 100 Christian books of the twentieth century. In 2005, Stott, though British, was named by *Time* magazine one of "The Twenty-five Most Influential Evangelicals in America." Later that year, *Time* recognized Stott as one of the "one hundred most influential people in the world." *New York Times* columnist David Brooks said, when John was still alive, "If the Evangelicals had a pope, it would be John Stott."

Stott said, "There are three things that Christianity is not, and three things that it is. First, Christianity is not a creed or an intellectual or philosophical system, not a set of beliefs like the Apostles' or Nicene Creeds. Beliefs are important, but one can recite the creeds and dogmas and not believe and live them out in their daily lives.

"Second, Christianity is not a system of behavior and ethics, like the Golden Rule. There are agnostics, humanists and others outside the kingdom who are upright in character and lead good, kind, helpful lives.

"Third, Christianity is more than being baptized, confirmed, teaching Sunday school classes and being part of a church community. Unfortunately, some think this makes them a Christian.

"The above 'nots' are important, but they are not the *essence* of Christianity. The essence is a person, Jesus Christ. Being a Christian means, first, knowing Jesus, which doesn't mean knowing something about him, as one might know about a public figure, but knowing him personally, as one would know a close friend.

"Second, it means trusting Jesus—trusting that believing in and following him will make us righteous in the sight and presence of God.

"Third, it means obeying Jesus—obeying his lordship over our family life, our sex life, our money, our work, our tax returns, even our leisure.

"When you boil Christianity down to its essence—to its 'irreducible minimum'—it is knowing, loving and growing closer to Jesus Christ; it is putting our full faith and trust in his promises; it is living under his lordship over our public and private lives every day of the year."

The First-Century World
of Palestine

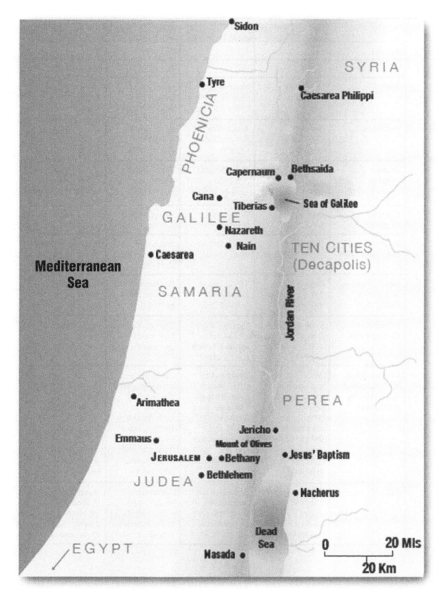

Summary Comparison of the Four Gospels

	MARK	MATTHEW	LUKE	JOHN
Verses	661	1,068	1,149	878
Date	65–70	Mid-80s	Mid-80s	Mid-90s
Author	John Mark, a follower of Peter	Matthew, the disciple, or his followers	Luke, a companion of the apostle Paul	John, the disciple and apostle
Audience	Gentile Christians in Rome	Jewish Christians in Galilee or Syria	Christians in the Greco-Roman world	Christian community in Ephesus
Jesus' Mission	"To give his life a ransom for many" (10:45)	"To fulfil what had been spoken" (1:22)	"To seek out and to save the lost" (19:10)	"To do the will of him who sent me" (6:39)
Portrait of Jesus	Crucified Son of God	Promised Messiah	Universal Savior	The Word Incarnate
Beginning of the Jesus Story	Baptism by John the Baptist (1:9-11)	Jesus' family tree (1:1-16)	Jesus' virginal conception (1:16-38)	Before creation (the divine logos) (1:1-2, 14)
Jesus' First Important Public Act	Capernaum: Jesus' first healing (1:21-28)	Sea of Galilee: Jesus' first sermon (5-7)	Nazareth: Jesus' first self claim (4:16-21)	Cana: Jesus' first sign (2:7-11)
Structural Center Point	Peter's confession of Jesus as the Messiah (8:27-30)	Peter's confession of Jesus as the Messiah (16:13-21)	Start of Jesus' final journey to Jerusalem (9:51)	Jesus' washing the disciples' feet (13:1)
Unique Jesus Materials and Stories in the Narratives	Jesus' action and straight forwardness; Jesus' humanness; Jesus' miracles (one third of Gospel); Jesus' passion (first written account)	Jesus as the fulfillment of Israel's hopes; Jesus' Sermon on the Mount; Jesus' end-time discourse (24-25); Jesus' Great Commission	Jesus' birth narrative; Jesus' concern for sinners, outcasts and women; Jesus' parables (the most and most unique); Jesus' ascension	Jesus as "the Word made flesh"; Jesus' "born again" dialogue with Nicodemus; Jesus' seven signs; Jesus' seven "I am" sayings
Special Features	Earliest Gospel; shortest; most urgent ("immediately"); two endings	Pride of place; systematic; OT references and citations; catechetical	Historical; sophisticated; Holy Spirit; Acts of the Apostles sequel	Independent of Synoptics; eyewitness; theological; most popular

Judeo-Christian Timeline: 2000 BC–AD 2000

BC/BCE

(Before Christ; BCE: Before the Common Era)

2000 God calls Abraham to "Go from your country and your kin-dred . . . to the land that I will show you" (Canaan)

1290 Moses leads the Israelites through the "Red Sea" in their exodus from Egypt

1250 Joshua leads the Israelites in their invasion of Canaan, the land promised to Abraham's descendants

1250 The beginning of the period of the Judges (1250-1000)

1000 The beginning of the reign of David, Israel's greatest king, from whose "house" the Messiah was to come

587 The destruction of Jerusalem and the temple by the Babylonians

586 The beginning of the Judean exile in Babylon (586-538)

538 The return of the exiles, the rebuilding of Jerusalem under Governor Nehemiah, and the reinstitution of Jewish life by the priest-scribe Ezra

332 Alexander the Great moves east and Israel becomes, again, a subject people

164 The Maccabeans defeat the Syrians and cleanse and rededicate the temple (*Hanukkah*)

63 The Roman army under Pompey invades Palestine and Israel becomes, yet again, a subject people

37 Herod the Great, with Marc Antony's backing, becomes the King of the Jews

6/5 Jesus of Nazareth is born in Bethlehem, where he is visited by shepherds and the maji

AD/CE

(Anno Domini: "In the year of the Lord"; CE: in the Common Era)

27 Jesus is baptized in the River Jordan by John the Baptist
and begins his public ministry in Galilee

30 Jesus' death and resurrection and the commissioning of his disciples
to take the gospel "to the ends of the earth"

30 Pentecost and the coming of the Holy Spirit in Jerusalem:
the "birthday" of the Christian church

33 The call of Paul, the early church's greatest theologian and church-
planter, on the road to Damascus

46 The first of Paul's three reported missionary journeys, accompanied
by Barnabas and Mark, to Asia Minor

57 Paul's letter to the church in Rome, his last will and
testament to the church

64 Nero's burning of Rome, the persecution of Christians
and the martyrdoms of Peter and Paul

66 The Gospel of Mark (ca. 65–67), which most scholars
believe was the first Gospel

70 The Roman army destroys Jerusalem and the temple
during the First Jewish War (66–70)

312 The conversion of Constantine the Great, the first
Christian emperor of the Roman Empire

325 The Council of Nicaea (Constantinople), the first great
church council, formulates the Nicene Creed

367 Athanasius's letter to bishops of the church listing
the twenty-seven books in the New Testament canon

405 Jerome completes the translation of the Hebrew and
Greek Scriptures into Latin (the *Vulgate*)

1054 The church splits into Roman Catholic in the West
and Eastern Orthodox in the East

1095 Pope Urban II, promising a pardon for sins, launches
a crusade to retake the Holy Land from the Muslims

1382 John Wycliffe translates the Latin Vulgate into English
so that it can be read by the people

1456   Johan Gutenberg invents the movable-type printing press, which launches the first "information age"

1492   Christopher Columbus sails to the New World, opening the Americas to Christianity

1517   Martin Luther's *95 Theses Against Indulgences* splits the Western Church into Catholic and Protestant

1536   Calvin's *Institutes of the Christian Religion* systematizes Protestant theology and doctrines

1545   The Council of Trent (1545-1563) affirms Roman Catholic teachings and doctrines

1611   The *King James Bible* becomes the "authorized" Bible of Protestantism

1620   The *Mayflower Pact*, the Pilgrims belief that they were launching "A new colony for the glory of God"

1647   The Westminster Confession calls Christians "To glorify God and enjoy him forever"

1793   William Carey launches the Protestant missionary movement in India, claiming that his mission was "From God, for God"

1859   Charles Darwin's *Origin of Species* challenges the opening chapters in the book of Genesis

1906   The Azusa Street (Los Angeles) Revival launches Pentecostalism, Christianity's fastest-growing movement

1910   *The Fundamentals: A Testimony to the Faith*, the beginning of "fundamentalism"

1942   The National Association of Evangelicals launches the evangelical movement in the United States

1947   The discovery of the Dead Sea Scrolls (900 scrolls), the most important manuscript find of the twentieth century

1949   Billy Graham's first crusade in Los Angeles (Graham has preached the gospel to an estimated 215 million people)

1962   Pope John XXIII calls Vatican II (1962–1965), the beginning of Catholic modernism

1991   The dissolution of the Union of Soviet Socialist Republics and the reinstatement of religions freedoms

2000   The *Amsterdam Declaration on Evangelism*

Index of Names

About the Author

 John Schwarz has academic degrees in business management and law and spent thirty years in the corporate business world. He also has a Masters in Christian Studies from Regent College, a non-denominational graduate school of theology in Vancouver, British Columbia. Schwarz took early retirement and went to Nairobi, Kenya, where he taught and started an MBA program at Daystar University, the largest Christian college in Africa; taught the Bible for two years in an indigenous Pentecostal church in a large slum; and, with his wife, started a K-12 school and a clinic-based community health care program in two other slums.

Schwarz was raised Episcopalian. As an adult, he and his wife and children were members in a Congregational church; while in seminary, he and his wife attended a Plymouth Brethren chapel; when they lived in Nairobi, they worshiped in an African Baptist church; for many years they attended an inner-city Methodist church in Minneapolis; today they are members of their home church and Presbyterian churches in Minneapolis and Scottsdale. Their ten children are members of churches in different denominations, including a son who spent ten years in a Catholic order.

Schwarz's other books include *Word Alive! An Introduction to the Christian Faith*, a resource guide for a DVD program by the same name; *A Handbook of the Christian Faith*, which has been translated into several foreign languages; and *Why Do You Believe That?*, a conversation with a Catholic scholar and writer.

Lightning Source UK Ltd.
Milton Keynes UK
UKOW06f1922230816

281282UK00001BA/59/P